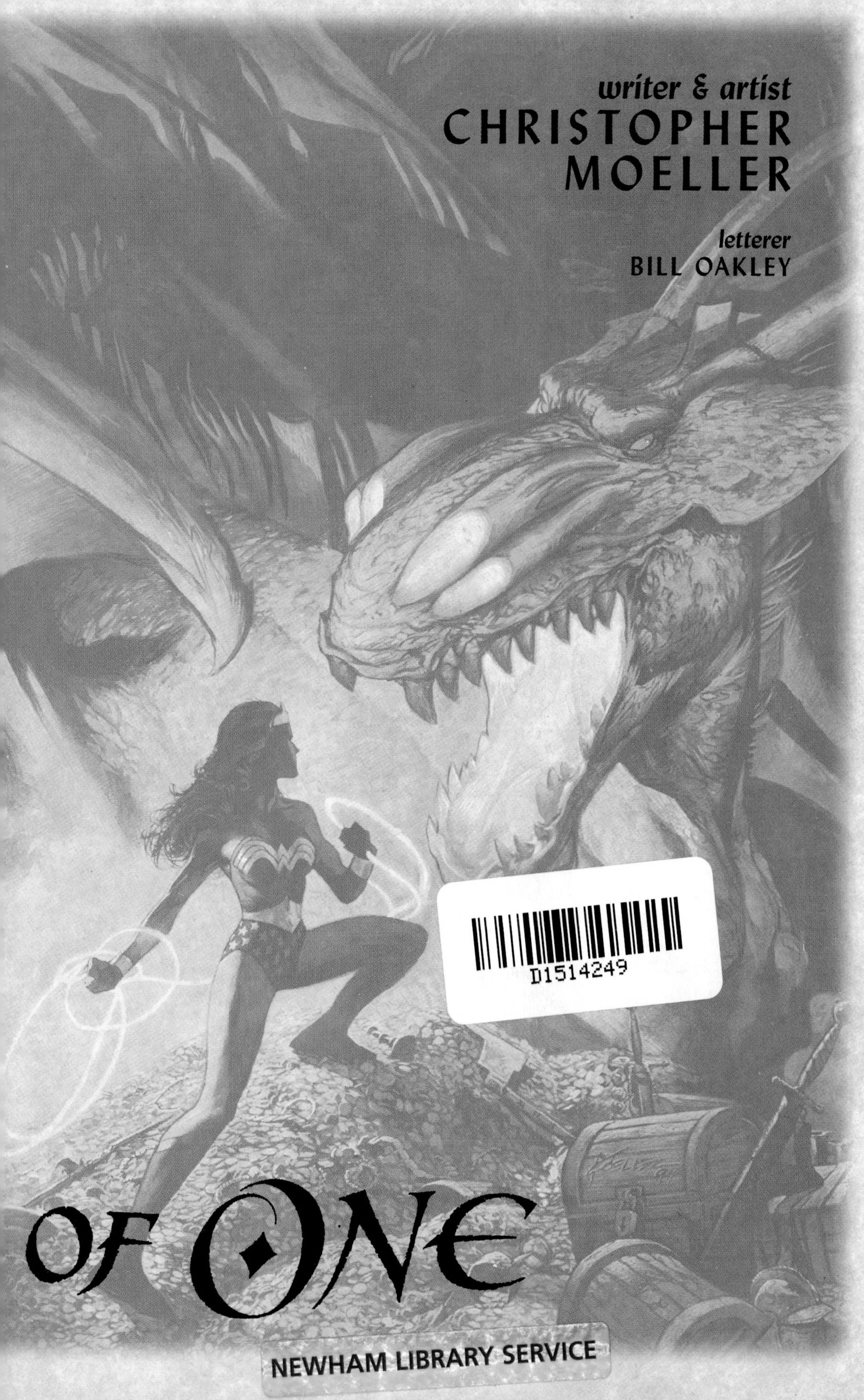

writer & artist
CHRISTOPHER
MOELLER

letterer
BILL OAKLEY

OF ONE

for
TESSA

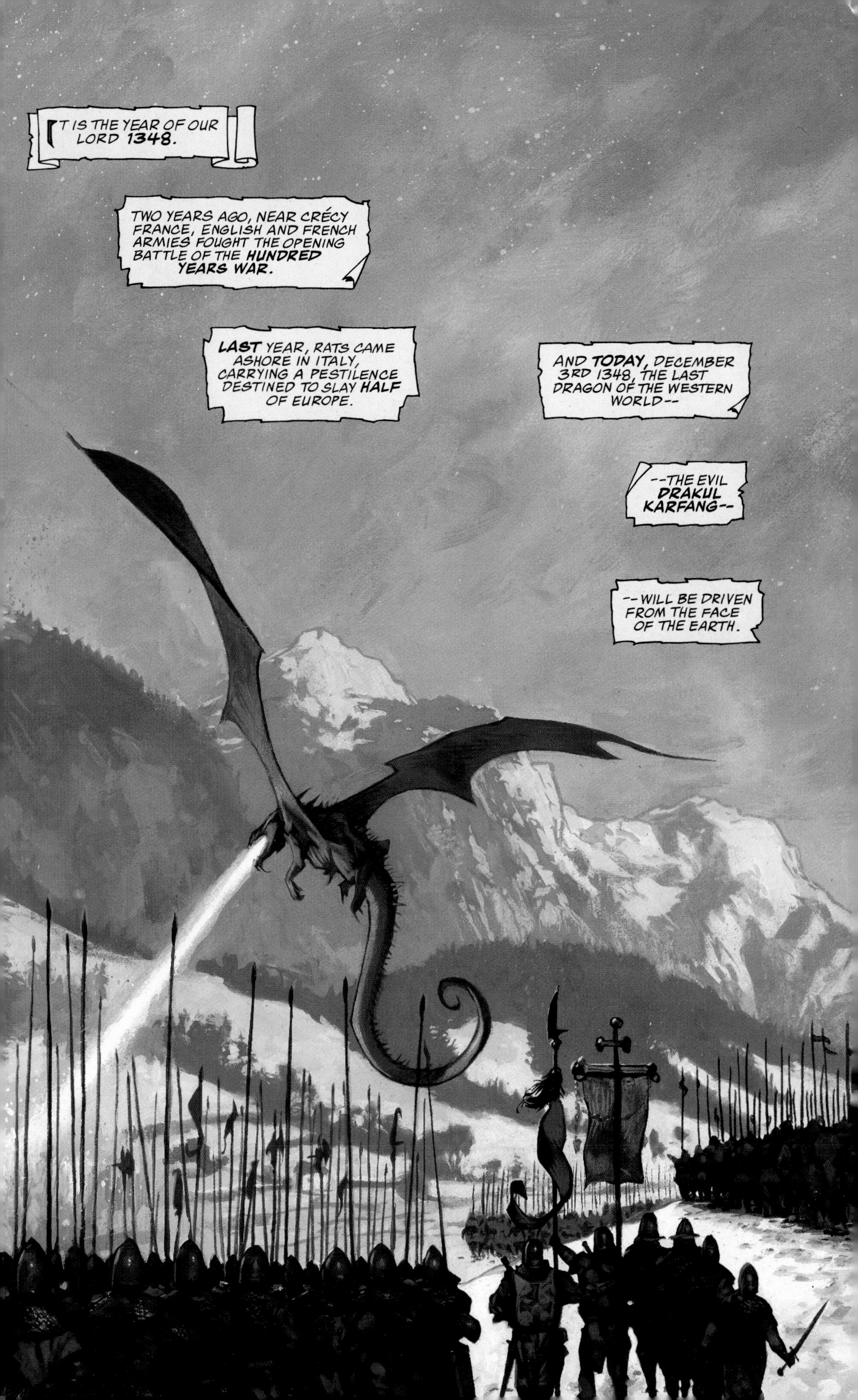
IT IS THE YEAR OF OUR LORD 1348.
TWO YEARS AGO, NEAR CRÉCY FRANCE, ENGLISH AND FRENCH ARMIES FOUGHT THE OPENING BATTLE OF THE HUNDRED YEARS WAR.
LAST YEAR, RATS CAME ASHORE IN ITALY, CARRYING A PESTILENCE DESTINED TO SLAY HALF OF EUROPE.
AND TODAY, DECEMBER 3RD 1348, THE LAST DRAGON OF THE WESTERN WORLD--
--THE EVIL DRAKUL KARFANG--
--WILL BE DRIVEN FROM THE FACE OF THE EARTH.

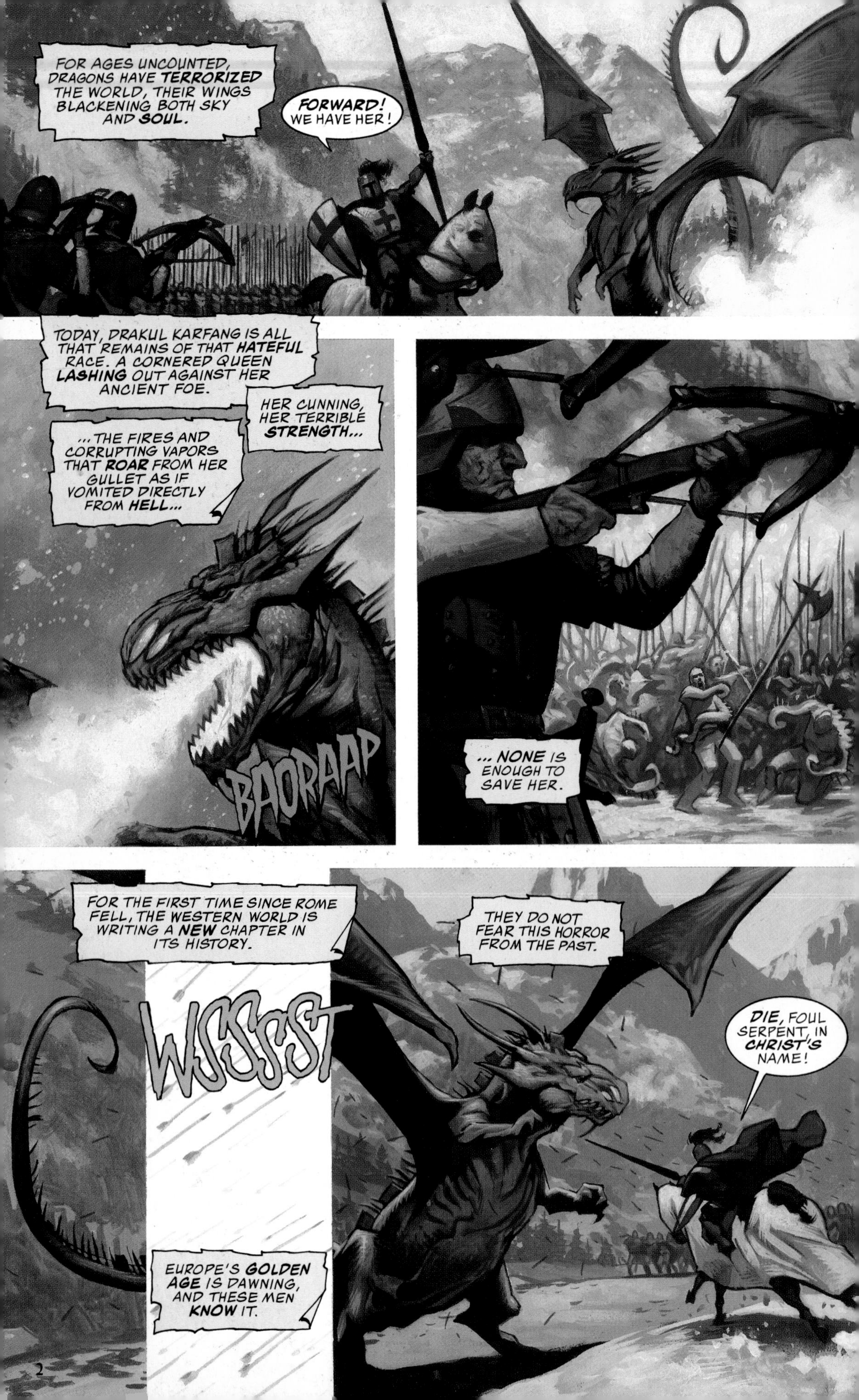

FOR AGES UNCOUNTED, DRAGONS HAVE **TERRORIZED** THE WORLD, THEIR WINGS BLACKENING BOTH SKY AND **SOUL.**
FORWARD! WE HAVE HER!
TODAY, DRAKUL KARFANG IS ALL THAT REMAINS OF THAT **HATEFUL** RACE. A CORNERED QUEEN **LASHING** OUT AGAINST HER ANCIENT FOE.
HER CUNNING, HER TERRIBLE **STRENGTH...**
...THE FIRES AND CORRUPTING VAPORS THAT **ROAR** FROM HER GULLET AS IF VOMITED DIRECTLY FROM **HELL...**
BAORAAP
... NONE IS ENOUGH TO SAVE HER.
FOR THE FIRST TIME SINCE ROME FELL, THE WESTERN WORLD IS WRITING A **NEW** CHAPTER IN ITS HISTORY.
THEY DO NOT FEAR THIS HORROR FROM THE PAST.
WSSSST
DIE, FOUL SERPENT, IN **CHRIST'S** NAME!
EUROPE'S **GOLDEN AGE** IS DAWNING, AND THESE MEN **KNOW** IT.

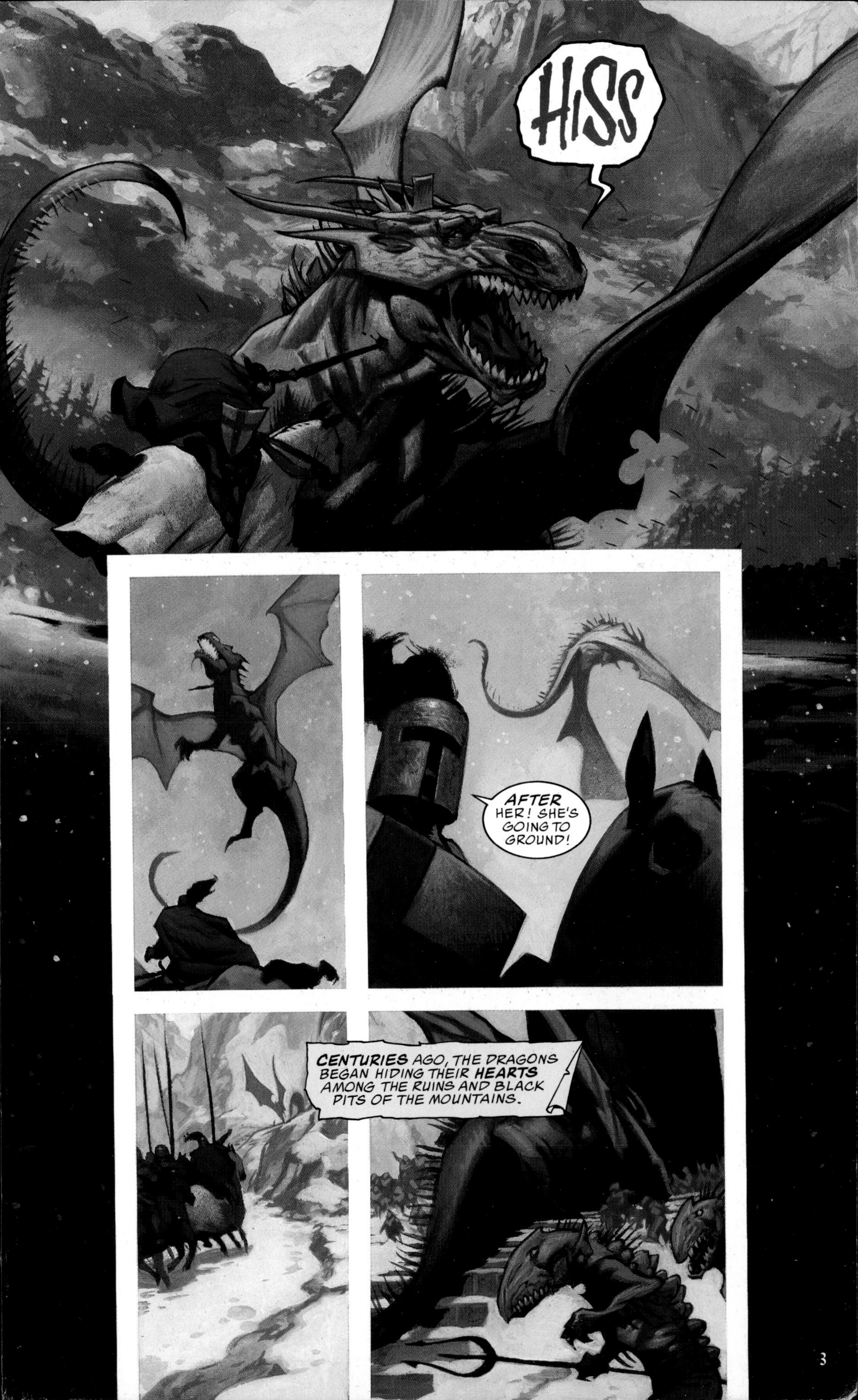
HISS
AFTER HER! SHE'S GOING TO GROUND!
CENTURIES AGO, THE DRAGONS BEGAN HIDING THEIR HEARTS AMONG THE RUINS AND BLACK PITS OF THE MOUNTAINS.

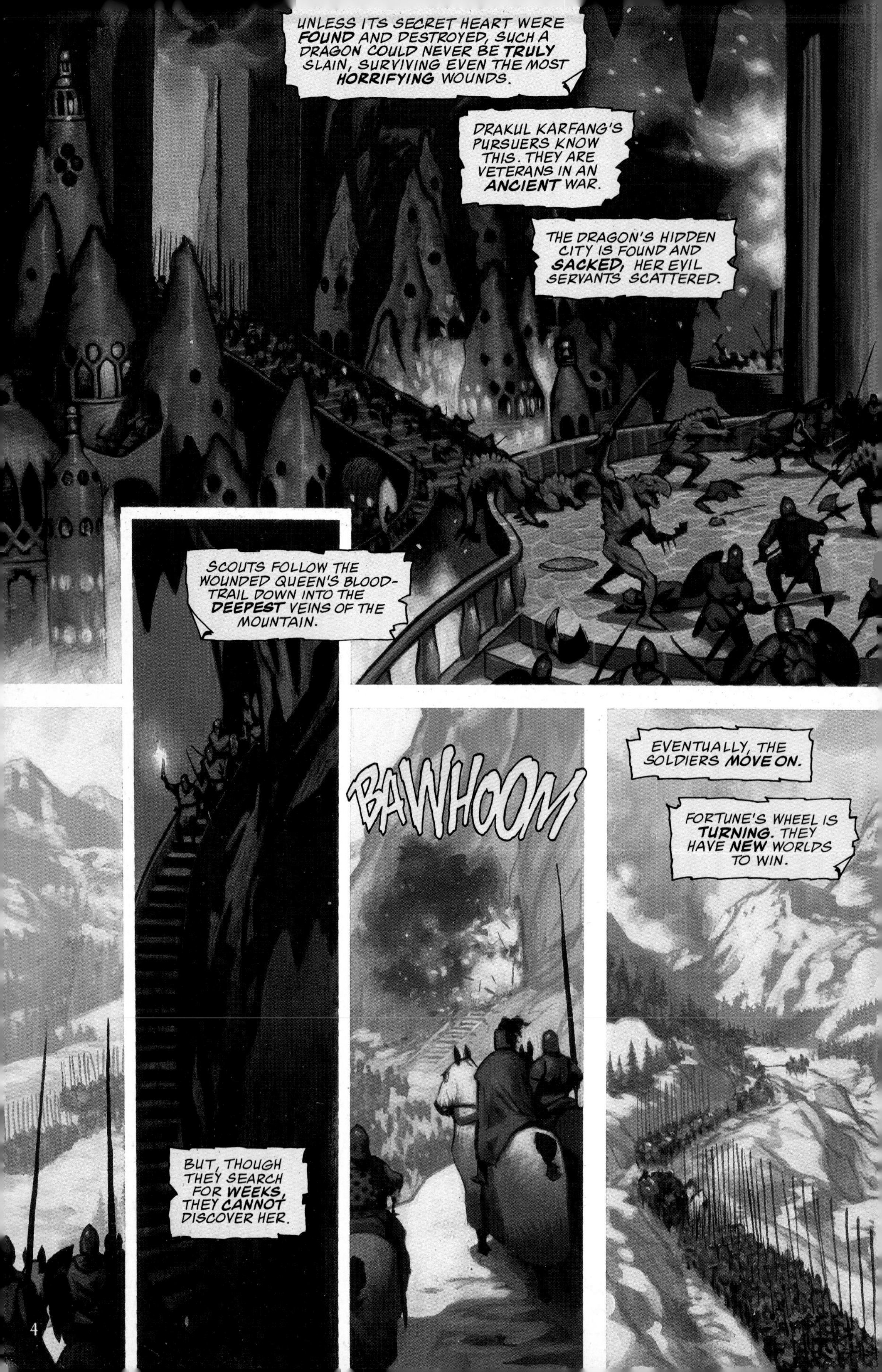
UNLESS ITS SECRET HEART WERE FOUND AND DESTROYED, SUCH A DRAGON COULD NEVER BE TRULY SLAIN, SURVIVING EVEN THE MOST HORRIFYING WOUNDS.
DRAKUL KARFANG'S PURSUERS KNOW THIS. THEY ARE VETERANS IN AN ANCIENT WAR.
THE DRAGON'S HIDDEN CITY IS FOUND AND SACKED, HER EVIL SERVANTS SCATTERED.
SCOUTS FOLLOW THE WOUNDED QUEEN'S BLOOD-TRAIL DOWN INTO THE DEEPEST VEINS OF THE MOUNTAIN.
BUT, THOUGH THEY SEARCH FOR WEEKS, THEY CANNOT DISCOVER HER.
BAWHOOM
EVENTUALLY, THE SOLDIERS MOVE ON.
FORTUNE'S WHEEL IS TURNING. THEY HAVE NEW WORLDS TO WIN.

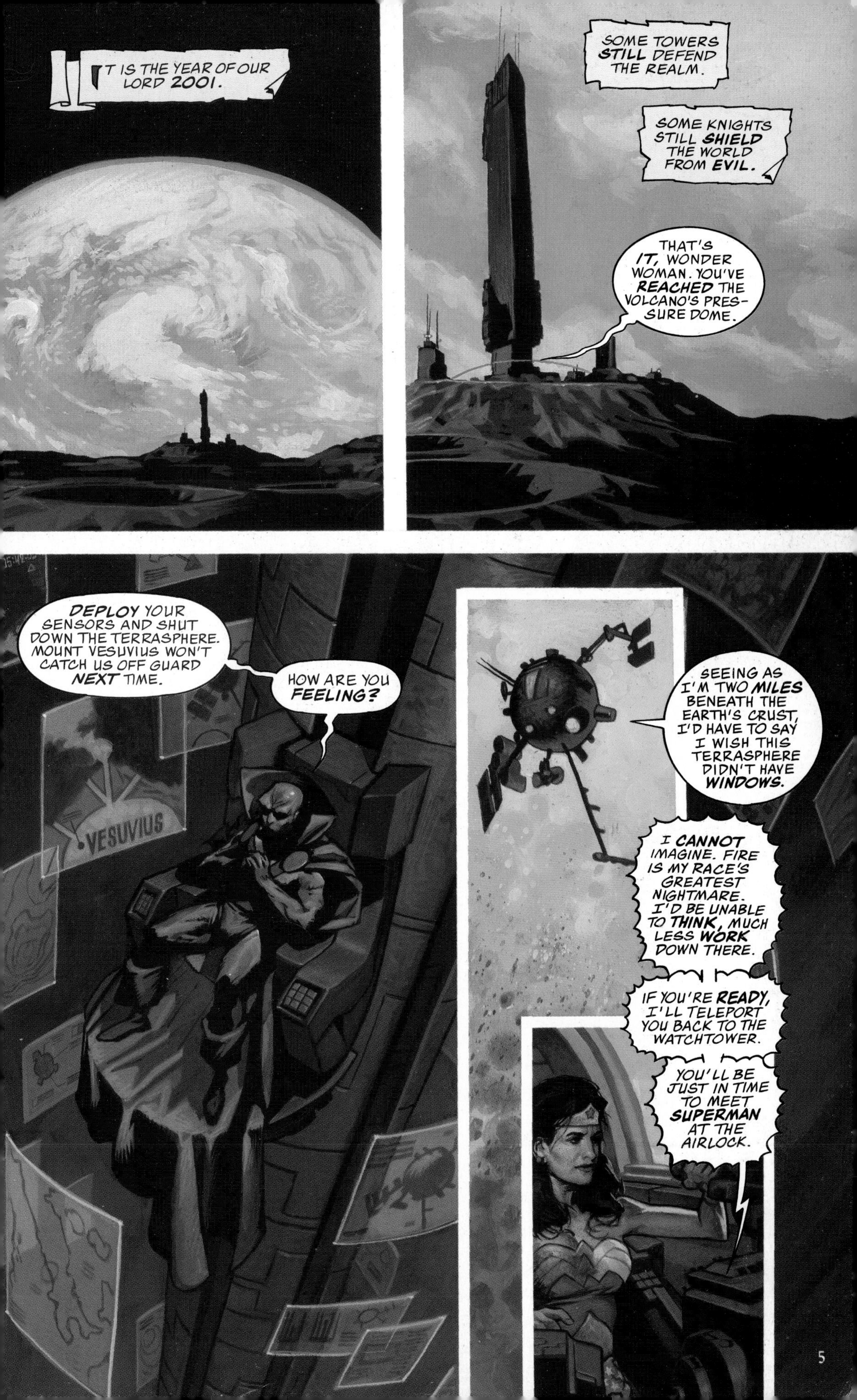

IT IS THE YEAR OF OUR LORD 2001.
SOME TOWERS STILL DEFEND THE REALM.
SOME KNIGHTS STILL SHIELD THE WORLD FROM EVIL.
THAT'S IT, WONDER WOMAN. YOU'VE REACHED THE VOLCANO'S PRESSURE DOME.
DEPLOY YOUR SENSORS AND SHUT DOWN THE TERRASPHERE. MOUNT VESUVIUS WON'T CATCH US OFF GUARD NEXT TIME.
HOW ARE YOU FEELING?
VESUVIUS
SEEING AS I'M TWO MILES BENEATH THE EARTH'S CRUST, I'D HAVE TO SAY I WISH THIS TERRASPHERE DIDN'T HAVE WINDOWS.
I CANNOT IMAGINE. FIRE IS MY RACE'S GREATEST NIGHTMARE. I'D BE UNABLE TO THINK, MUCH LESS WORK DOWN THERE.
IF YOU'RE READY, I'LL TELEPORT YOU BACK TO THE WATCHTOWER.
YOU'LL BE JUST IN TIME TO MEET SUPERMAN AT THE AIRLOCK.

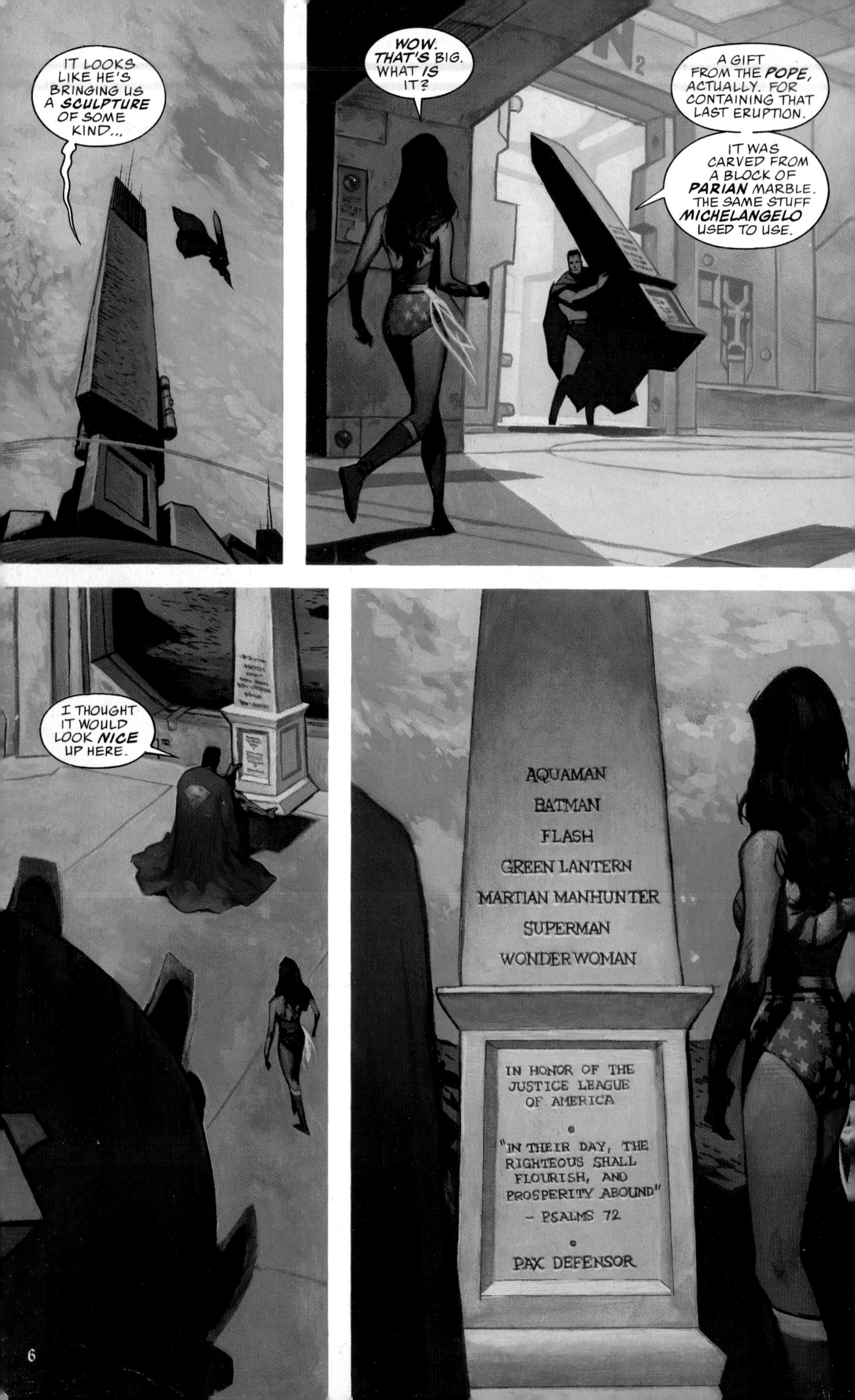
IT LOOKS LIKE HE'S BRINGING US A ***SCULPTURE*** OF SOME KIND...
WOW. THAT'S BIG. WHAT ***IS*** IT?
A GIFT FROM THE ***POPE,*** ACTUALLY. FOR CONTAINING THAT LAST ERUPTION.
IT WAS CARVED FROM A BLOCK OF ***PARIAN*** MARBLE. THE SAME STUFF ***MICHELANGELO*** USED TO USE.
I THOUGHT IT WOULD LOOK ***NICE*** UP HERE.
AQUAMAN
BATMAN
FLASH
GREEN LANTERN
MARTIAN MANHUNTER
SUPERMAN
WONDER WOMAN
IN HONOR OF THE JUSTICE LEAGUE OF AMERICA
"IN THEIR DAY, THE RIGHTEOUS SHALL FLOURISH, AND PROSPERITY ABOUND"
- PSALMS 72
PAX DEFENSOR

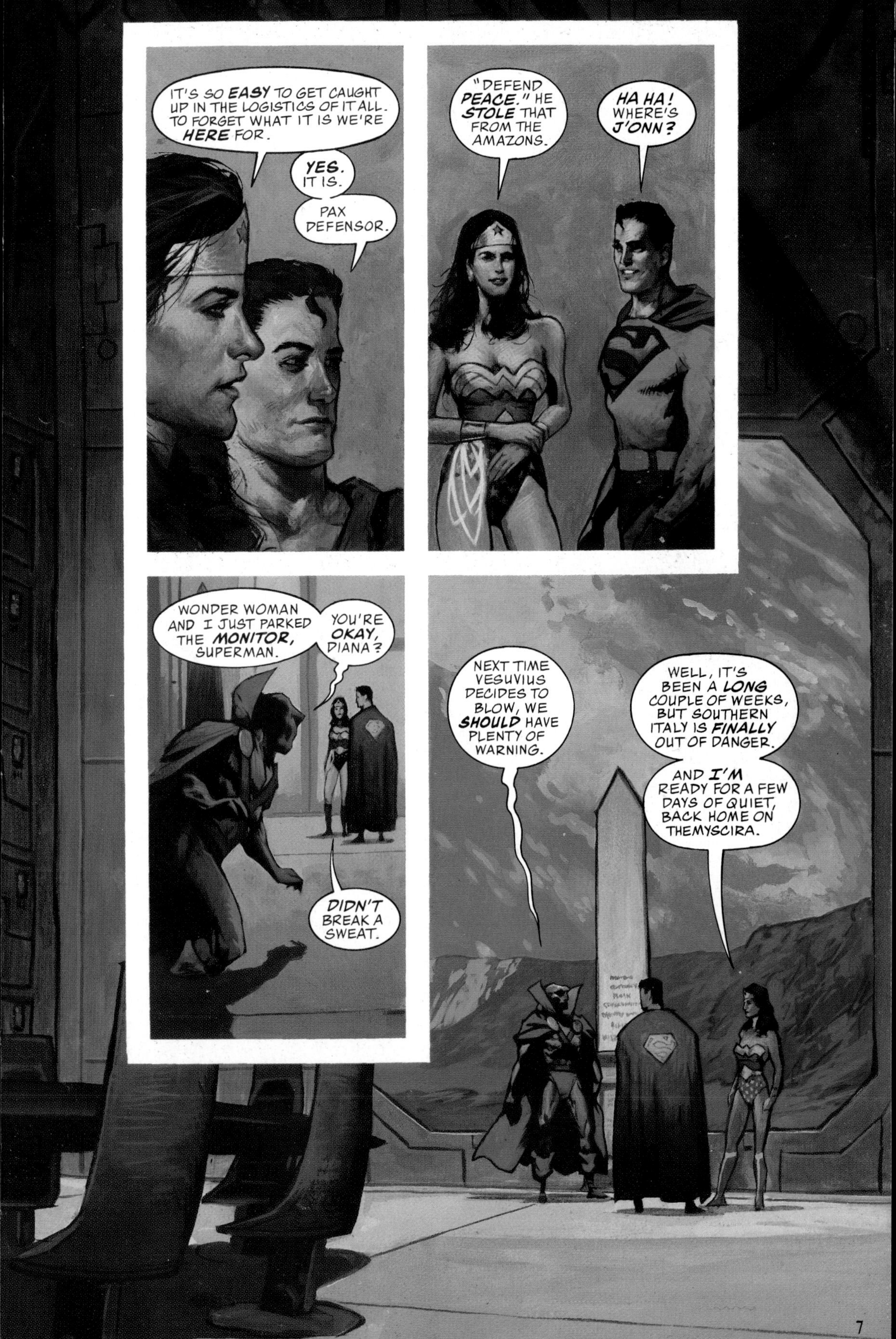
IT'S SO EASY TO GET CAUGHT UP IN THE LOGISTICS OF IT ALL. TO FORGET WHAT IT IS WE'RE HERE FOR.
YES. IT IS.
PAX DEFENSOR.
"DEFEND PEACE." HE STOLE THAT FROM THE AMAZONS.
HA HA! WHERE'S J'ONN?
WONDER WOMAN AND I JUST PARKED THE MONITOR, SUPERMAN.
YOU'RE OKAY, DIANA?
DIDN'T BREAK A SWEAT.
NEXT TIME VESUVIUS DECIDES TO BLOW, WE SHOULD HAVE PLENTY OF WARNING.
WELL, IT'S BEEN A LONG COUPLE OF WEEKS, BUT SOUTHERN ITALY IS FINALLY OUT OF DANGER.
AND I'M READY FOR A FEW DAYS OF QUIET, BACK HOME ON THEMYSCIRA.

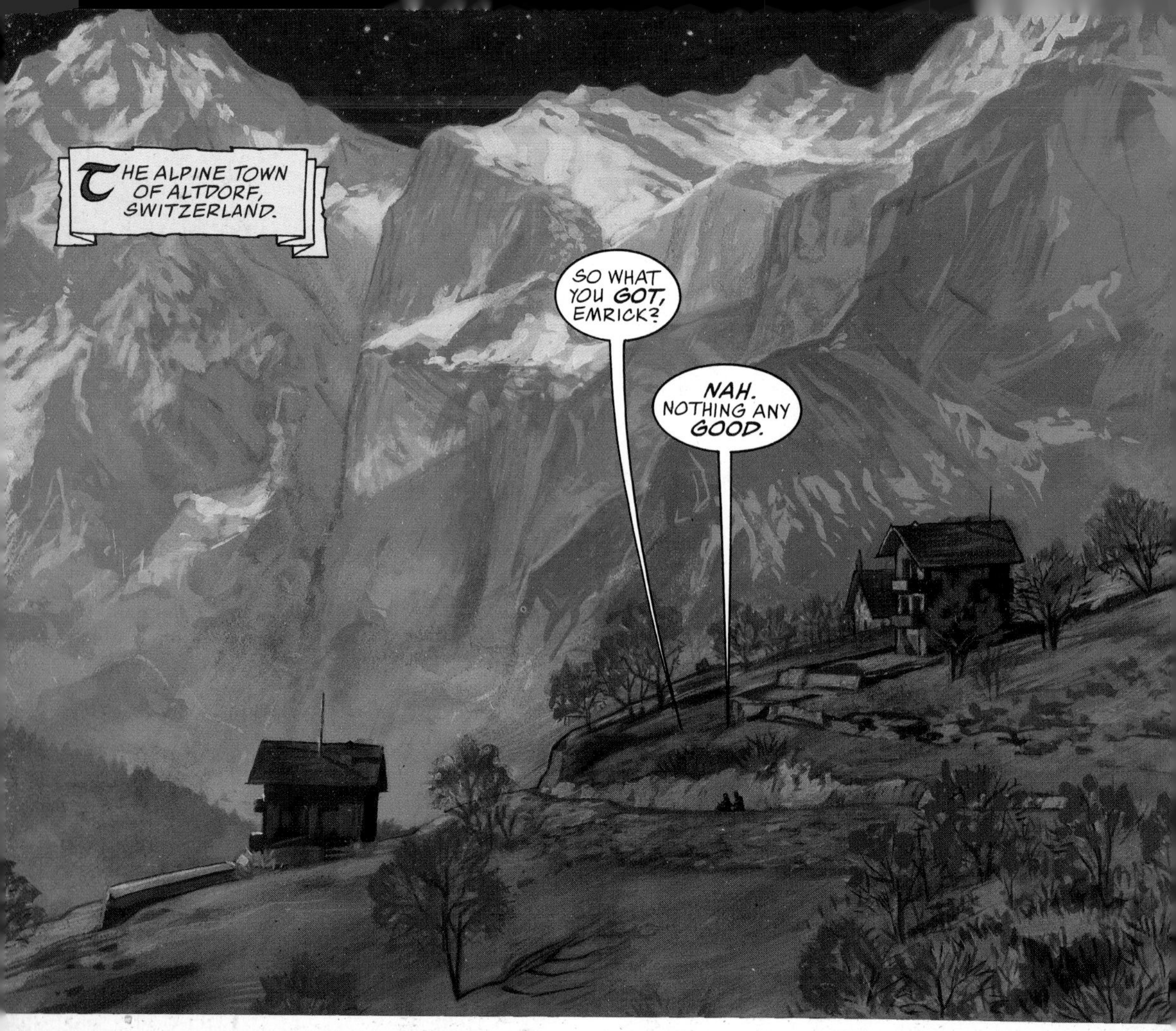
THE ALPINE TOWN OF ALTDORF, SWITZERLAND.
SO WHAT YOU GOT, EMRICK?
NAH. NOTHING ANY GOOD.

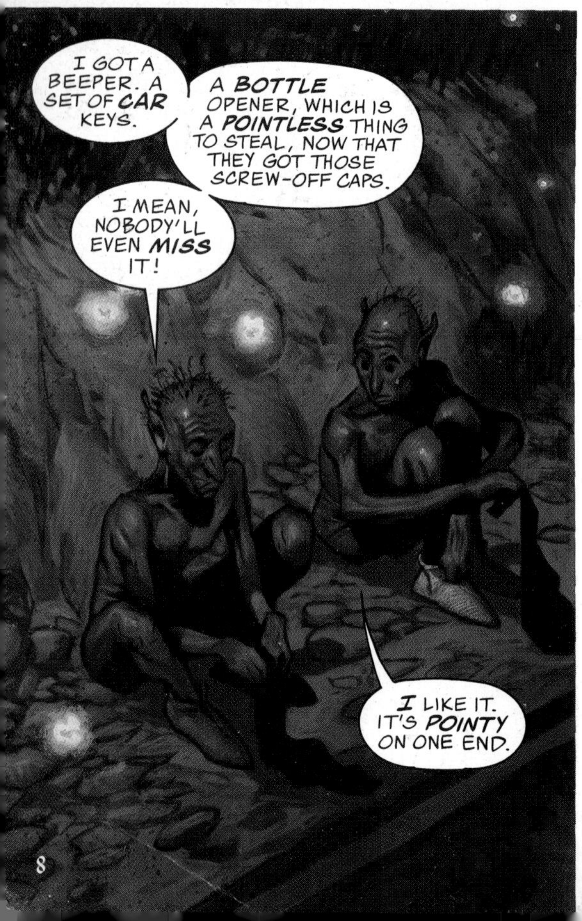
I GOT A BEEPER. A SET OF CAR KEYS.
A BOTTLE OPENER, WHICH IS A POINTLESS THING TO STEAL, NOW THAT THEY GOT THOSE SCREW-OFF CAPS.
I MEAN, NOBODY'LL EVEN MISS IT!
I LIKE IT. IT'S POINTY ON ONE END.

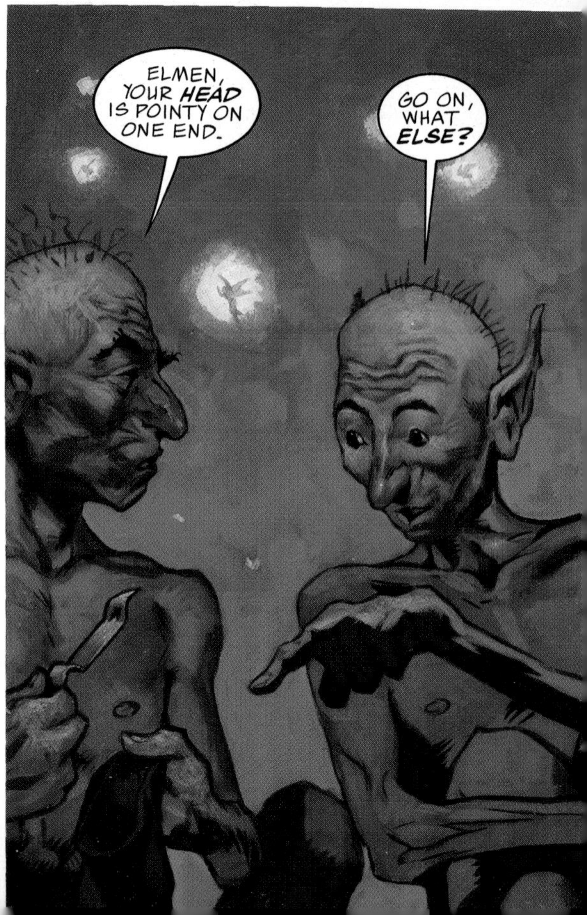
ELMEN, YOUR HEAD IS POINTY ON ONE END.
GO ON, WHAT ELSE?

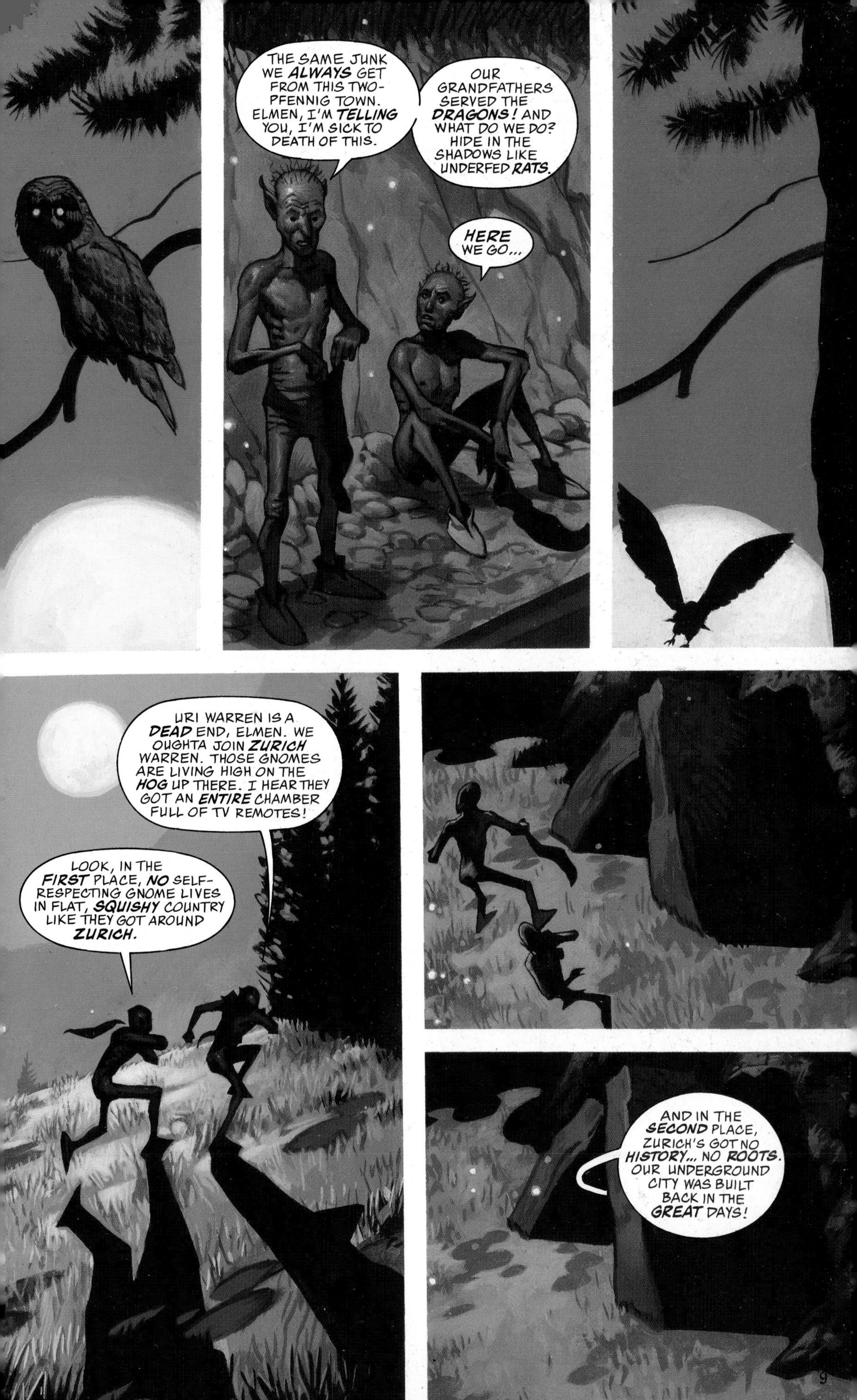
THE SAME JUNK WE ALWAYS GET FROM THIS TWO-PFENNIG TOWN. ELMEN, I'M TELLING YOU, I'M SICK TO DEATH OF THIS.
OUR GRANDFATHERS SERVED THE DRAGONS! AND WHAT DO WE DO? HIDE IN THE SHADOWS LIKE UNDERFED RATS.
HERE WE GO...
URI WARREN IS A DEAD END, ELMEN. WE OUGHTA JOIN ZURICH WARREN. THOSE GNOMES ARE LIVING HIGH ON THE HOG UP THERE. I HEAR THEY GOT AN ENTIRE CHAMBER FULL OF TV REMOTES!
LOOK, IN THE FIRST PLACE, NO SELF-RESPECTING GNOME LIVES IN FLAT, SQUISHY COUNTRY LIKE THEY GOT AROUND ZURICH.
AND IN THE SECOND PLACE, ZURICH'S GOT NO HISTORY... NO ROOTS. OUR UNDERGROUND CITY WAS BUILT BACK IN THE GREAT DAYS!

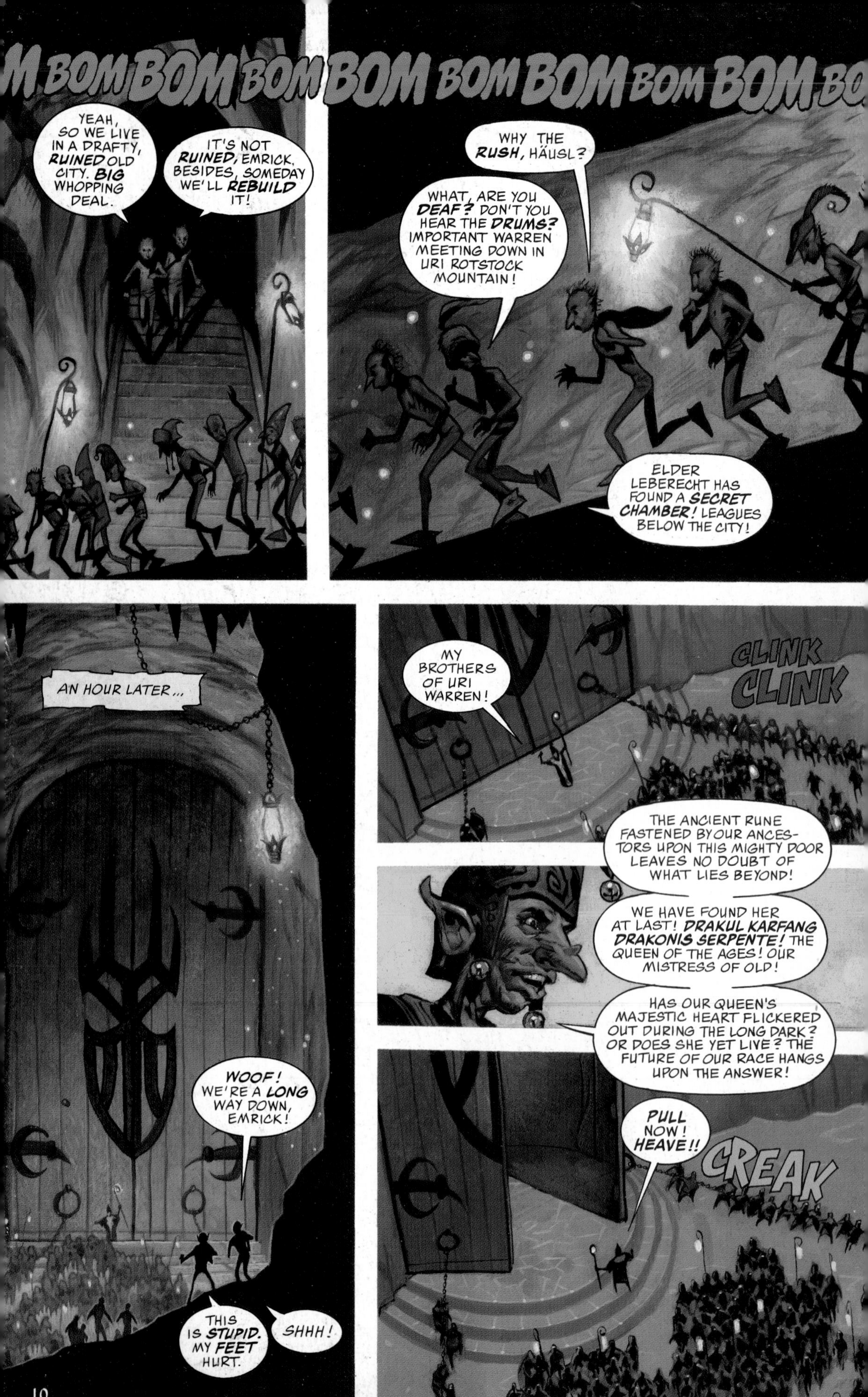
M BOM BOM BOM BOM BOM BOM BOM BOM BOM BO
YEAH, SO WE LIVE IN A DRAFTY, RUINED OLD CITY. BIG WHOPPING DEAL.
IT'S NOT RUINED, EMRICK. BESIDES, SOMEDAY WE'LL REBUILD IT!
WHY THE RUSH, HÄUSL?
WHAT, ARE YOU DEAF? DON'T YOU HEAR THE DRUMS? IMPORTANT WARREN MEETING DOWN IN URI ROTSTOCK MOUNTAIN!
ELDER LEBERECHT HAS FOUND A SECRET CHAMBER! LEAGUES BELOW THE CITY!
AN HOUR LATER...
WOOF! WE'RE A LONG WAY DOWN, EMRICK!
THIS IS STUPID. MY FEET HURT.
SHHH!
MY BROTHERS OF URI WARREN!
CLINK CLINK
THE ANCIENT RUNE FASTENED BY OUR ANCESTORS UPON THIS MIGHTY DOOR LEAVES NO DOUBT OF WHAT LIES BEYOND!
WE HAVE FOUND HER AT LAST! DRAKUL KARFANG DRAKONIS SERPENTE! THE QUEEN OF THE AGES! OUR MISTRESS OF OLD!
HAS OUR QUEEN'S MAJESTIC HEART FLICKERED OUT DURING THE LONG DARK? OR DOES SHE YET LIVE? THE FUTURE OF OUR RACE HANGS UPON THE ANSWER!
PULL NOW! HEAVE!!
CREAK

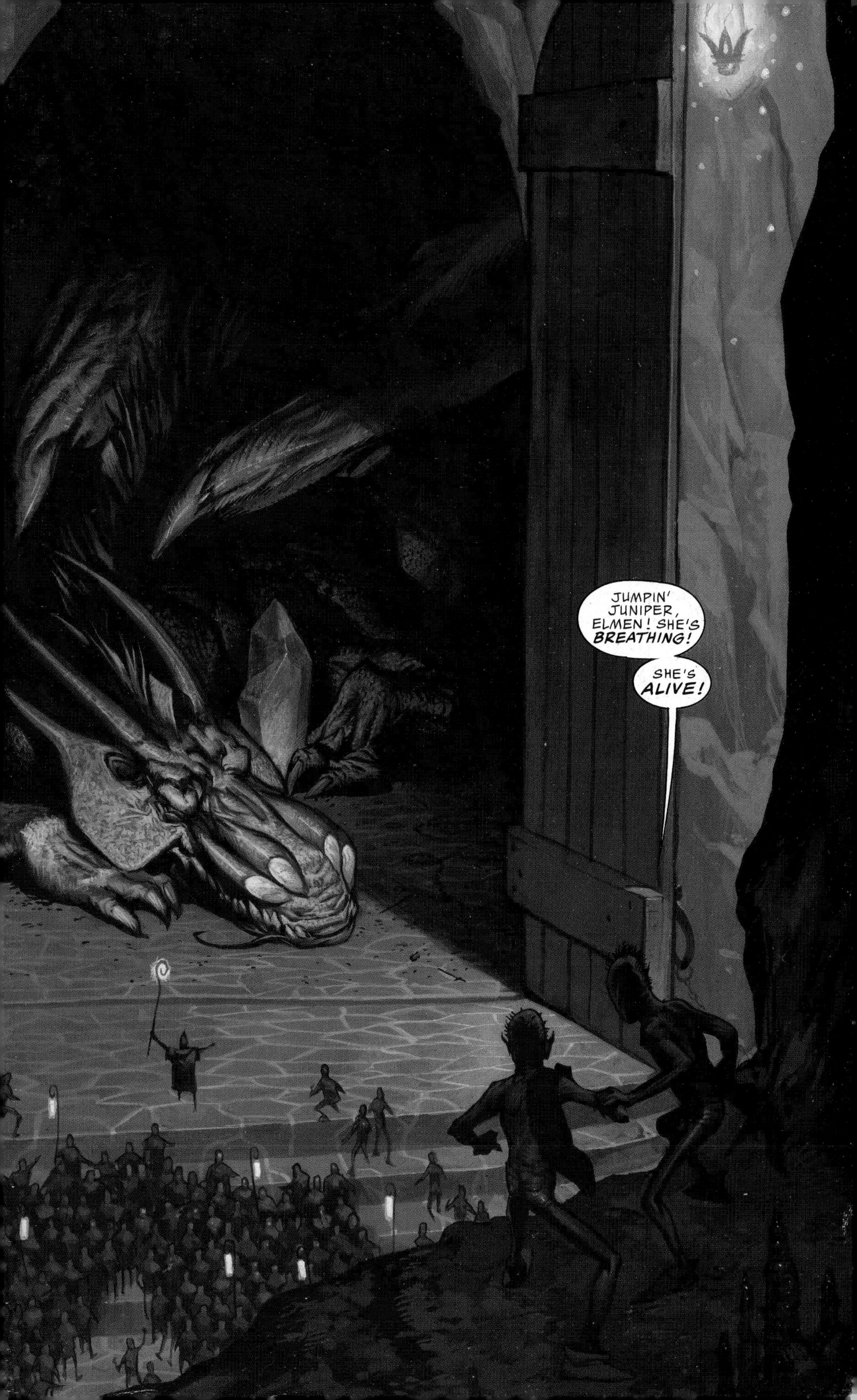
JUMPIN' JUNIPER, ELMEN! SHE'S BREATHING!
SHE'S ALIVE!

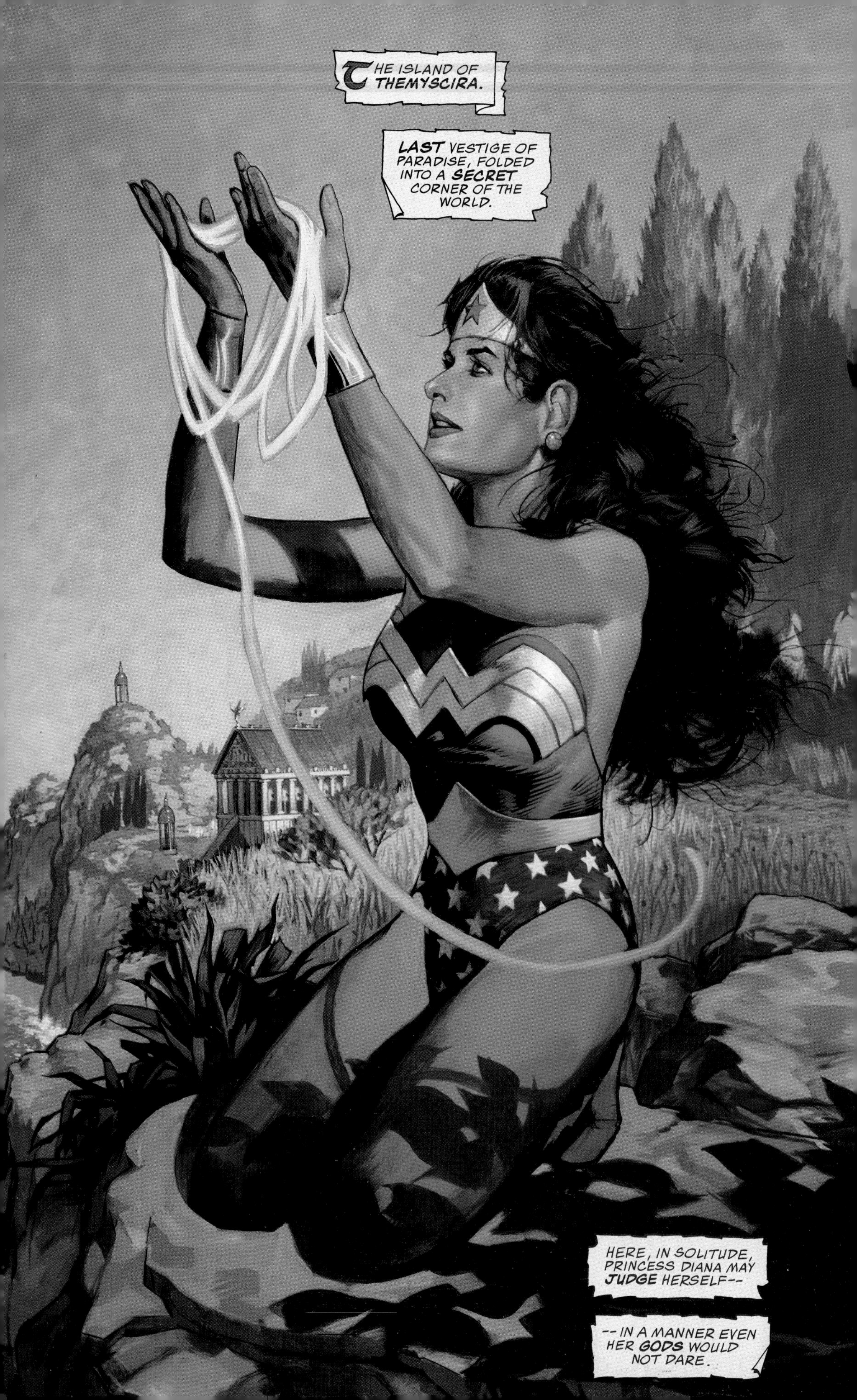
THE ISLAND OF THEMYSCIRA.
LAST VESTIGE OF PARADISE, FOLDED INTO A SECRET CORNER OF THE WORLD.
HERE, IN SOLITUDE, PRINCESS DIANA MAY JUDGE HERSELF--
--IN A MANNER EVEN HER GODS WOULD NOT DARE.

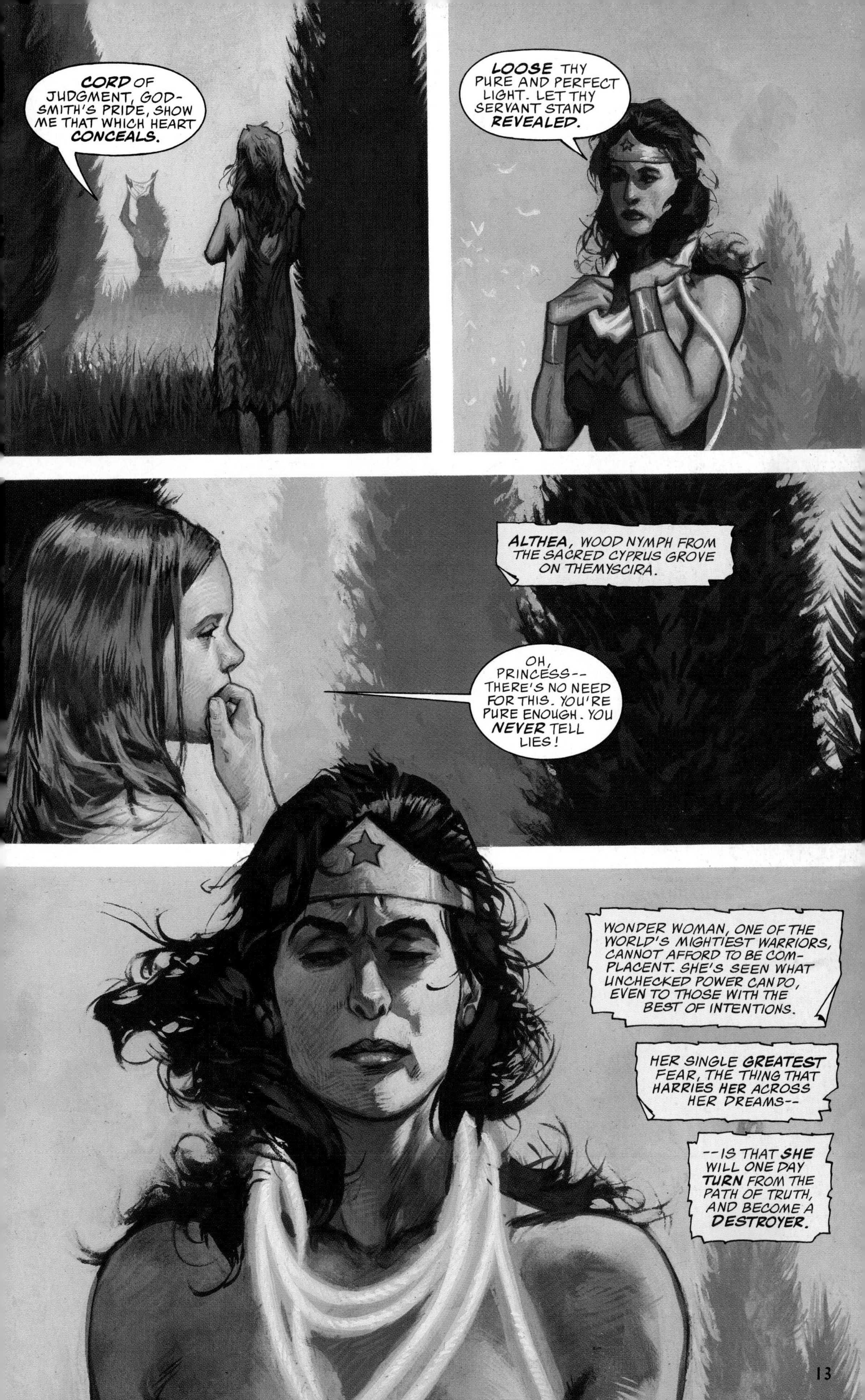
CORD OF JUDGMENT, GOD-SMITH'S PRIDE, SHOW ME THAT WHICH HEART CONCEALS.
LOOSE THY PURE AND PERFECT LIGHT. LET THY SERVANT STAND REVEALED.
ALTHEA, WOOD NYMPH FROM THE SACRED CYPRUS GROVE ON THEMYSCIRA.
OH, PRINCESS--THERE'S NO NEED FOR THIS. YOU'RE PURE ENOUGH. YOU NEVER TELL LIES!
WONDER WOMAN, ONE OF THE WORLD'S MIGHTIEST WARRIORS, CANNOT AFFORD TO BE COMPLACENT. SHE'S SEEN WHAT UNCHECKED POWER CAN DO, EVEN TO THOSE WITH THE BEST OF INTENTIONS.
HER SINGLE GREATEST FEAR, THE THING THAT HARRIES HER ACROSS HER DREAMS--
--IS THAT SHE WILL ONE DAY TURN FROM THE PATH OF TRUTH, AND BECOME A DESTROYER.

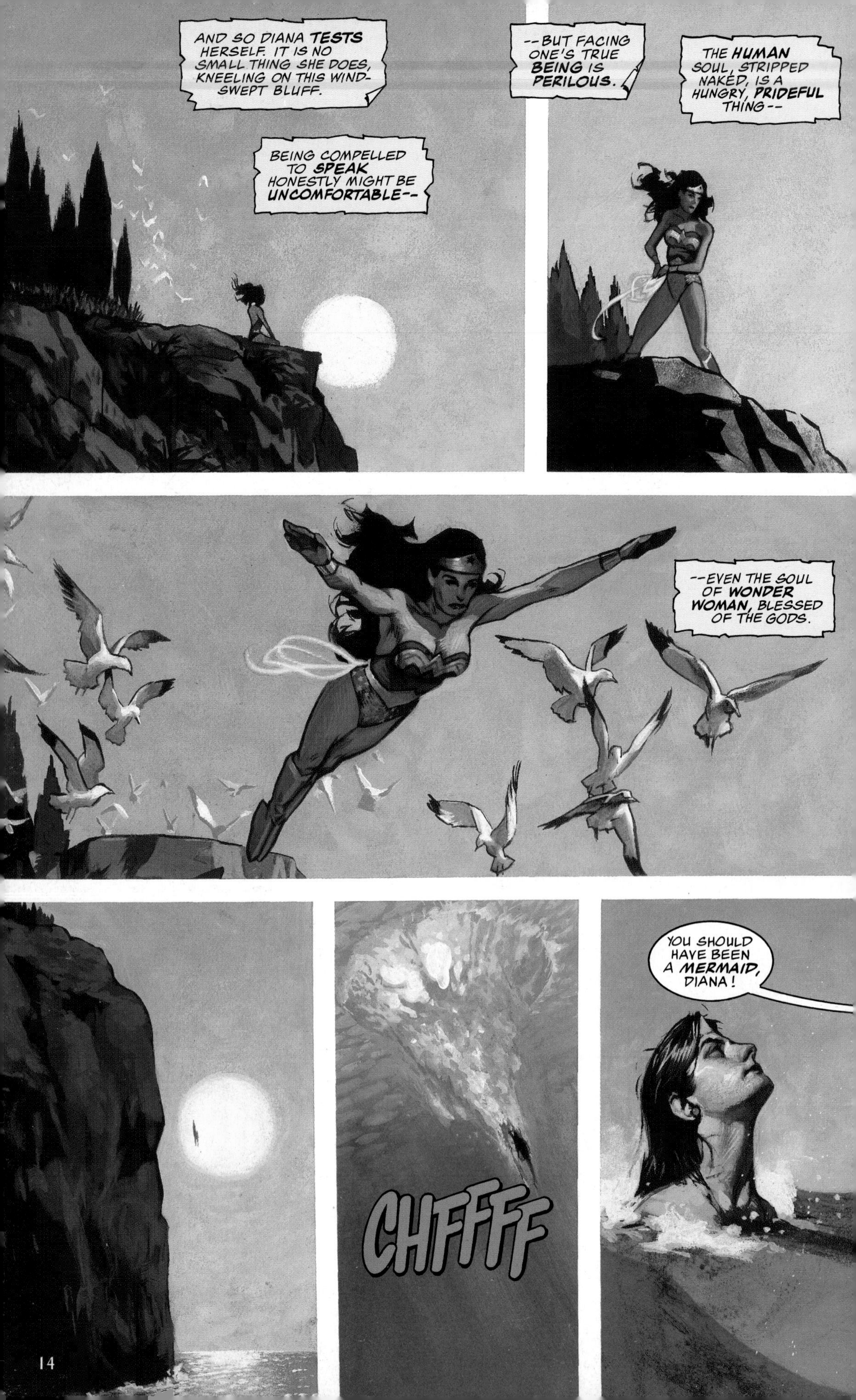

AND SO DIANA TESTS HERSELF. IT IS NO SMALL THING SHE DOES, KNEELING ON THIS WIND-SWEPT BLUFF.
BEING COMPELLED TO SPEAK HONESTLY MIGHT BE UNCOMFORTABLE--
--BUT FACING ONE'S TRUE BEING IS PERILOUS.
THE HUMAN SOUL, STRIPPED NAKED, IS A HUNGRY, PRIDEFUL THING--
--EVEN THE SOUL OF WONDER WOMAN, BLESSED OF THE GODS.
CHFFFF
YOU SHOULD HAVE BEEN A MERMAID, DIANA!

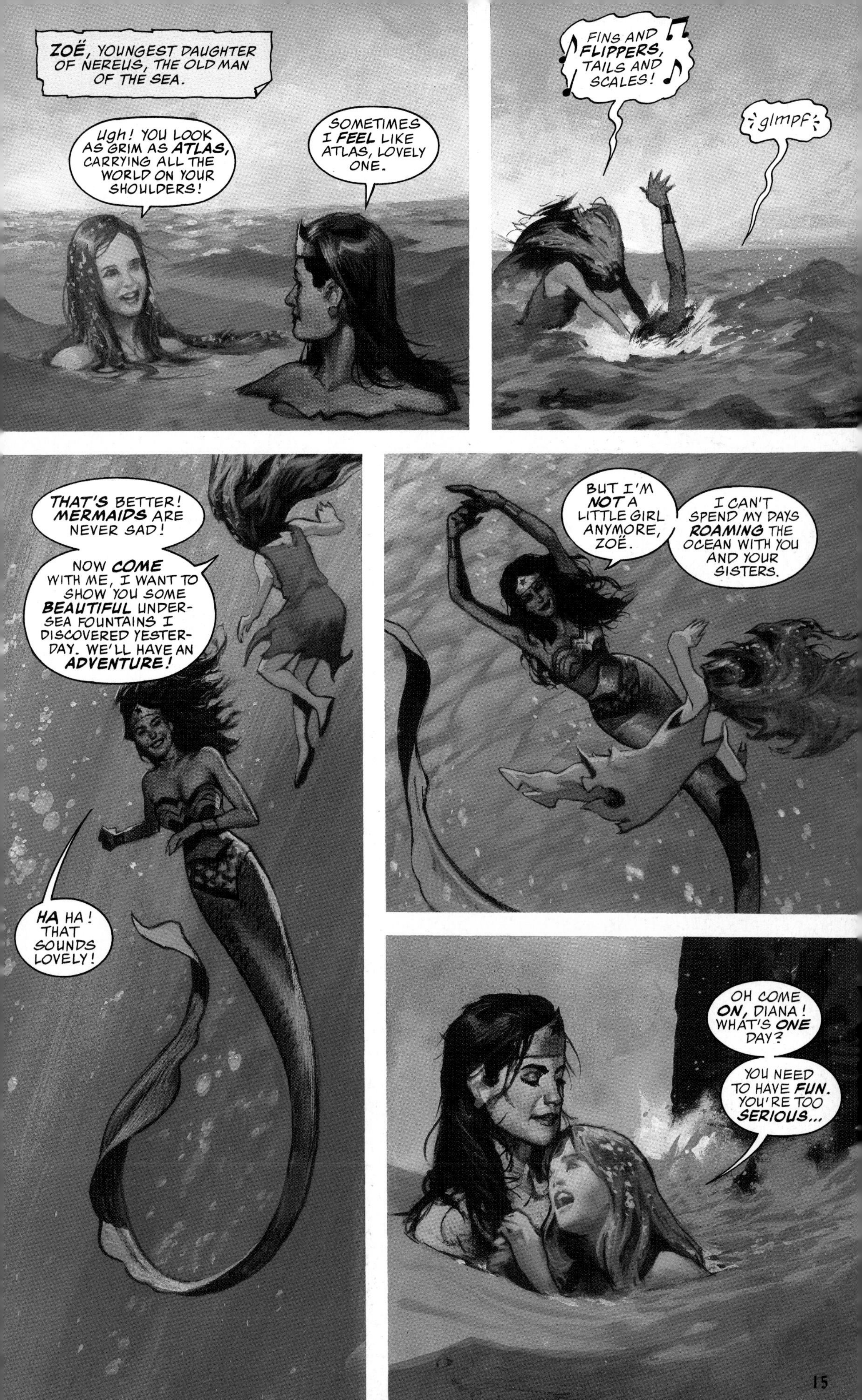
ZOË, YOUNGEST DAUGHTER OF NEREUS, THE OLD MAN OF THE SEA.
Ugh! YOU LOOK AS GRIM AS ATLAS, CARRYING ALL THE WORLD ON YOUR SHOULDERS!
SOMETIMES I FEEL LIKE ATLAS, LOVELY ONE.
FINS AND FLIPPERS, TAILS AND SCALES!
glmpf
THAT'S BETTER! MERMAIDS ARE NEVER SAD!
NOW COME WITH ME, I WANT TO SHOW YOU SOME BEAUTIFUL UNDER-SEA FOUNTAINS I DISCOVERED YESTER-DAY. WE'LL HAVE AN ADVENTURE!
HA HA! THAT SOUNDS LOVELY!
BUT I'M NOT A LITTLE GIRL ANYMORE, ZOË.
I CAN'T SPEND MY DAYS ROAMING THE OCEAN WITH YOU AND YOUR SISTERS.
OH COME ON, DIANA! WHAT'S ONE DAY?
YOU NEED TO HAVE FUN. YOU'RE TOO SERIOUS...

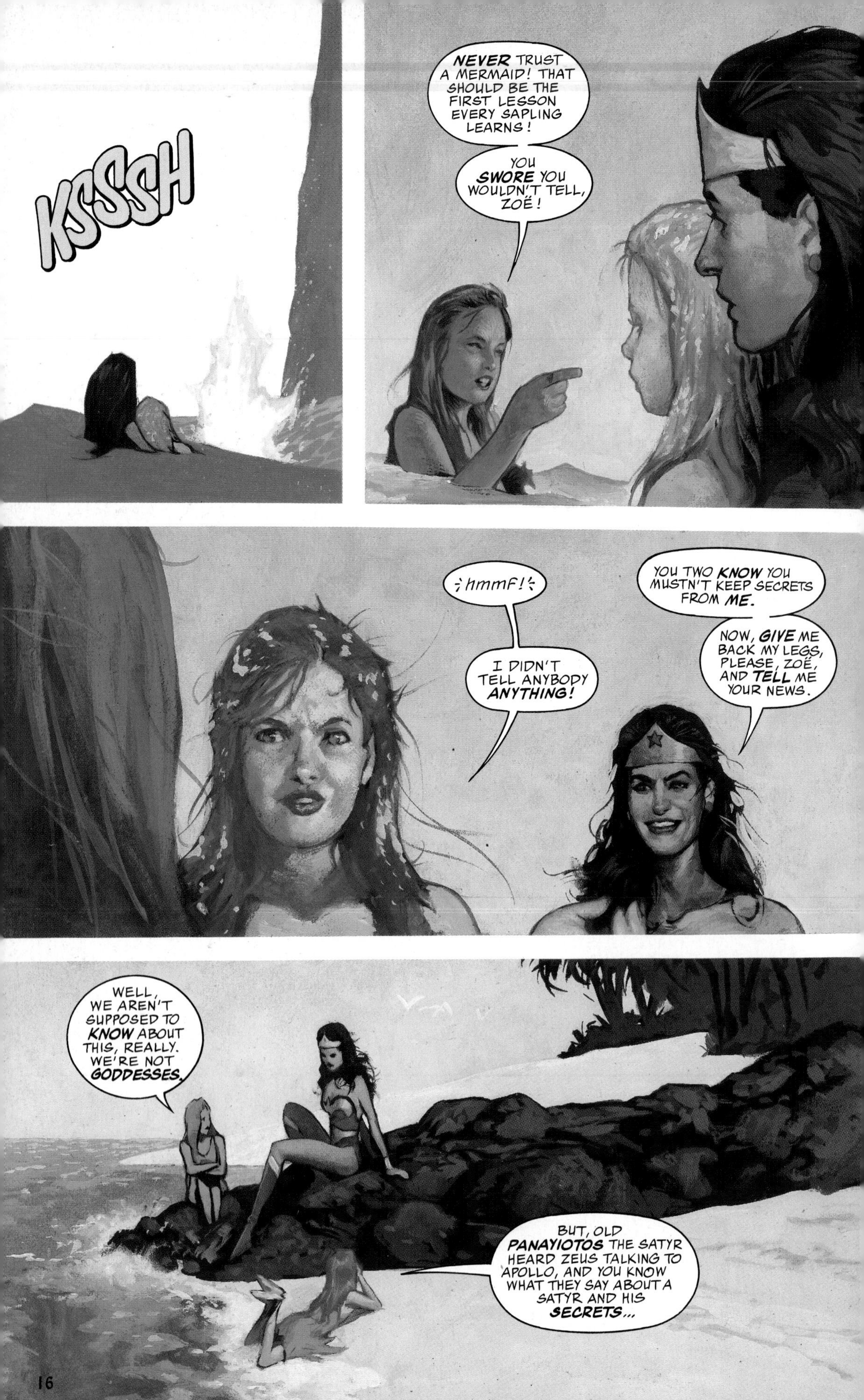
KSSSH
NEVER TRUST A MERMAID! THAT SHOULD BE THE FIRST LESSON EVERY SAPLING LEARNS!
YOU SWORE YOU WOULDN'T TELL, ZOË!
hmmf!
I DIDN'T TELL ANYBODY ANYTHING!
YOU TWO KNOW YOU MUSTN'T KEEP SECRETS FROM ME.
NOW, GIVE ME BACK MY LEGS, PLEASE, ZOË, AND TELL ME YOUR NEWS.
WELL, WE AREN'T SUPPOSED TO KNOW ABOUT THIS, REALLY. WE'RE NOT GODDESSES.
BUT, OLD PANAYIOTOS THE SATYR HEARD ZEUS TALKING TO APOLLO, AND YOU KNOW WHAT THEY SAY ABOUT A SATYR AND HIS SECRETS...

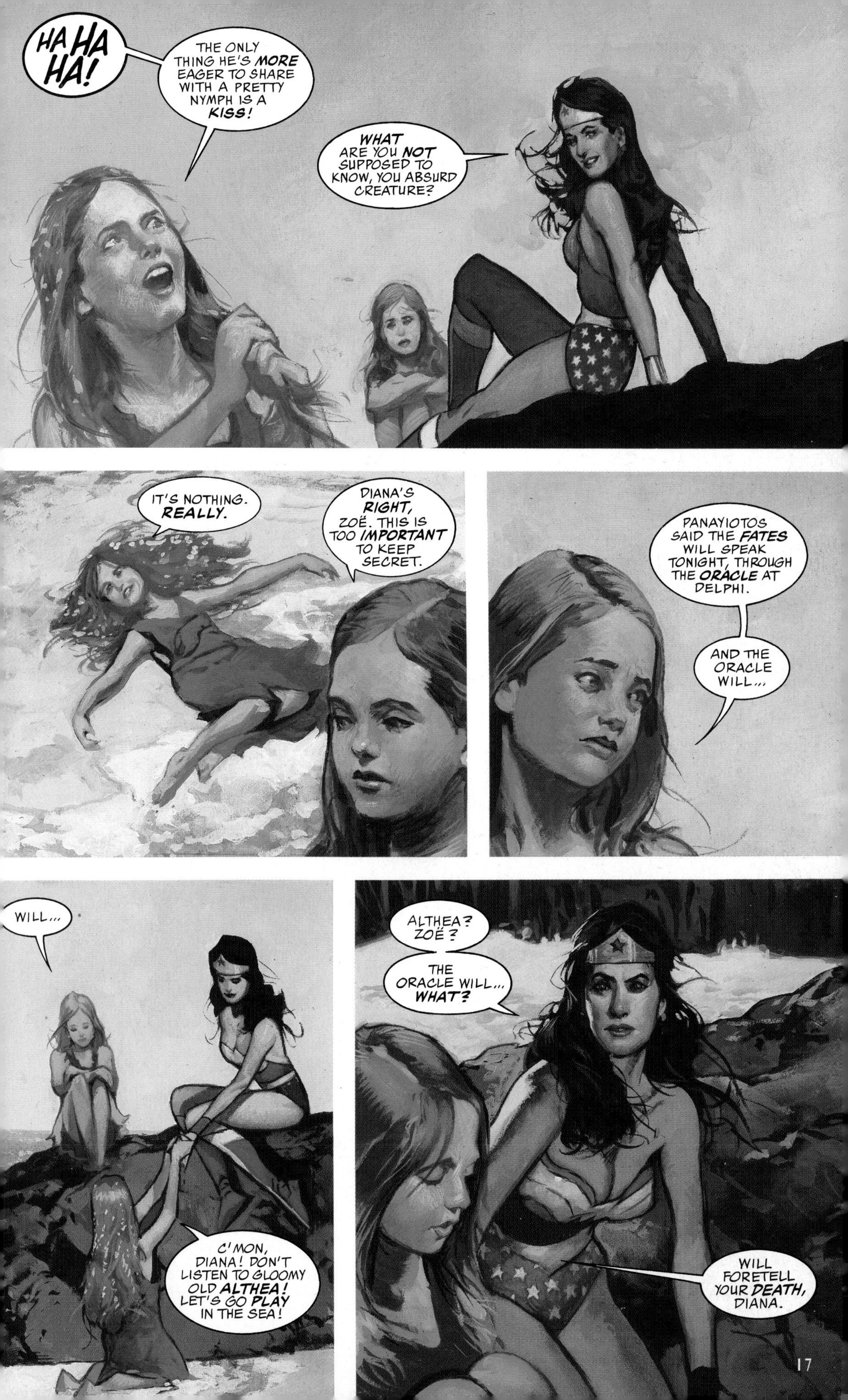
HA HA HA!
THE ONLY THING HE'S **MORE** EAGER TO SHARE WITH A PRETTY NYMPH IS A **KISS!**
WHAT ARE YOU **NOT** SUPPOSED TO KNOW, YOU ABSURD CREATURE?
IT'S NOTHING. **REALLY.**
DIANA'S **RIGHT,** ZOË. THIS IS TOO **IMPORTANT** TO KEEP SECRET.
PANAYIOTOS SAID THE **FATES** WILL SPEAK TONIGHT, THROUGH THE **ORACLE** AT DELPHI.
AND THE ORACLE WILL...
WILL...
C'MON, DIANA! DON'T LISTEN TO GLOOMY OLD **ALTHEA!** LET'S GO **PLAY** IN THE SEA!
ALTHEA? ZOË?
THE ORACLE WILL... **WHAT?**
WILL FORETELL YOUR **DEATH,** DIANA.

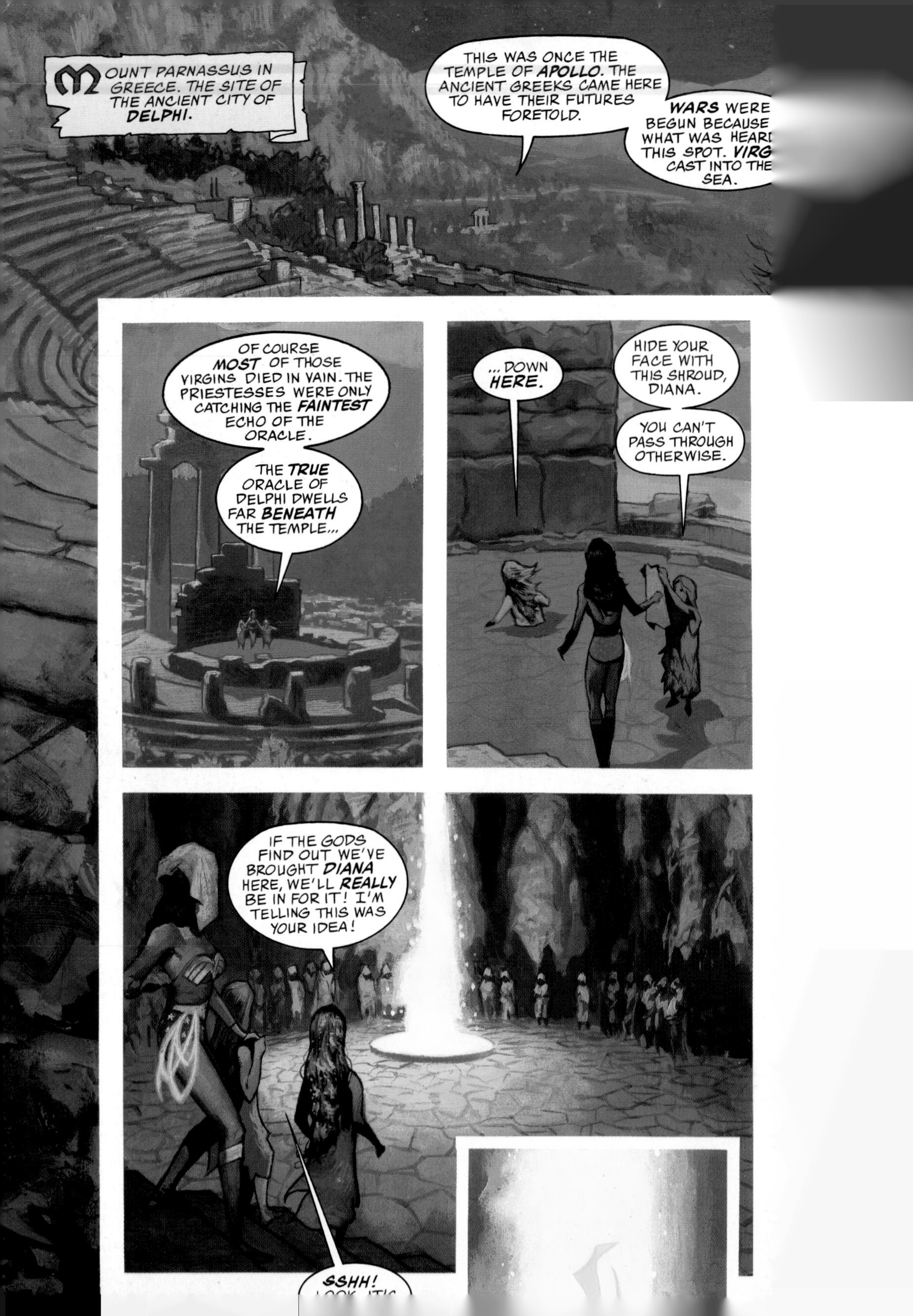
MOUNT PARNASSUS IN GREECE. THE SITE OF THE ANCIENT CITY OF DELPHI.
THIS WAS ONCE THE TEMPLE OF APOLLO. THE ANCIENT GREEKS CAME HERE TO HAVE THEIR FUTURES FORETOLD.
WARS WERE BEGUN BECAUSE WHAT WAS HEAR THIS SPOT. VIRG CAST INTO THE SEA.
OF COURSE MOST OF THOSE VIRGINS DIED IN VAIN. THE PRIESTESSES WERE ONLY CATCHING THE FAINTEST ECHO OF THE ORACLE.
THE TRUE ORACLE OF DELPHI DWELLS FAR BENEATH THE TEMPLE...
...DOWN HERE.
HIDE YOUR FACE WITH THIS SHROUD, DIANA.
YOU CAN'T PASS THROUGH OTHERWISE.
IF THE GODS FIND OUT WE'VE BROUGHT DIANA HERE, WE'LL REALLY BE IN FOR IT! I'M TELLING THIS WAS YOUR IDEA!
SSHH!

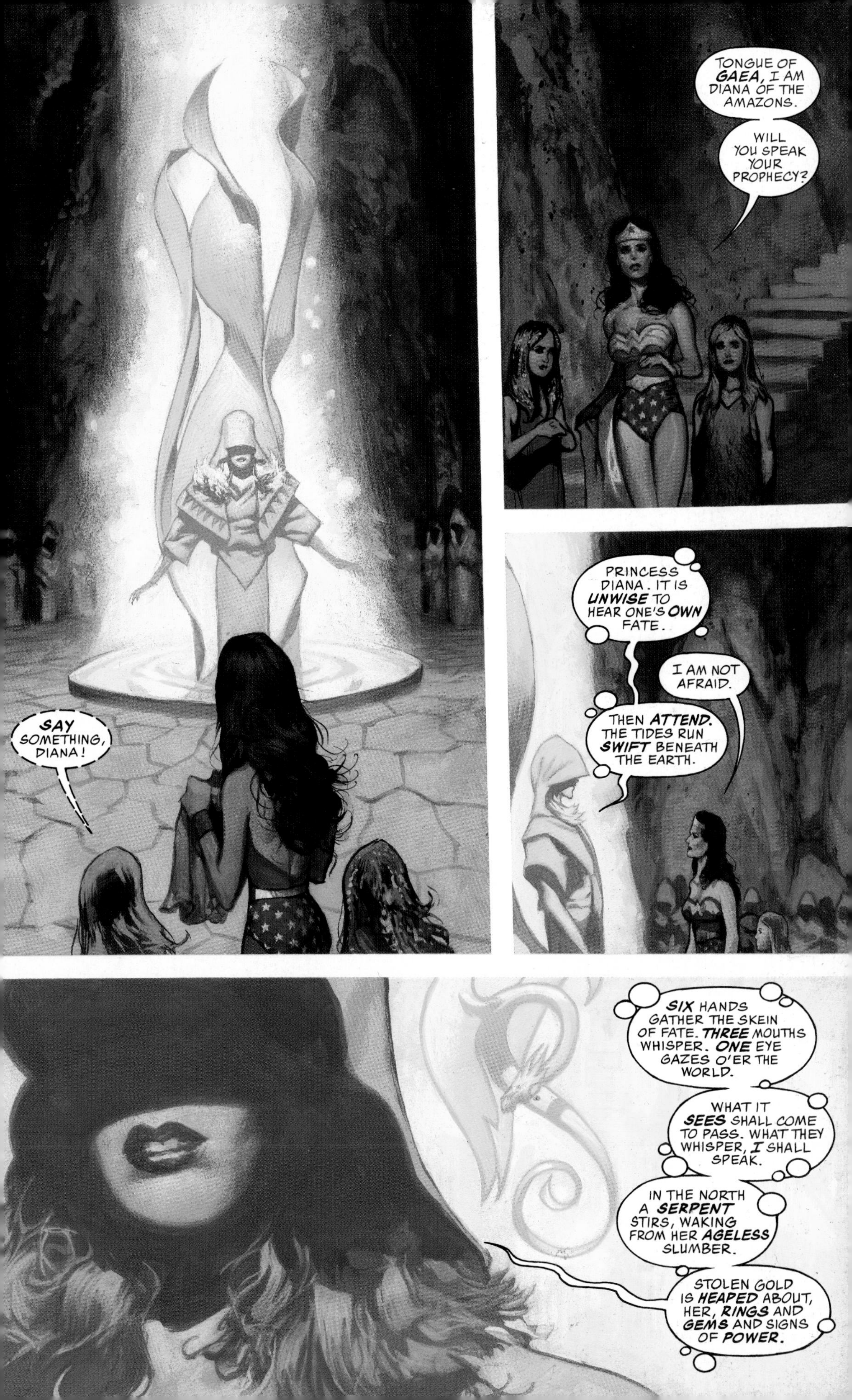
SAY SOMETHING, DIANA!
TONGUE OF GAEA, I AM DIANA OF THE AMAZONS.
WILL YOU SPEAK YOUR PROPHECY?
PRINCESS DIANA. IT IS UNWISE TO HEAR ONE'S OWN FATE.
I AM NOT AFRAID.
THEN ATTEND. THE TIDES RUN SWIFT BENEATH THE EARTH.
SIX HANDS GATHER THE SKEIN OF FATE. THREE MOUTHS WHISPER. ONE EYE GAZES O'ER THE WORLD.
WHAT IT SEES SHALL COME TO PASS. WHAT THEY WHISPER, I SHALL SPEAK.
IN THE NORTH A SERPENT STIRS, WAKING FROM HER AGELESS SLUMBER.
STOLEN GOLD IS HEAPED ABOUT, HER, RINGS AND GEMS AND SIGNS OF POWER.

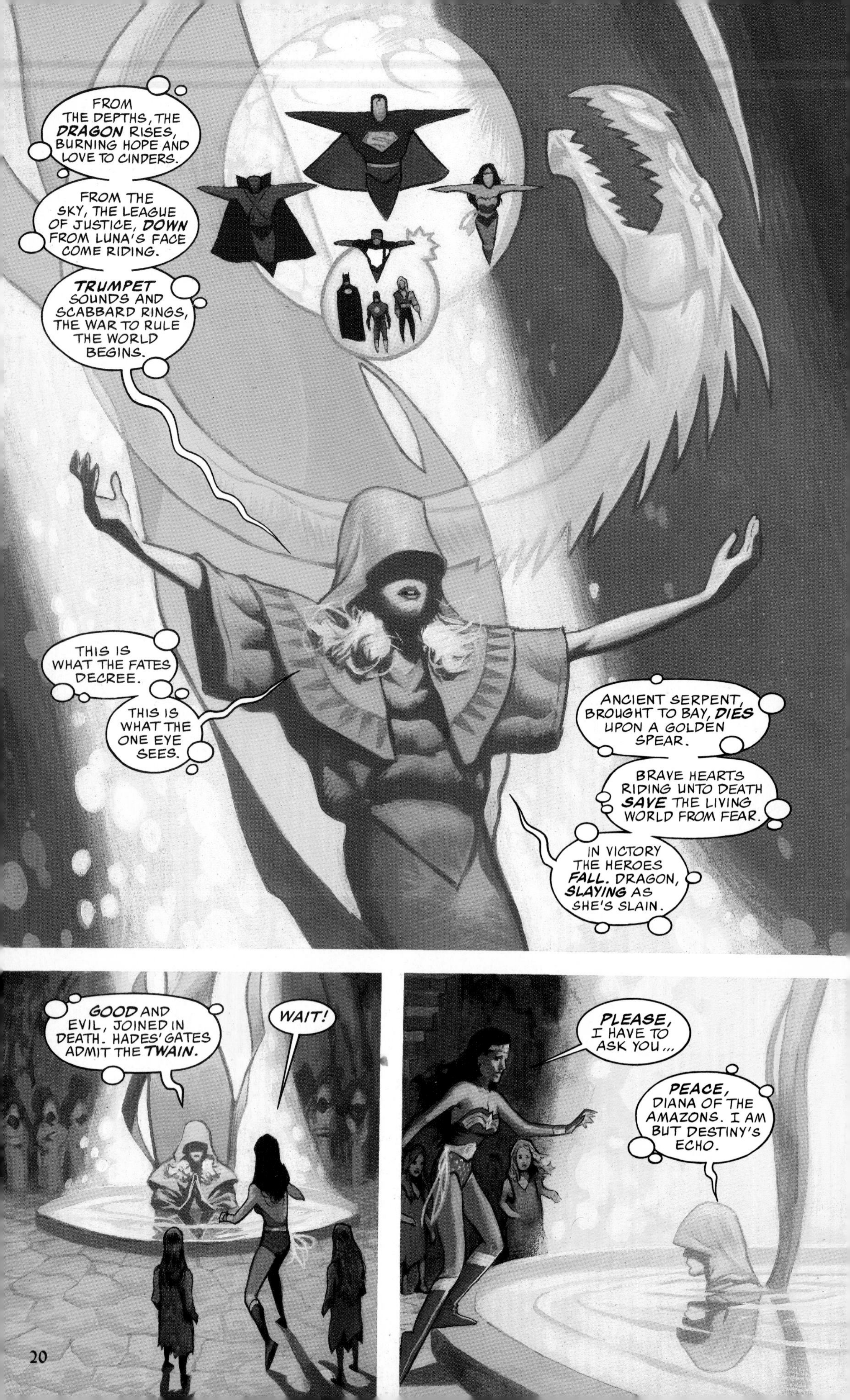
FROM THE DEPTHS, THE DRAGON RISES, BURNING HOPE AND LOVE TO CINDERS.
FROM THE SKY, THE LEAGUE OF JUSTICE, DOWN FROM LUNA'S FACE COME RIDING.
TRUMPET SOUNDS AND SCABBARD RINGS, THE WAR TO RULE THE WORLD BEGINS.
THIS IS WHAT THE FATES DECREE.
THIS IS WHAT THE ONE EYE SEES.
ANCIENT SERPENT, BROUGHT TO BAY, DIES UPON A GOLDEN SPEAR.
BRAVE HEARTS RIDING UNTO DEATH SAVE THE LIVING WORLD FROM FEAR.
IN VICTORY THE HEROES FALL. DRAGON, SLAYING AS SHE'S SLAIN.
GOOD AND EVIL, JOINED IN DEATH. HADES' GATES ADMIT THE TWAIN.
WAIT!
PLEASE, I HAVE TO ASK YOU...
PEACE, DIANA OF THE AMAZONS. I AM BUT DESTINY'S ECHO.

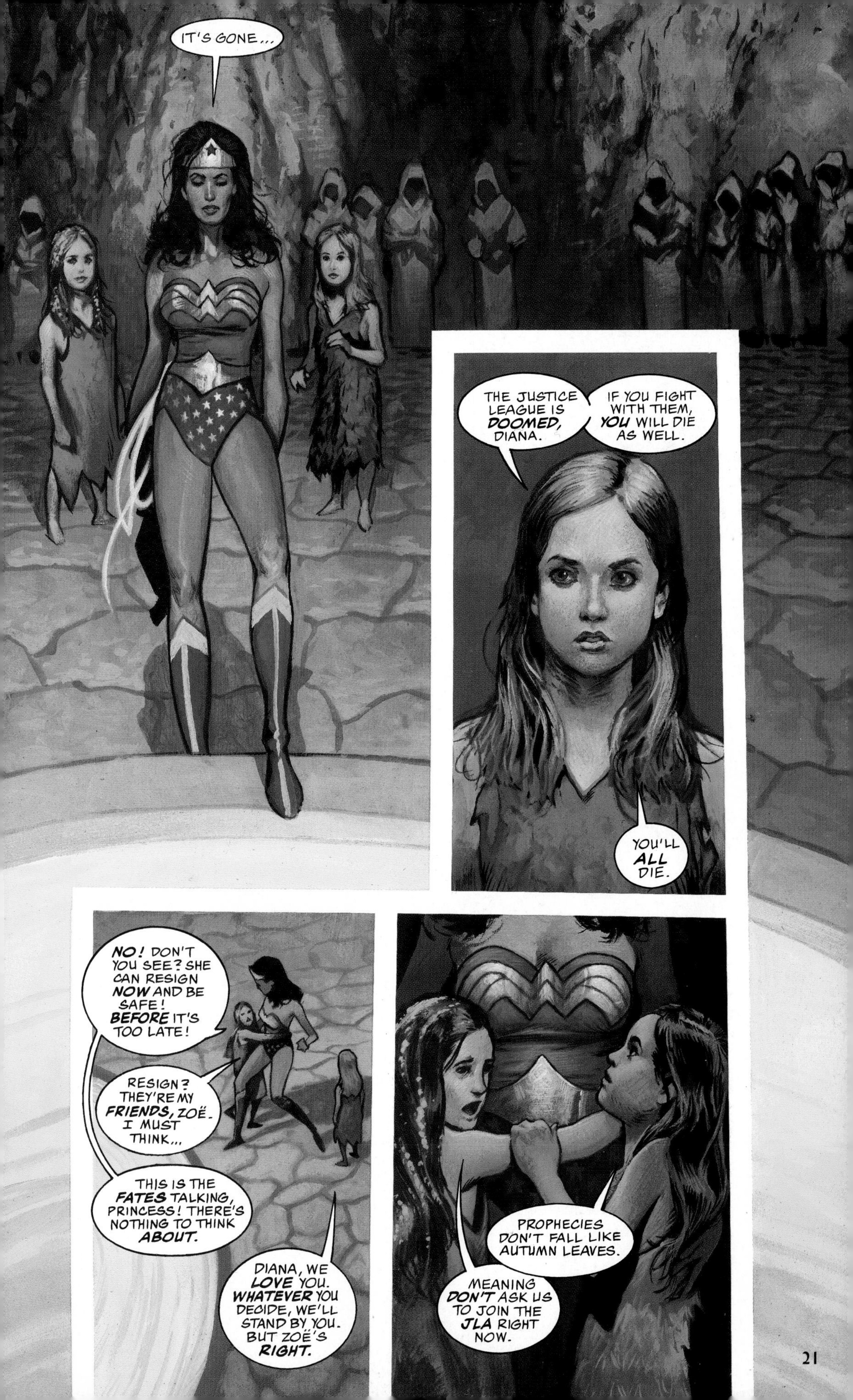
IT'S GONE...
THE JUSTICE LEAGUE IS **DOOMED,** DIANA.
IF YOU FIGHT WITH THEM, **YOU** WILL DIE AS WELL.
YOU'LL **ALL** DIE.
NO! DON'T YOU SEE? SHE CAN RESIGN **NOW** AND BE SAFE! **BEFORE** IT'S TOO LATE!
RESIGN? THEY'RE MY **FRIENDS,** ZOË. I MUST THINK...
THIS IS THE **FATES** TALKING, PRINCESS! THERE'S NOTHING TO THINK **ABOUT.**
DIANA, WE **LOVE** YOU. **WHATEVER** YOU DECIDE, WE'LL STAND BY YOU. BUT ZOË'S **RIGHT.**
PROPHECIES DON'T FALL LIKE AUTUMN LEAVES.
MEANING **DON'T** ASK US TO JOIN THE **JLA** RIGHT NOW.

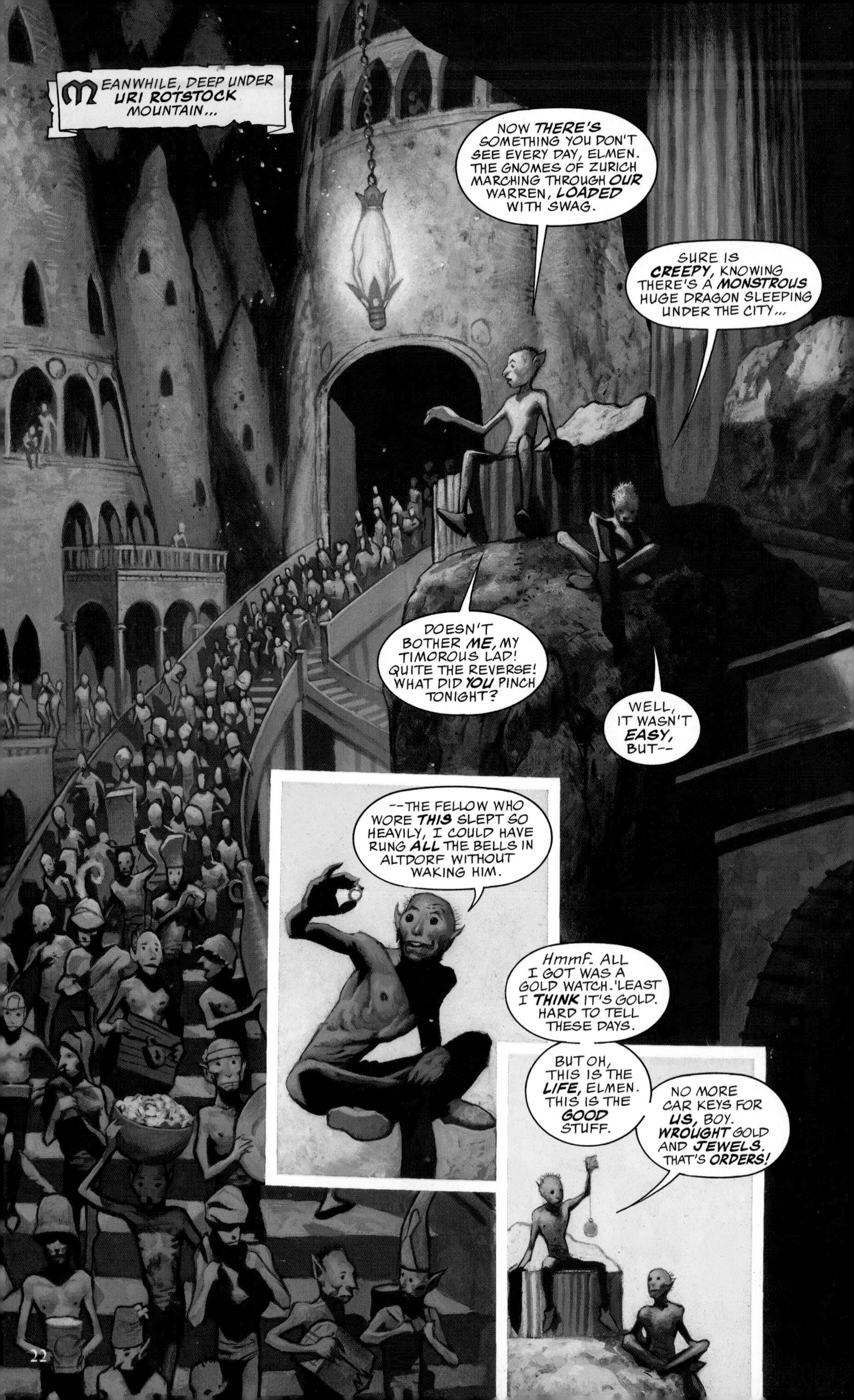
MEANWHILE, DEEP UNDER URI ROTSTOCK MOUNTAIN...
NOW THERE'S SOMETHING YOU DON'T SEE EVERY DAY, ELMEN. THE GNOMES OF ZURICH MARCHING THROUGH OUR WARREN, LOADED WITH SWAG.
SURE IS CREEPY, KNOWING THERE'S A MONSTROUS HUGE DRAGON SLEEPING UNDER THE CITY...
DOESN'T BOTHER ME, MY TIMOROUS LAD! QUITE THE REVERSE! WHAT DID YOU PINCH TONIGHT?
WELL, IT WASN'T EASY, BUT--
--THE FELLOW WHO WORE THIS SLEPT SO HEAVILY, I COULD HAVE RUNG ALL THE BELLS IN ALTDORF WITHOUT WAKING HIM.
HmmF. ALL I GOT WAS A GOLD WATCH. 'LEAST I THINK IT'S GOLD. HARD TO TELL THESE DAYS.
BUT OH, THIS IS THE LIFE, ELMEN. THIS IS THE GOOD STUFF.
NO MORE CAR KEYS FOR US, BOY. WROUGHT GOLD AND JEWELS. THAT'S ORDERS!

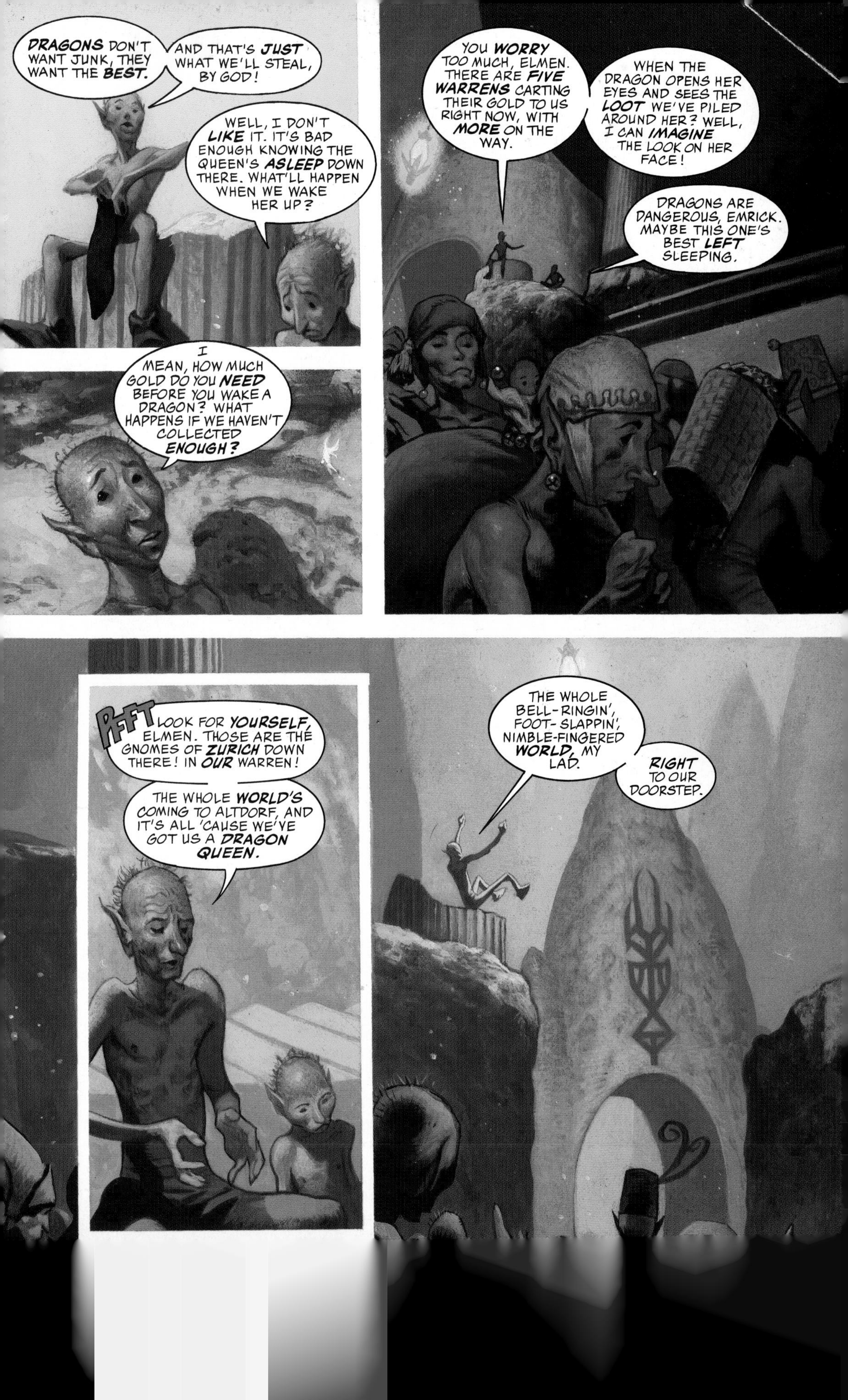
DRAGONS DON'T WANT JUNK, THEY WANT THE BEST.
AND THAT'S JUST WHAT WE'LL STEAL, BY GOD!
WELL, I DON'T LIKE IT. IT'S BAD ENOUGH KNOWING THE QUEEN'S ASLEEP DOWN THERE. WHAT'LL HAPPEN WHEN WE WAKE HER UP?
I MEAN, HOW MUCH GOLD DO YOU NEED BEFORE YOU WAKE A DRAGON? WHAT HAPPENS IF WE HAVEN'T COLLECTED ENOUGH?
YOU WORRY TOO MUCH, ELMEN. THERE ARE FIVE WARRENS CARTING THEIR GOLD TO US RIGHT NOW, WITH MORE ON THE WAY.
WHEN THE DRAGON OPENS HER EYES AND SEES THE LOOT WE'VE PILED AROUND HER? WELL, I CAN IMAGINE THE LOOK ON HER FACE!
DRAGONS ARE DANGEROUS, EMRICK. MAYBE THIS ONE'S BEST LEFT SLEEPING.
PFFT
LOOK FOR YOURSELF, ELMEN. THOSE ARE THE GNOMES OF ZURICH DOWN THERE! IN OUR WARREN!
THE WHOLE WORLD'S COMING TO ALTDORF, AND IT'S ALL 'CAUSE WE'VE GOT US A DRAGON QUEEN.
THE WHOLE BELL-RINGIN', FOOT-SLAPPIN', NIMBLE-FINGERED WORLD, MY LAD.
RIGHT TO OUR DOORSTEP.

FIVE DAYS LATER.

TWO HUNDRED THIRTY THOUSAND MILES **STRAIGHT UP.**

THE **WATCHTOWER.**

IF YOU'VE ALL SETTLED IN, LET'S GET **STARTED.**

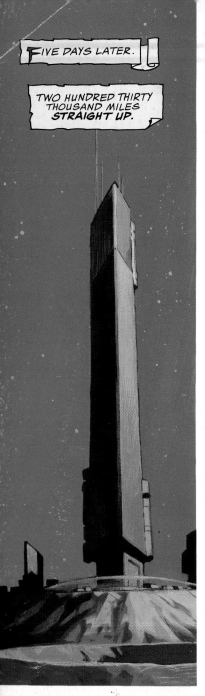

THERE ARE SEVERAL CRISES THAT DESERVE OUR ATTENTION. **NONE** REQUIRE OUR **UNIFIED** STRENGTH.

FIRST, IT SEEMS THE **AMAZON RIVER** IS BEING CHOKED BY SOME SORT OF **FAST-GROWING** WATER PLANT.

FLOODING NEAR THE RIVER'S HEADWATERS IS THREATENING A **NUMBER** OF LOW-LYING TOWNS AND VILLAGES.

THE ARCH VILLAIN **POISON IVY** HAS BEEN SIGHTED IN THE AREA, AND IS SUS-PECTED OF HAVING **ENGINEERED** THE FLOODING.

SECOND, A **SUPER-TANKER** HAS RUN AGROUND NEAR MESSINA, SICILY. THE SEA'S GETTING ROUGH, AND THERE IS CONCERN THAT THE SHIP'S **CARGO** MAY BEGIN LEAKING.

DIANA IS ONLY **DIMLY** AWARE OF THE MARTIAN MANHUNTER'S VOICE.

EVER SINCE HER ENCOUNTER WITH THE **ORACLE,** SHE HAS BEEN **GRAPPLING** WITH THE TRUTH ...

... THAT HER **FRIENDS,** ALL THESE VIBRANT, HEROIC PEOPLE ARE LIVING ON **BORROWED** TIME.

AND YET, WHILE HER **CONSCIOUS** MIND IS OVERWHELMED BY GRIEF--

--THERE IS **ANOTHER** PART OF HER, **WALLED OFF** FROM DISTRACTIONS LIKE REGRET OR FEAR, WHICH SHOWS **NO** HESITATION.

THAT PART OF HER ALREADY KNOWS WHAT SHE MUST DO.

THIRD. FIGHTING'S BROKEN OUT AGAIN IN THE BALKANS. THERE ARE THE USUAL WORRIES ABOUT IT SPILLING OVER INTO NEIGHBORING NATIONS.

WONDER WOMAN...?

ON A LIGHTER NOTE, ASTRONOMERS HAVE RECORDED ERRATIC SOLAR FLARE ACTIVITY, ORIGINATING ON THE FAR SIDE OF THE SUN.

HEY, ARE YOU ALL RIGHT?

PROBABLY NOTHING SINISTER, BUT IT'S OUT OF CYCLE, AND BEARS CHECKING.

"LIGHTER NOTE"? WAS THAT SUPPOSED TO BE A JOKE?

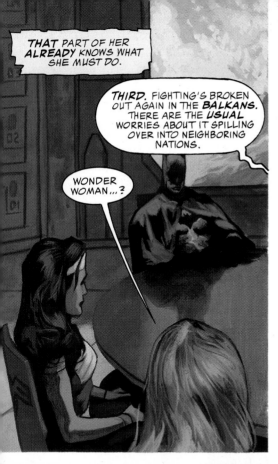

OH, AND THAT ASTEROID WE PICKED UP A FEW MONTHS BACK SHOULD BE DEFLECTED BEFORE IT GETS ANY DEEPER INTO EARTH'S GRAVITY WELL.

YEAH, I HAVE THAT ONE WORKED OUT. I'LL JUST BUMP IT INTO ONE OF THE TROJAN POINTS.

GOOD. FINALLY, THERE HAVEN'T BEEN ANY SPECTACULAR CRIMES RECENTLY--

--BUT THERE HAS BEEN A BIZARRE RASH OF BURGLARIES THROUGHOUT THE ALPINE REGIONS OF WESTERN EUROPE. MOSTLY GOLD AND JEWELRY.

INTERPOL IS PURSUING SOME LEADS, BUT HAVE NO REAL SUSPECTS. IT'S STRANGE ENOUGH THAT WE MIGHT WANT TO KEEP AN EYE ON THAT, TOO.

THAT'S IT. ANY QUESTIONS?

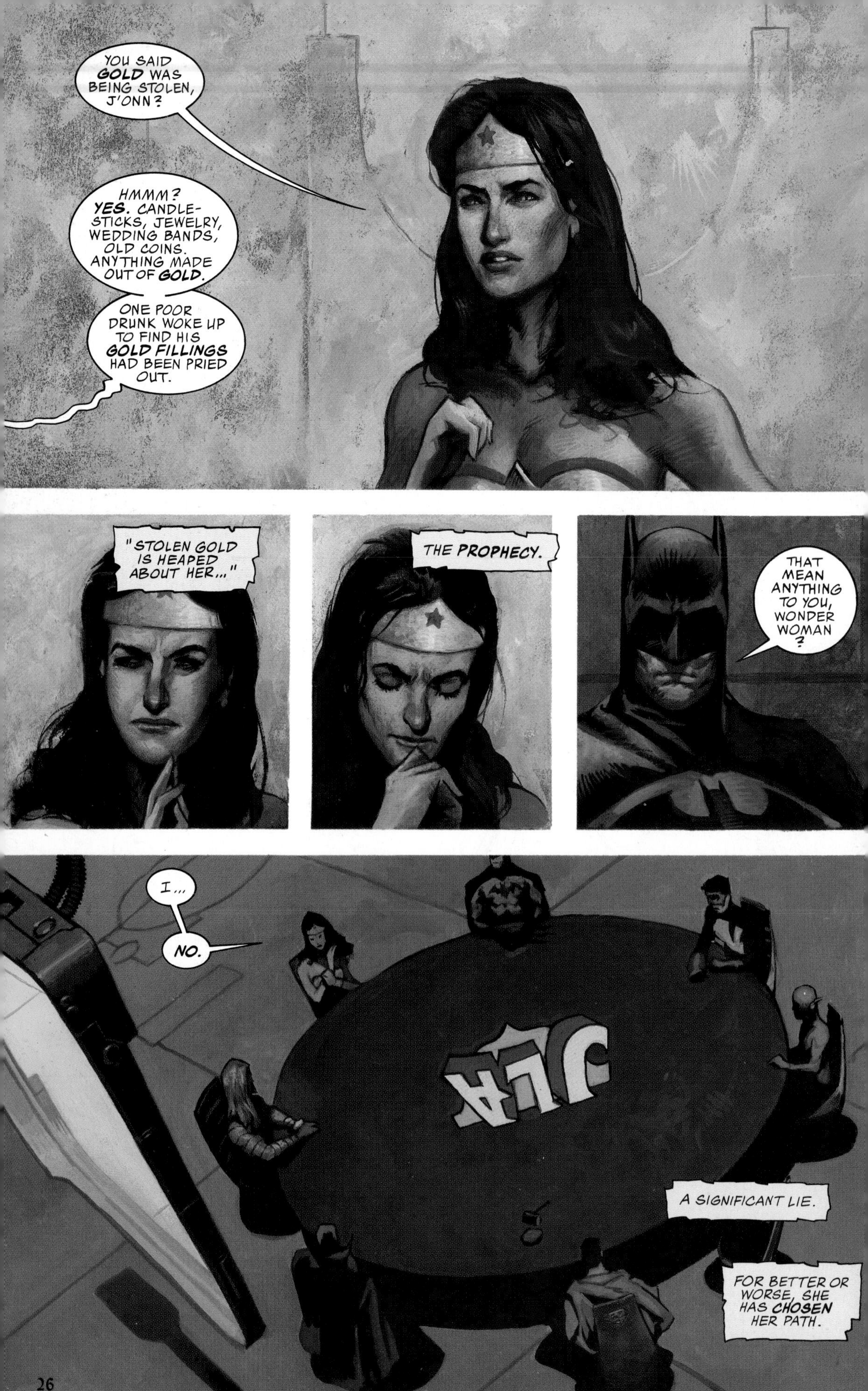
YOU SAID GOLD WAS BEING STOLEN, J'ONN?
HMMM? YES. CANDLE-STICKS, JEWELRY, WEDDING BANDS, OLD COINS. ANYTHING MADE OUT OF GOLD.
ONE POOR DRUNK WOKE UP TO FIND HIS GOLD FILLINGS HAD BEEN PRIED OUT.
"STOLEN GOLD IS HEAPED ABOUT HER..."
THE PROPHECY.
THAT MEAN ANYTHING TO YOU, WONDER WOMAN?
I...
NO.
JLA
A SIGNIFICANT LIE.
FOR BETTER OR WORSE, SHE HAS CHOSEN HER PATH.

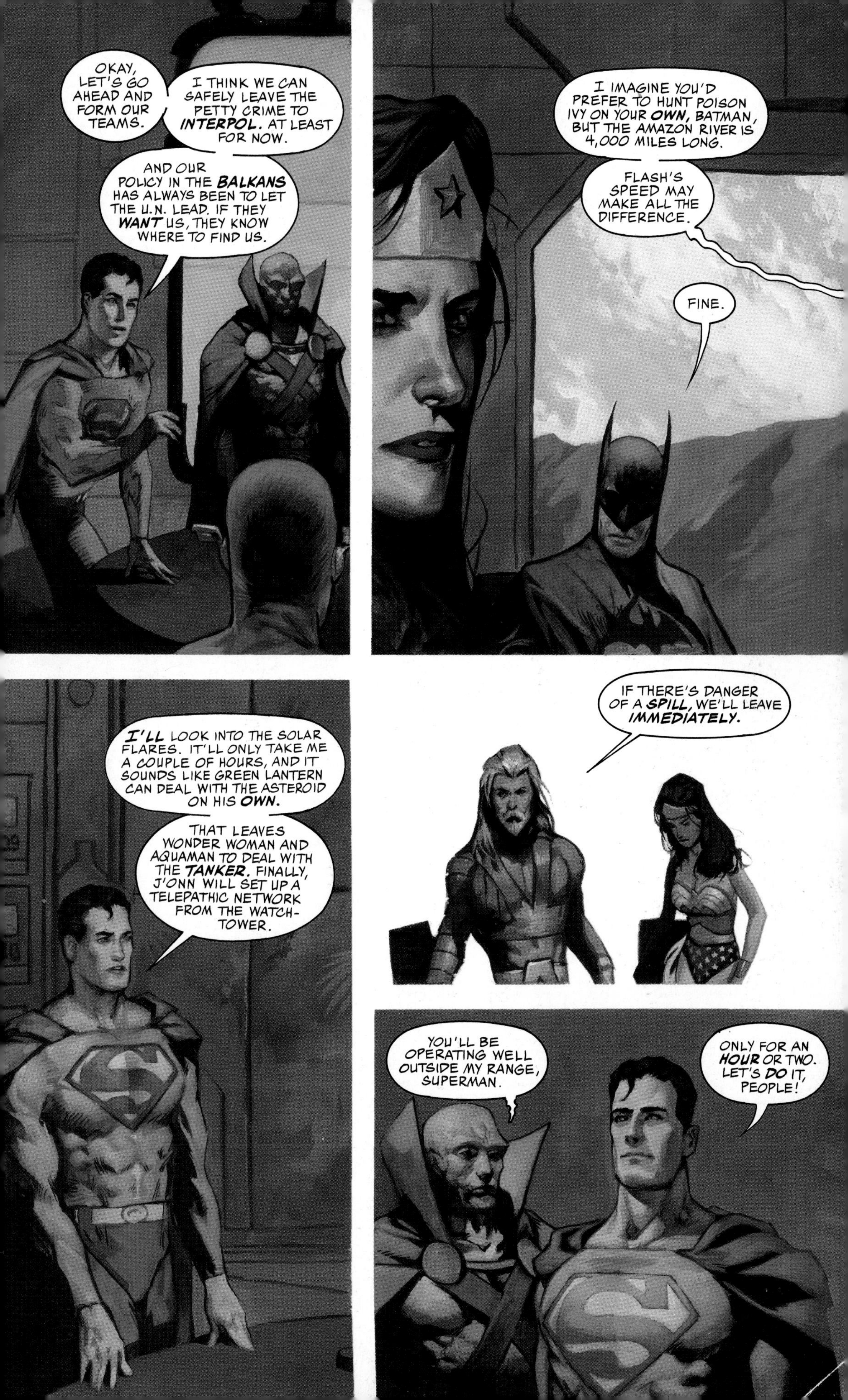
OKAY, LET'S GO AHEAD AND FORM OUR TEAMS.
I THINK WE CAN SAFELY LEAVE THE PETTY CRIME TO INTERPOL. AT LEAST FOR NOW.
AND OUR POLICY IN THE BALKANS HAS ALWAYS BEEN TO LET THE U.N. LEAD. IF THEY WANT US, THEY KNOW WHERE TO FIND US.
I IMAGINE YOU'D PREFER TO HUNT POISON IVY ON YOUR OWN, BATMAN, BUT THE AMAZON RIVER IS 4,000 MILES LONG.
FLASH'S SPEED MAY MAKE ALL THE DIFFERENCE.
FINE.
I'LL LOOK INTO THE SOLAR FLARES. IT'LL ONLY TAKE ME A COUPLE OF HOURS, AND IT SOUNDS LIKE GREEN LANTERN CAN DEAL WITH THE ASTEROID ON HIS OWN.
THAT LEAVES WONDER WOMAN AND AQUAMAN TO DEAL WITH THE TANKER. FINALLY, J'ONN WILL SET UP A TELEPATHIC NETWORK FROM THE WATCH-TOWER.
IF THERE'S DANGER OF A SPILL, WE'LL LEAVE IMMEDIATELY.
YOU'LL BE OPERATING WELL OUTSIDE MY RANGE, SUPERMAN.
ONLY FOR AN HOUR OR TWO. LET'S DO IT, PEOPLE!

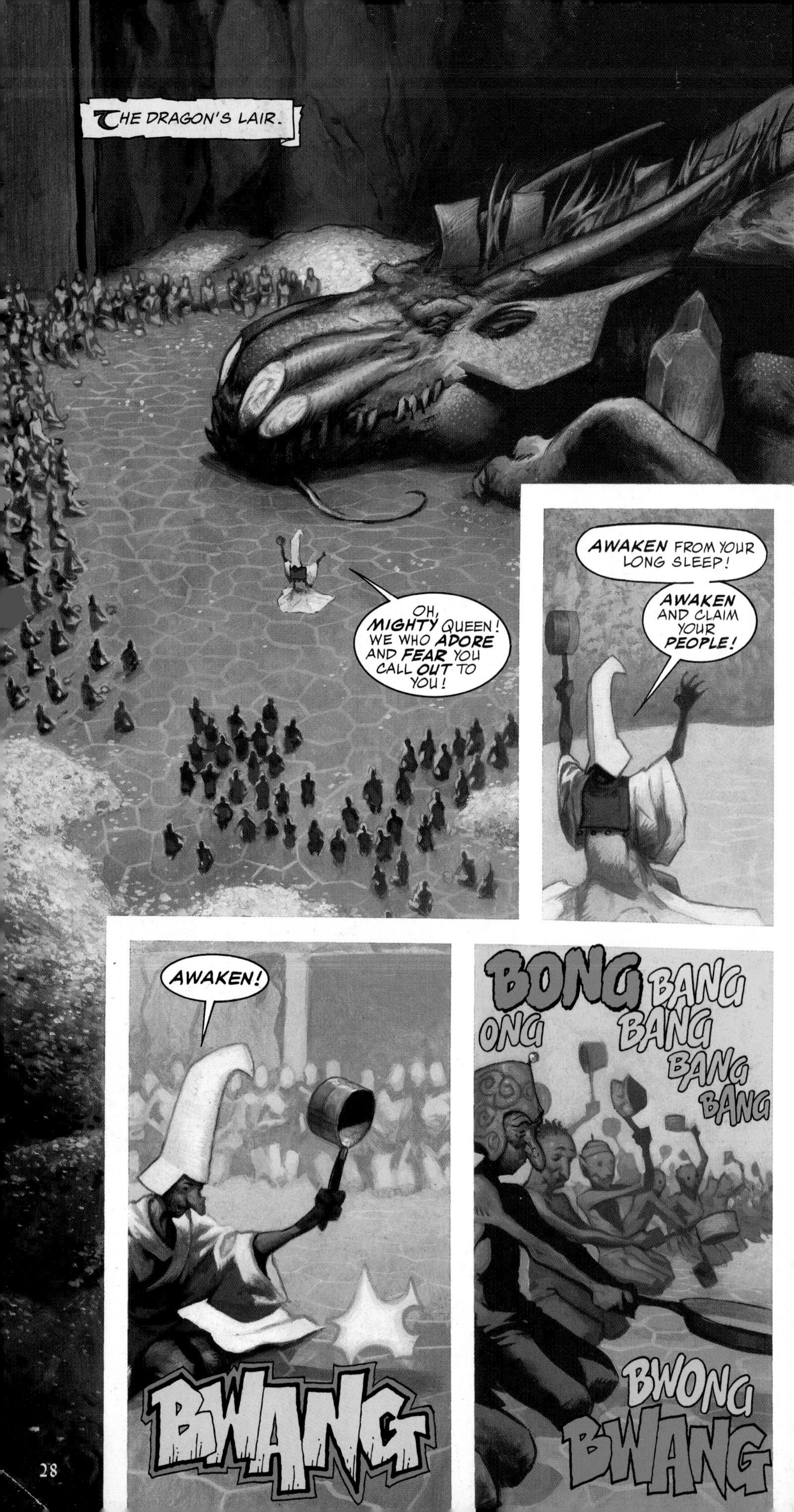
THE DRAGON'S LAIR.
OH, MIGHTY QUEEN! WE WHO ADORE AND FEAR YOU CALL OUT TO YOU!
AWAKEN FROM YOUR LONG SLEEP!
AWAKEN AND CLAIM YOUR PEOPLE!
AWAKEN!
BWANG
BONG BANG
ONG
BANG
BANG
BANG
BWONG
BWANG

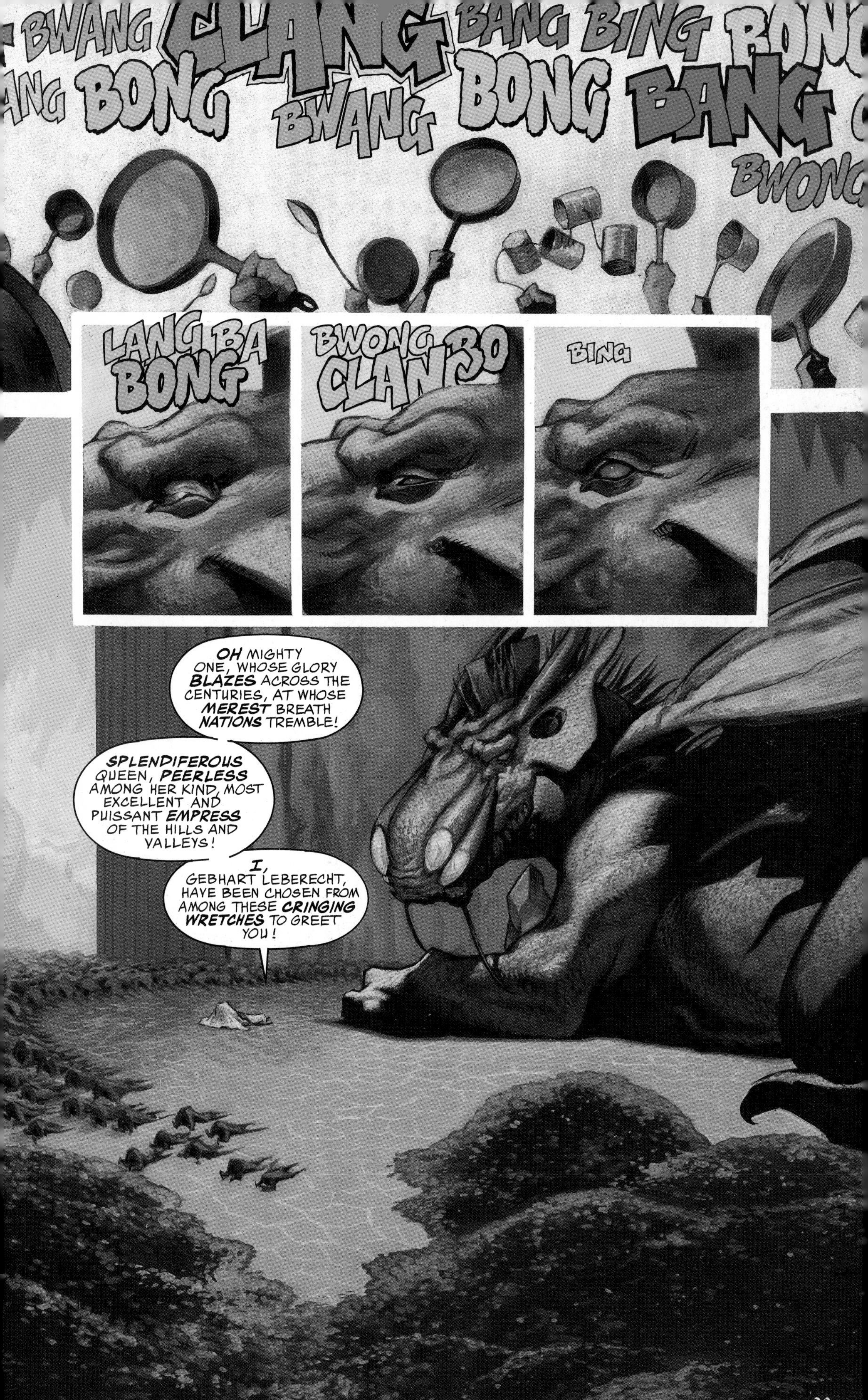
BWANG CLANG BANG BING BONG
BONG
BWANG BONG BANG
BWONG
LANG BA BONG
BWONG CLANGBO
BING
OH MIGHTY ONE, WHOSE GLORY BLAZES ACROSS THE CENTURIES, AT WHOSE MEREST BREATH NATIONS TREMBLE!
SPLENDIFEROUS QUEEN, PEERLESS AMONG HER KIND, MOST EXCELLENT AND PUISSANT EMPRESS OF THE HILLS AND VALLEYS!
I, GEBHART LEBERECHT, HAVE BEEN CHOSEN FROM AMONG THESE CRINGING WRETCHES TO GREET YOU!

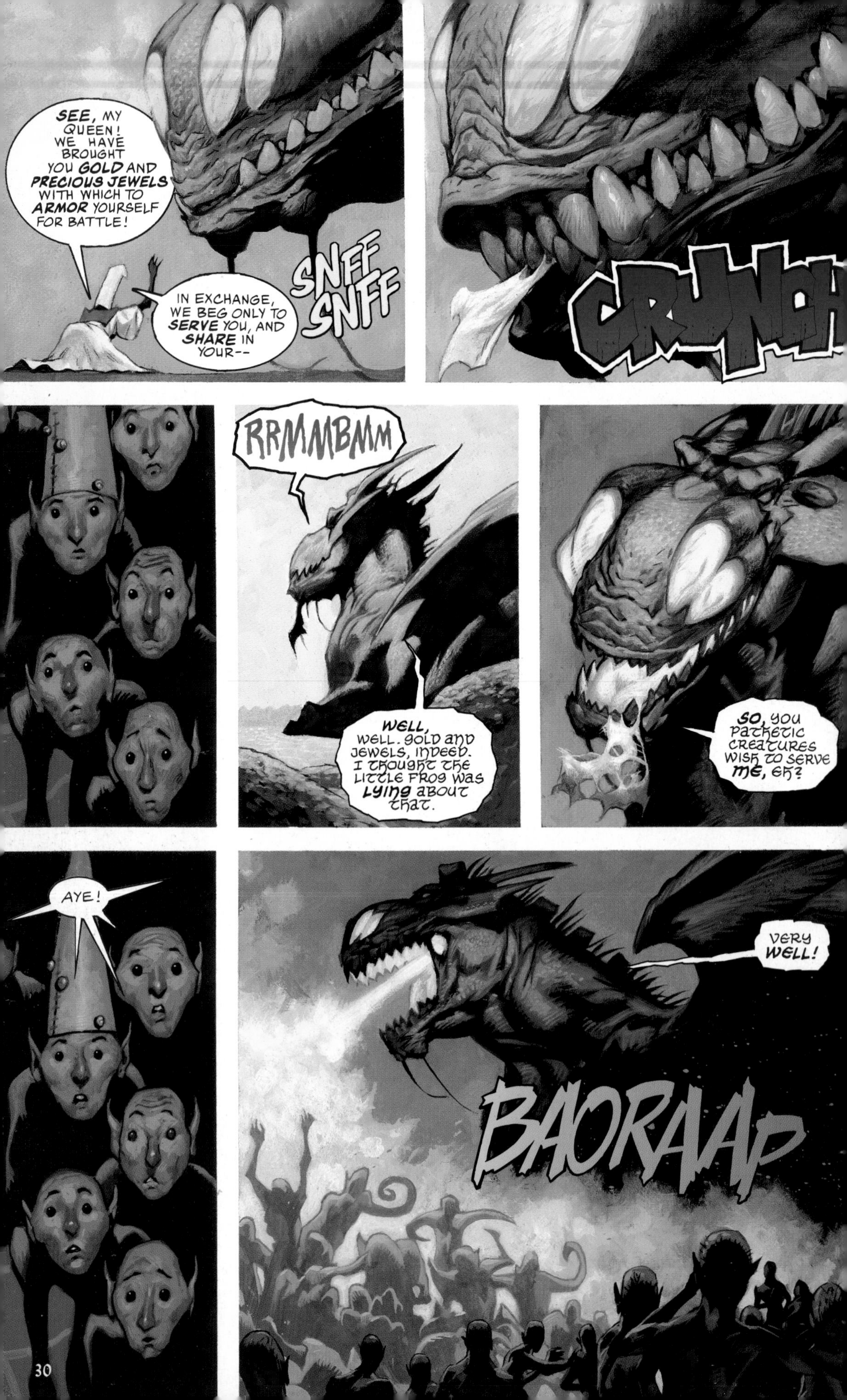
SEE, MY QUEEN! WE HAVE BROUGHT YOU GOLD AND PRECIOUS JEWELS WITH WHICH TO ARMOR YOURSELF FOR BATTLE!
IN EXCHANGE, WE BEG ONLY TO SERVE YOU, AND SHARE IN YOUR--
SNFF SNFF
CRUNCH
RRMMBMM
WELL, WELL. GOLD AND JEWELS, INDEED. I THOUGHT THE LITTLE FROG WAS LYING ABOUT THAT.
SO, YOU PATHETIC CREATURES WISH TO SERVE ME, EH?
AYE!
VERY WELL!
BAORAAP

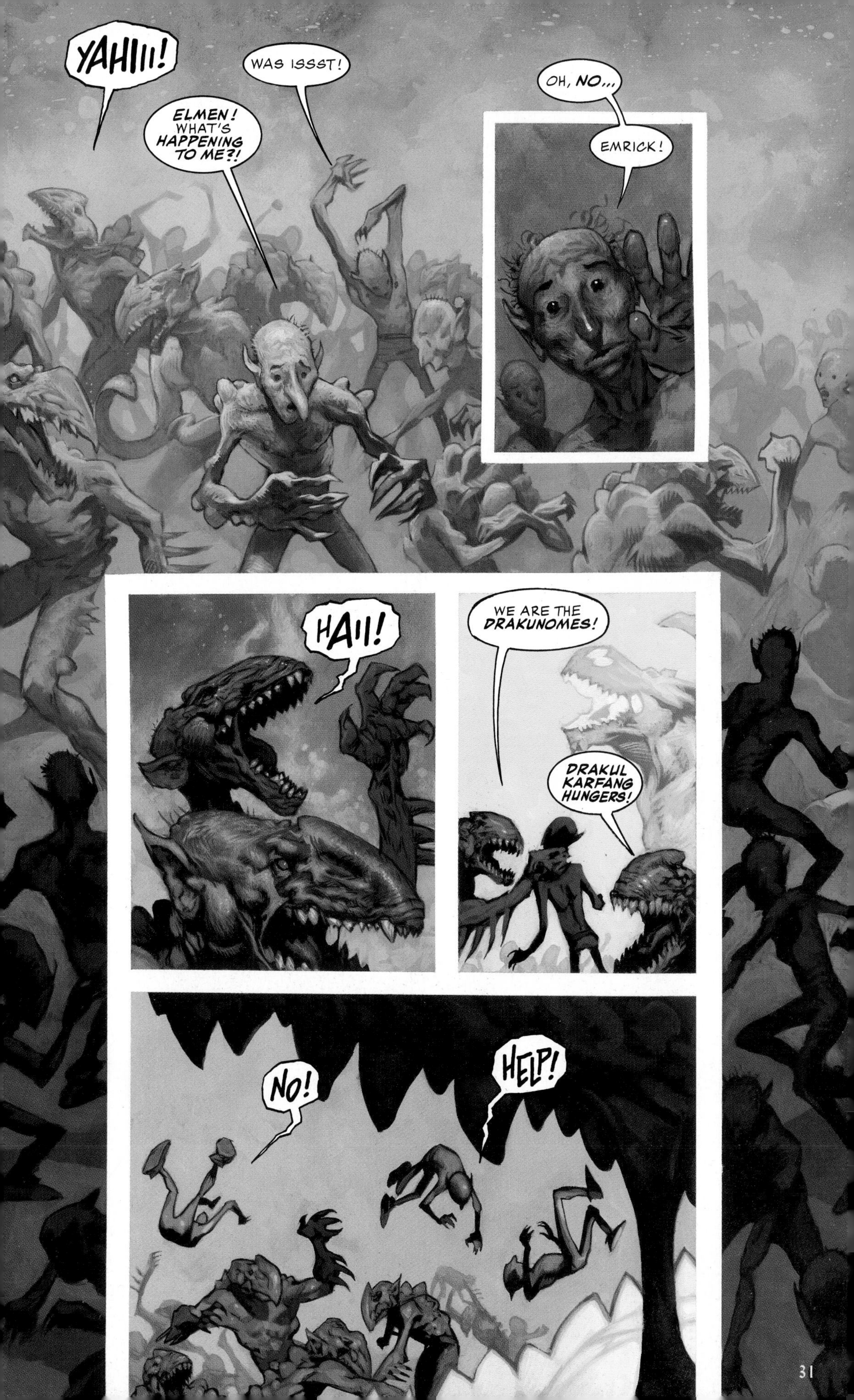
YAHIII!
ELMEN! WHAT'S HAPPENING TO ME?!
WAS ISSST!
OH, NO...
EMRICK!
HAII!
WE ARE THE DRAKUNOMES!
DRAKUL KARFANG HUNGERS!
NO!
HELP!

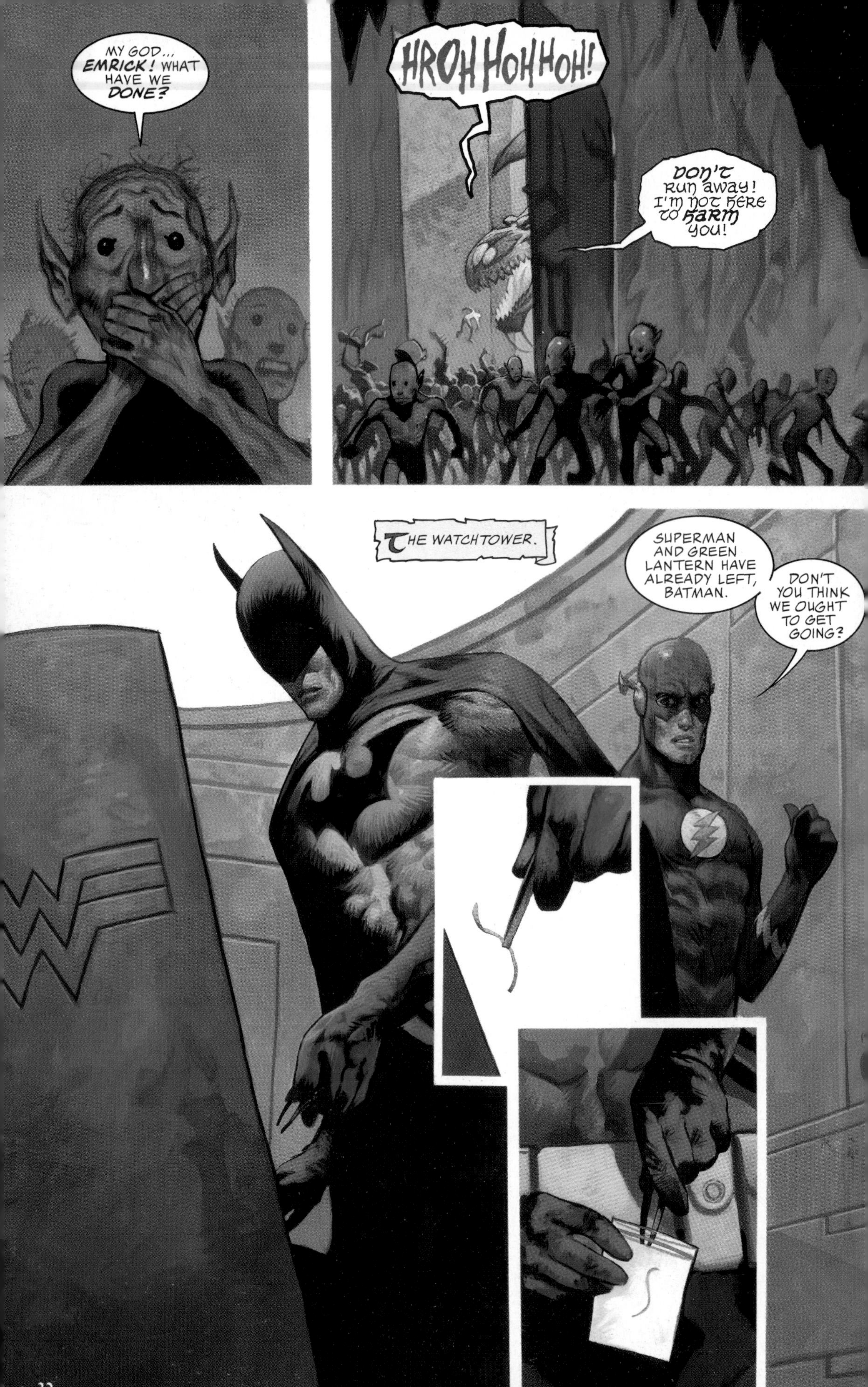
MY GOD... EMRICK! WHAT HAVE WE DONE?
HROH HOH HOH!
DON'T RUN AWAY! I'M NOT HERE TO HARM YOU!
THE WATCHTOWER.
SUPERMAN AND GREEN LANTERN HAVE ALREADY LEFT, BATMAN.
DON'T YOU THINK WE OUGHT TO GET GOING?

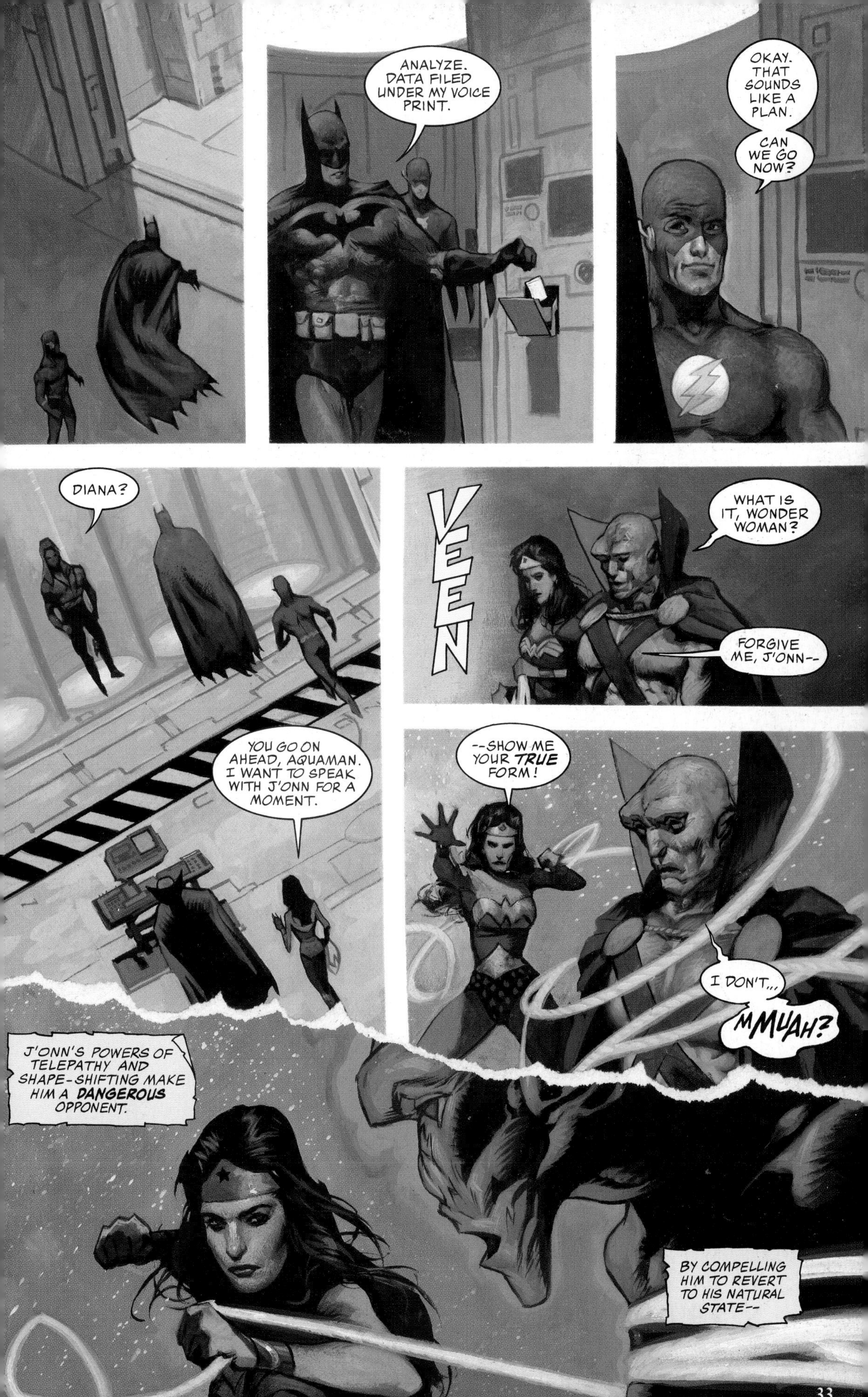
ANALYZE. DATA FILED UNDER MY VOICE PRINT.
OKAY. THAT SOUNDS LIKE A PLAN.
CAN WE GO NOW?
DIANA?
YOU GO ON AHEAD, AQUAMAN. I WANT TO SPEAK WITH J'ONN FOR A MOMENT.
VEEN
WHAT IS IT, WONDER WOMAN?
FORGIVE ME, J'ONN--
--SHOW ME YOUR TRUE FORM!
I DON'T...
MMUAH?
J'ONN'S POWERS OF TELEPATHY AND SHAPE-SHIFTING MAKE HIM A DANGEROUS OPPONENT.
BY COMPELLING HIM TO REVERT TO HIS NATURAL STATE--

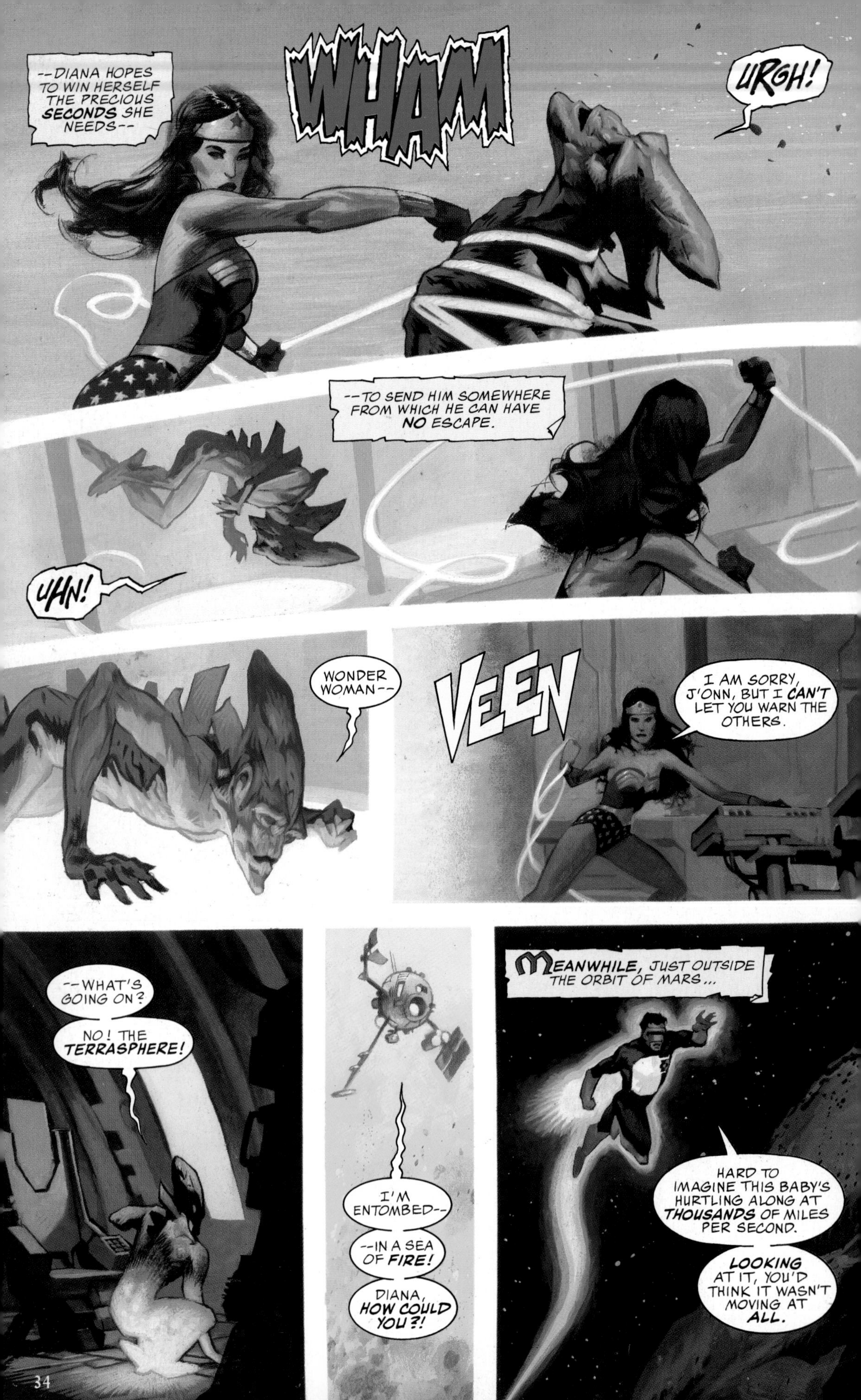
--DIANA HOPES TO WIN HERSELF THE PRECIOUS SECONDS SHE NEEDS--
WHAM
URGH!
--TO SEND HIM SOMEWHERE FROM WHICH HE CAN HAVE NO ESCAPE.
UHN!
WONDER WOMAN--
VEEN
I AM SORRY, J'ONN, BUT I CAN'T LET YOU WARN THE OTHERS.
--WHAT'S GOING ON?
NO! THE TERRASPHERE!
I'M ENTOMBED--
--IN A SEA OF FIRE!
DIANA, HOW COULD YOU?!
MEANWHILE, JUST OUTSIDE THE ORBIT OF MARS...
HARD TO IMAGINE THIS BABY'S HURTLING ALONG AT THOUSANDS OF MILES PER SECOND.
LOOKING AT IT, YOU'D THINK IT WASN'T MOVING AT ALL.

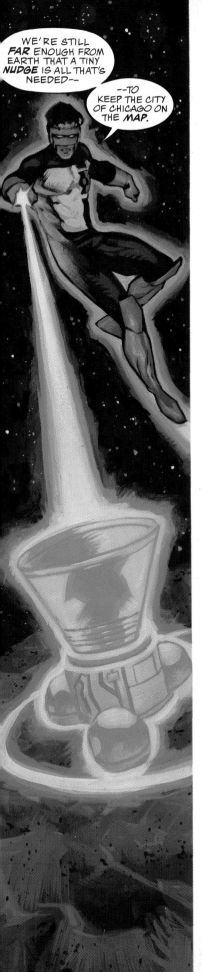

WE'RE STILL *FAR* ENOUGH FROM EARTH THAT A TINY *NUDGE* IS ALL THAT'S NEEDED--

--TO KEEP THE CITY OF CHICAGO ON THE *MAP.*

I *WONDER* WHAT'S KEEPING J'ONN?

HE'S USUALLY BUTTING IN ABOUT NOW, TELLING ME SIX WAYS *NOT* TO SCREW UP.

*T*HE AMAZON RIVER, DEEP IN THE BRAZILIAN RAIN FOREST.

MAN, J'ONN WASN'T *KIDDING.* IT'S WALL TO WALL LILY PADS DOWN THERE.

THAT'S HER. POISON IVY'S DOWN BY THAT WATER-FALL.

YOU DEAL WITH HER. *I'LL* LOOK INTO OUR *OTHER* LITTLE PROBLEM.

Huh? WHAT PROBLEM?

THE MARTIAN MANHUNTER'S TELEPATHIC LINK.

BUT... HE HASN'T SET IT *UP* YET.

THAT'S *RIGHT.*

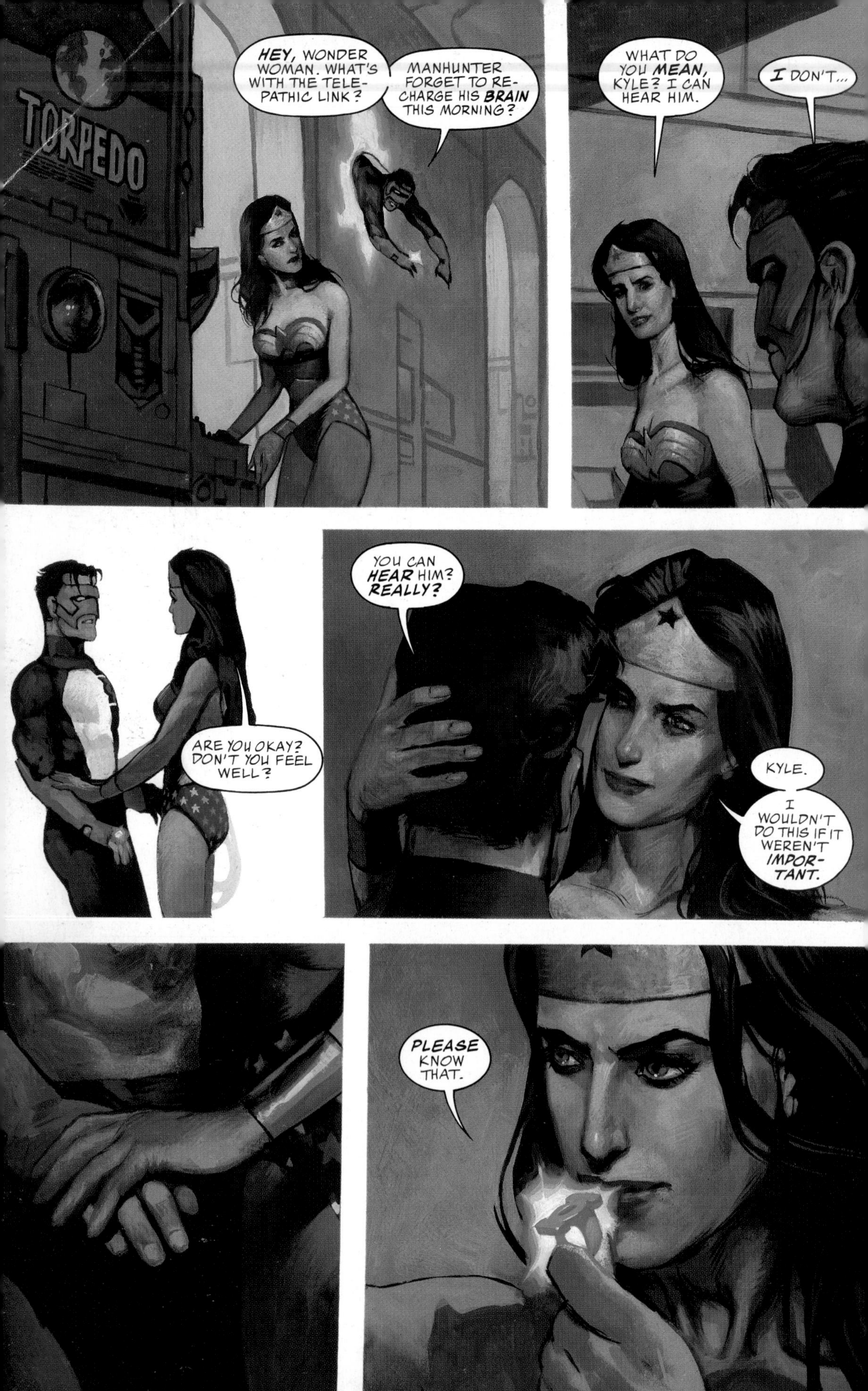
TORPEDO
HEY, WONDER WOMAN. WHAT'S WITH THE TELE-PATHIC LINK?
MANHUNTER FORGET TO RE-CHARGE HIS BRAIN THIS MORNING?
WHAT DO YOU MEAN, KYLE? I CAN HEAR HIM.
I DON'T...
ARE YOU OKAY? DON'T YOU FEEL WELL?
YOU CAN HEAR HIM? REALLY?
KYLE.
I WOULDN'T DO THIS IF IT WEREN'T IMPOR-TANT.
PLEASE KNOW THAT.

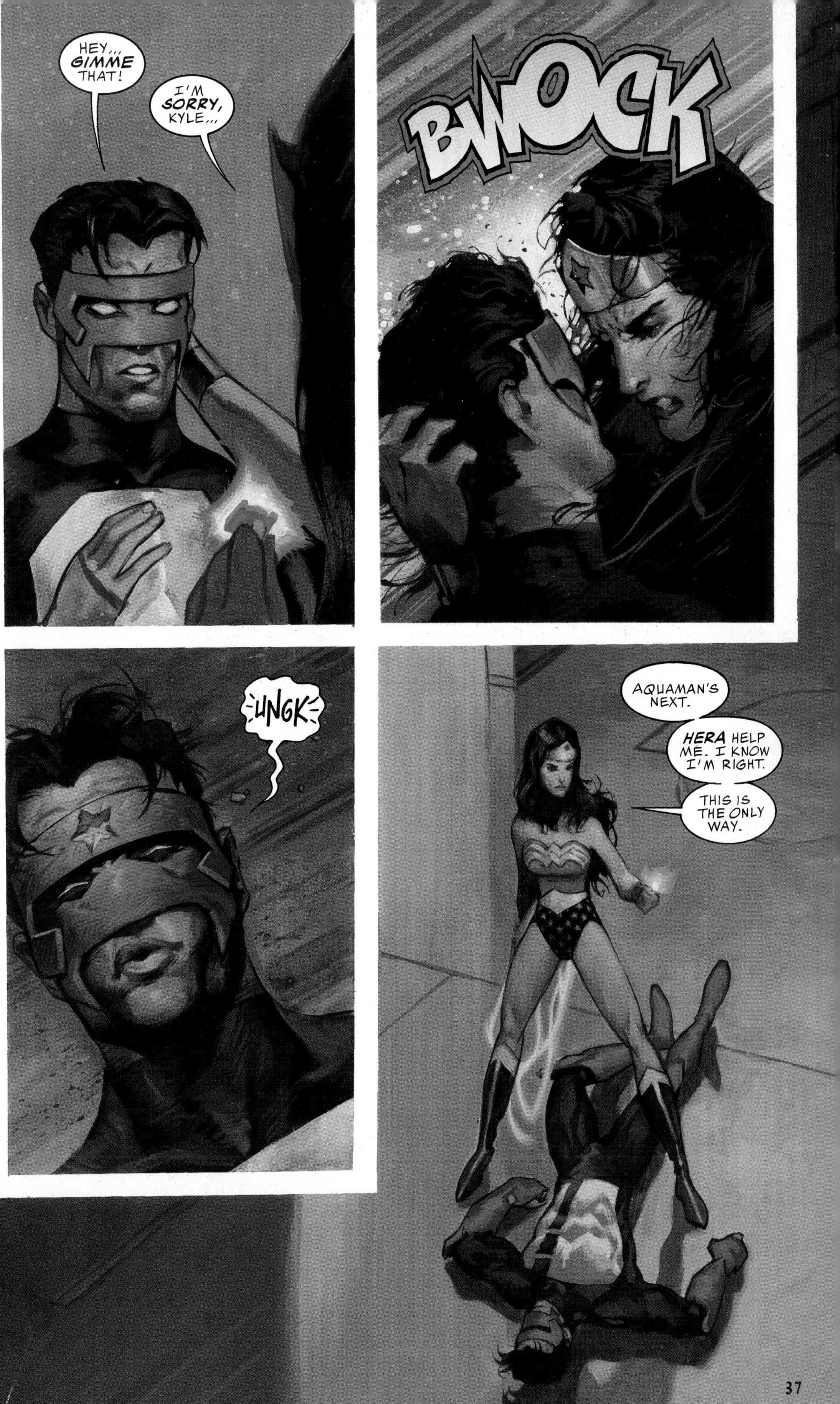

HEY... GIMME THAT!
I'M SORRY, KYLE...
BWOCK
UNGK
AQUAMAN'S NEXT.
HERA HELP ME. I KNOW I'M RIGHT.
THIS IS THE ONLY WAY.

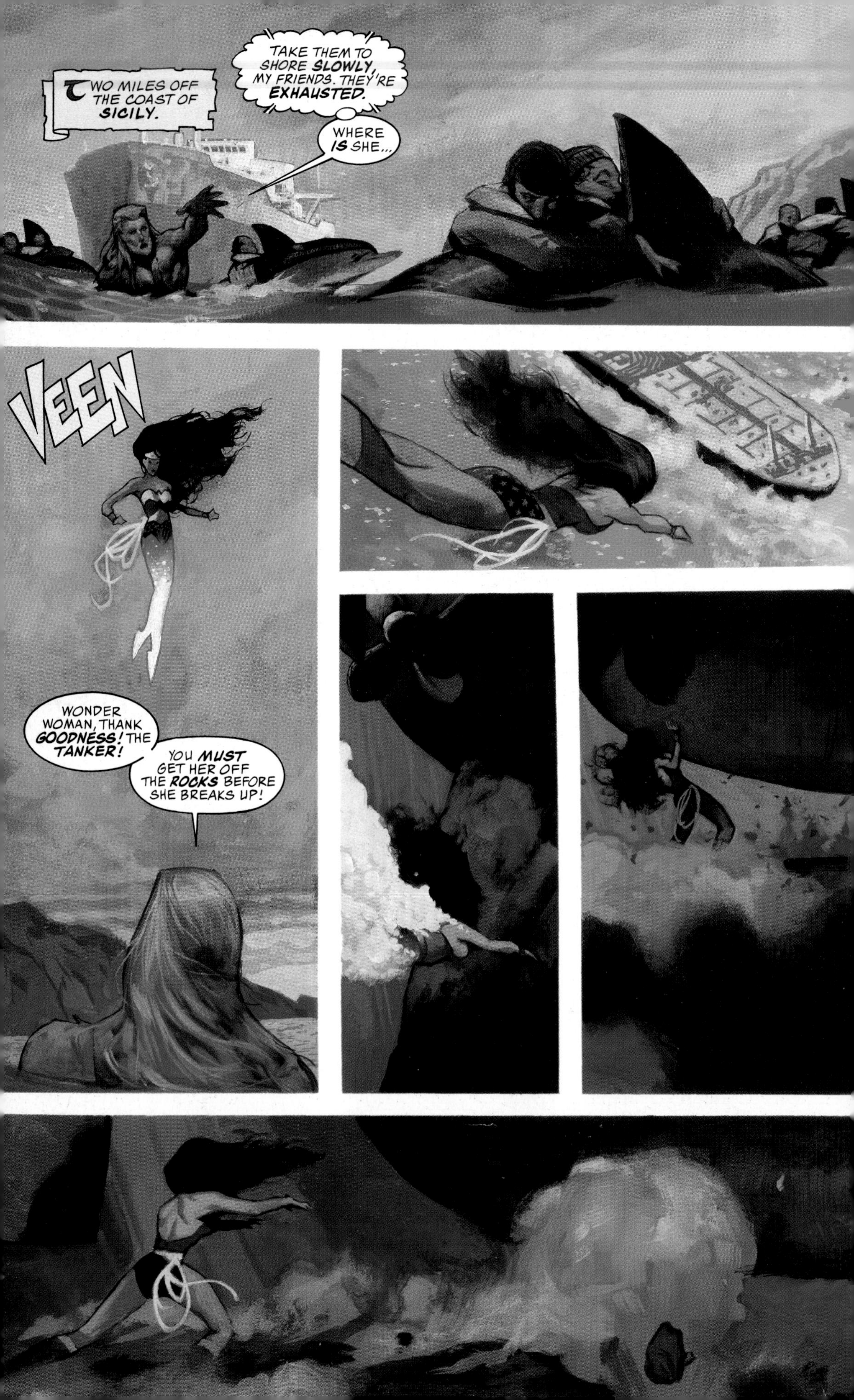
TWO MILES OFF THE COAST OF SICILY.
TAKE THEM TO SHORE SLOWLY, MY FRIENDS. THEY'RE EXHAUSTED.
WHERE IS SHE...
VEEN
WONDER WOMAN, THANK GOODNESS! THE TANKER!
YOU MUST GET HER OFF THE ROCKS BEFORE SHE BREAKS UP!

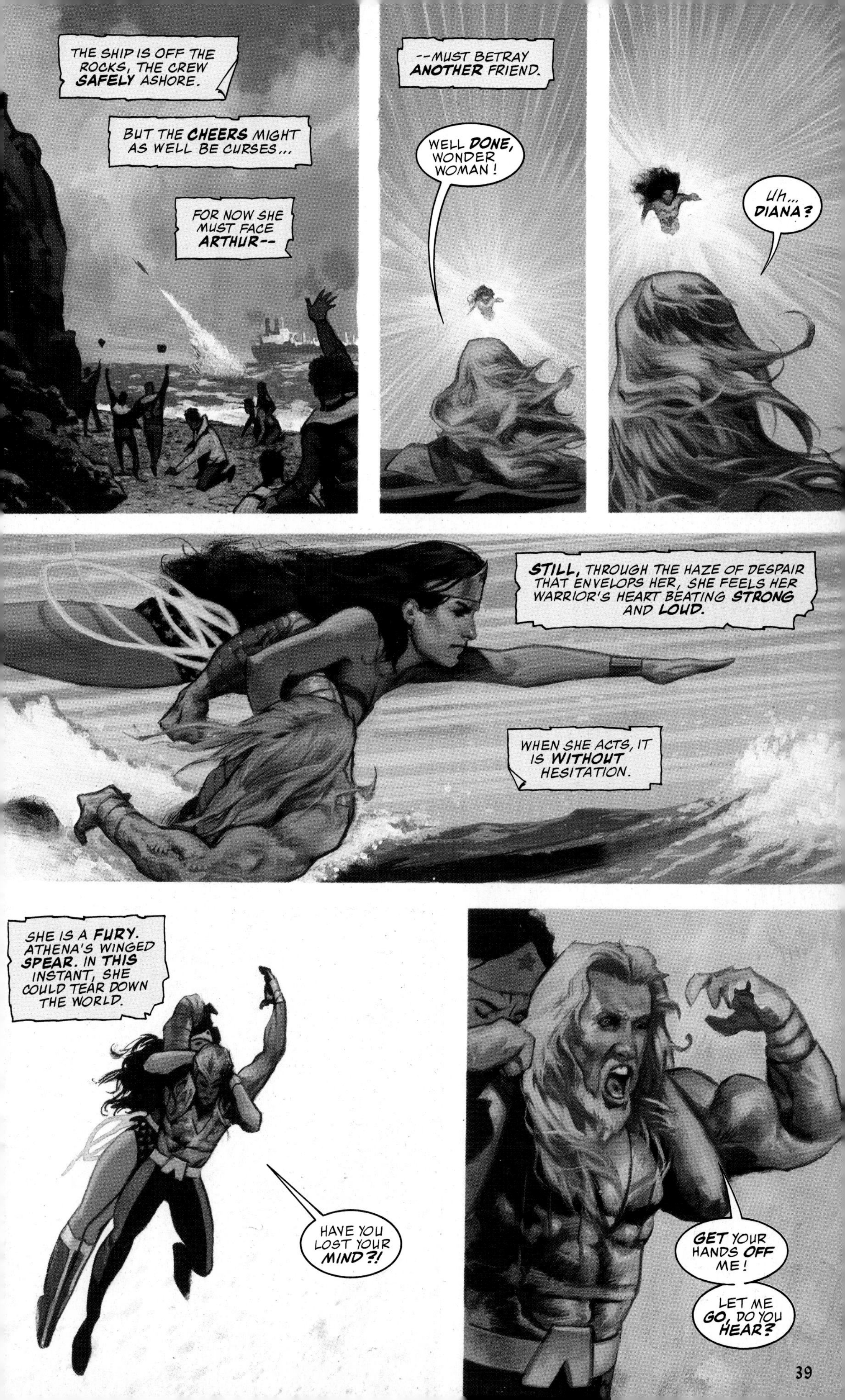
THE SHIP IS OFF THE ROCKS, THE CREW SAFELY ASHORE.
BUT THE CHEERS MIGHT AS WELL BE CURSES...
FOR NOW SHE MUST FACE ARTHUR--
--MUST BETRAY ANOTHER FRIEND.
WELL DONE, WONDER WOMAN!
UH... DIANA?
STILL, THROUGH THE HAZE OF DESPAIR THAT ENVELOPS HER, SHE FEELS HER WARRIOR'S HEART BEATING STRONG AND LOUD.
WHEN SHE ACTS, IT IS WITHOUT HESITATION.
SHE IS A FURY. ATHENA'S WINGED SPEAR. IN THIS INSTANT, SHE COULD TEAR DOWN THE WORLD.
HAVE YOU LOST YOUR MIND?!
GET YOUR HANDS OFF ME!
LET ME GO, DO YOU HEAR?

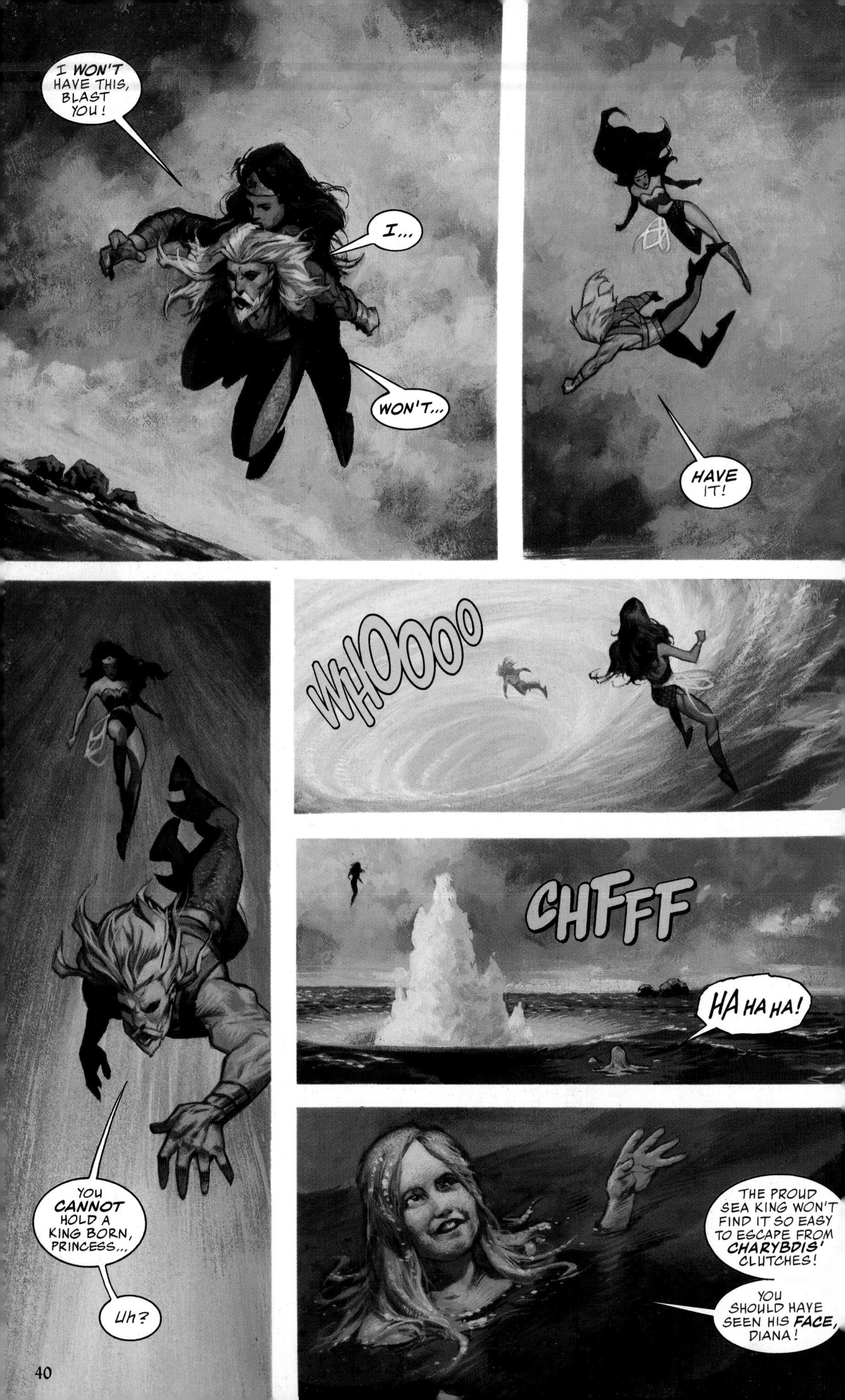

I WON'T HAVE THIS, BLAST YOU!
I...
WON'T...
HAVE IT!
YOU CANNOT HOLD A KING BORN, PRINCESS...
Uh?
WHOOOO
CHFFF
HA HA HA!
THE PROUD SEA KING WON'T FIND IT SO EASY TO ESCAPE FROM CHARYBDIS' CLUTCHES!
YOU SHOULD HAVE SEEN HIS FACE, DIANA!

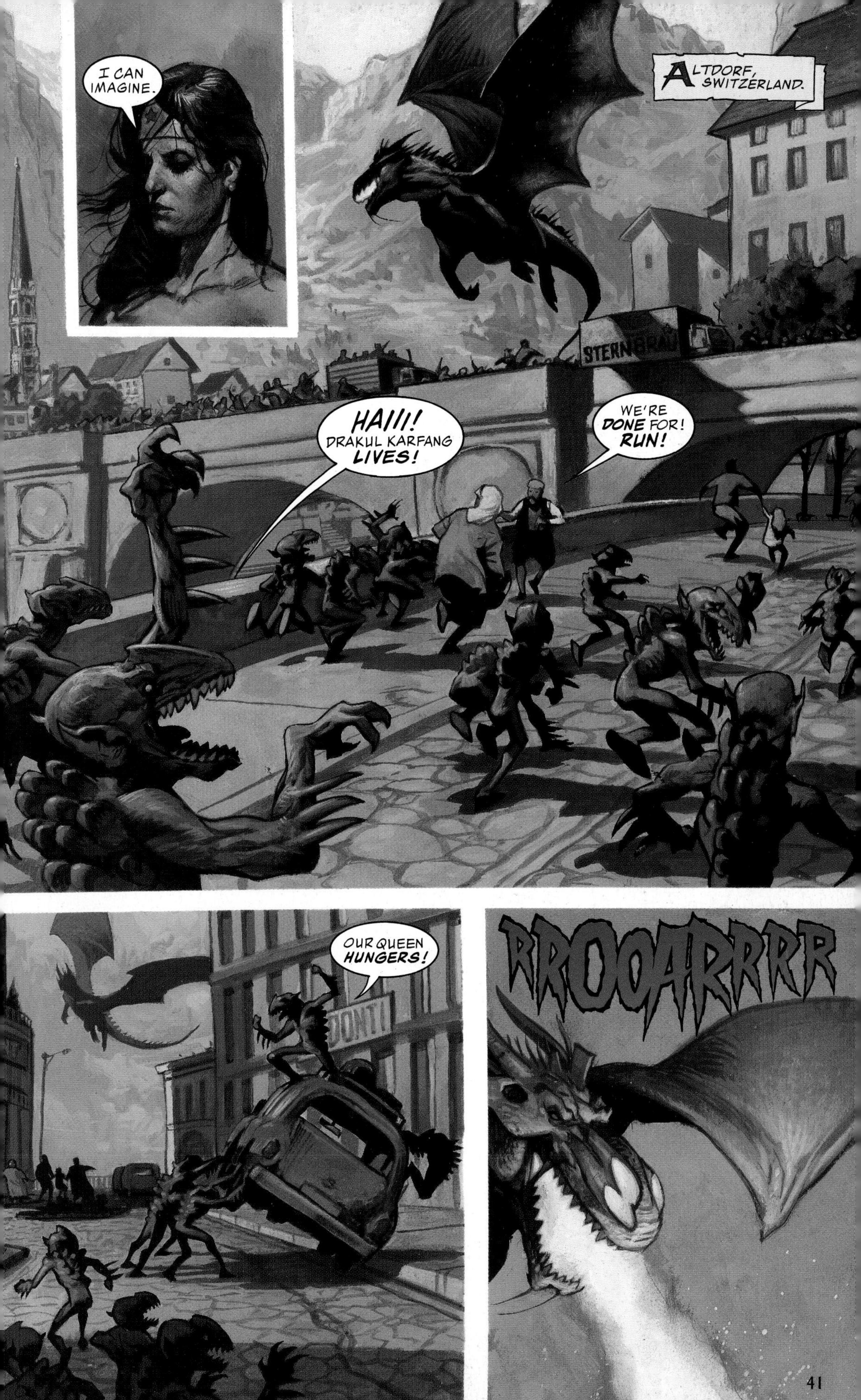
I CAN IMAGINE.
ALTDORF, SWITZERLAND.
HAIII! DRAKUL KARFANG LIVES!
WE'RE DONE FOR! RUN!
OUR QUEEN HUNGERS!
RROOARRRR

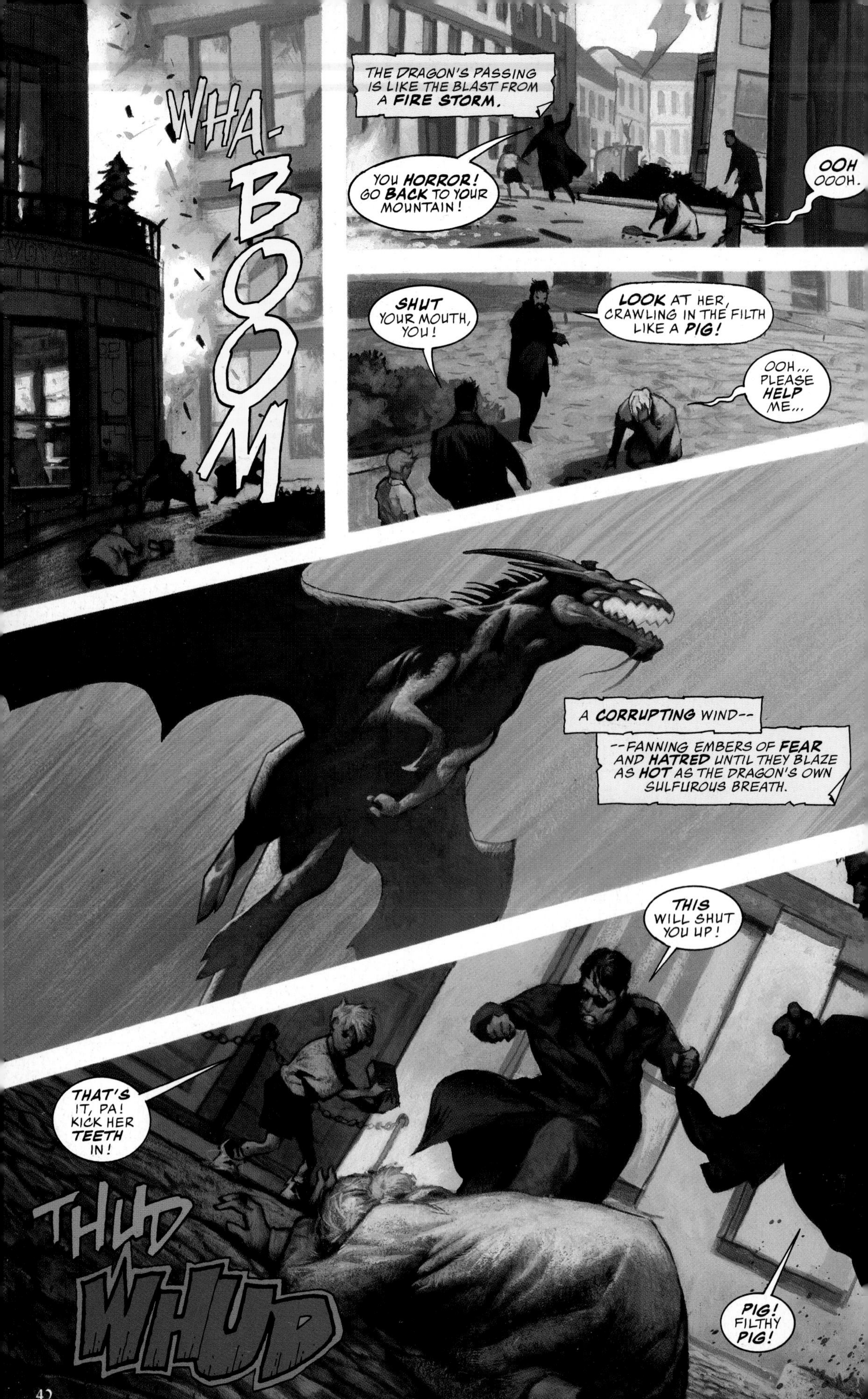
WHA-BOOM
THE DRAGON'S PASSING IS LIKE THE BLAST FROM A FIRE STORM.
YOU HORROR! GO BACK TO YOUR MOUNTAIN!
OOH OOOH.
SHUT YOUR MOUTH, YOU!
LOOK AT HER, CRAWLING IN THE FILTH LIKE A PIG!
OOH... PLEASE HELP ME...
A CORRUPTING WIND--
--FANNING EMBERS OF FEAR AND HATRED UNTIL THEY BLAZE AS HOT AS THE DRAGON'S OWN SULFUROUS BREATH.
THIS WILL SHUT YOU UP!
THAT'S IT, PA! KICK HER TEETH IN!
THUD
WHUD
PIG! FILTHY PIG!

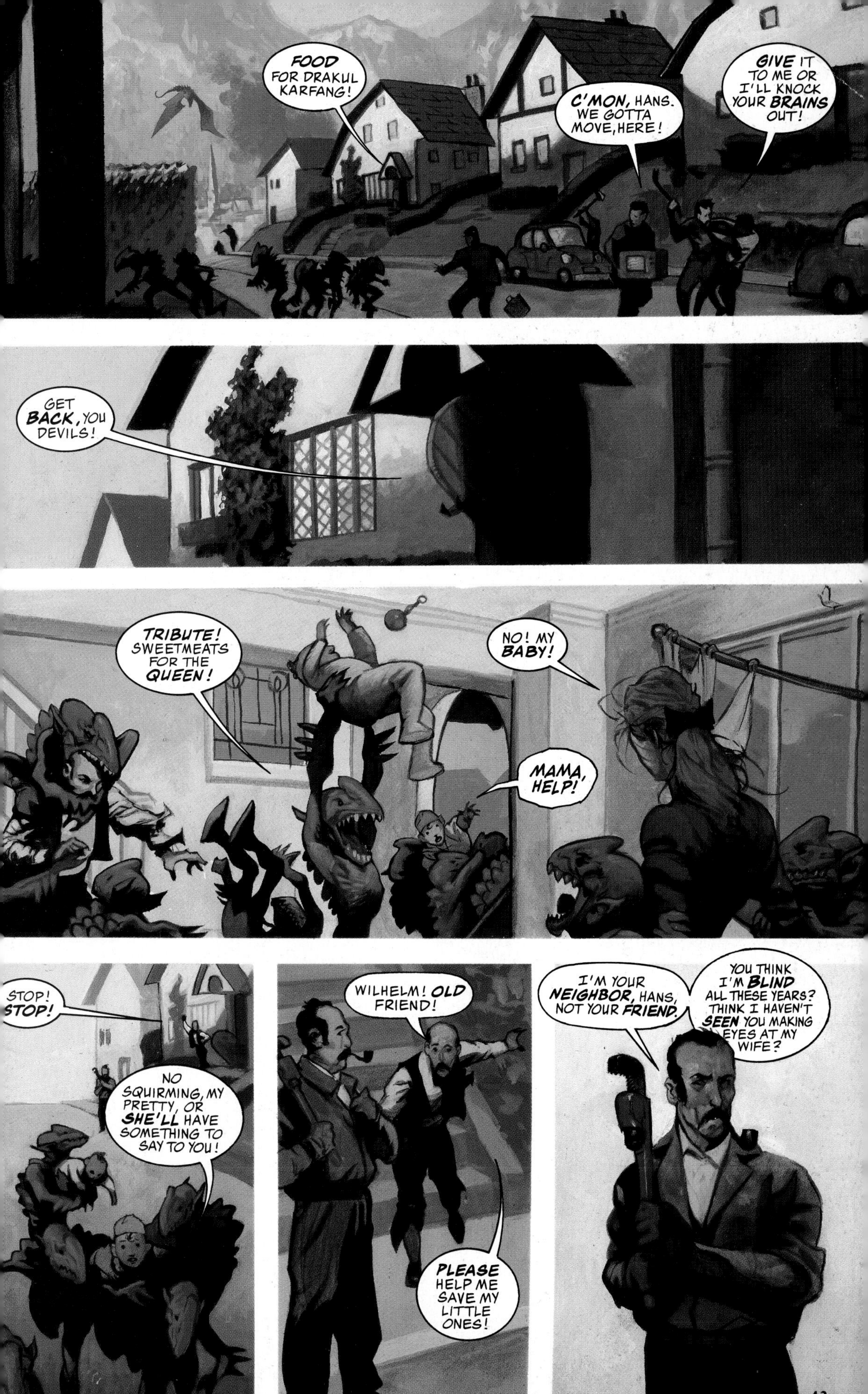
FOOD FOR DRAKUL KARFANG!
C'MON, HANS. WE GOTTA MOVE, HERE!
GIVE IT TO ME OR I'LL KNOCK YOUR BRAINS OUT!
GET BACK, YOU DEVILS!
TRIBUTE! SWEETMEATS FOR THE QUEEN!
NO! MY BABY!
MAMA, HELP!
STOP! STOP!
NO SQUIRMING, MY PRETTY, OR SHE'LL HAVE SOMETHING TO SAY TO YOU!
WILHELM! OLD FRIEND!
PLEASE HELP ME SAVE MY LITTLE ONES!
I'M YOUR NEIGHBOR, HANS, NOT YOUR FRIEND.
YOU THINK I'M BLIND ALL THESE YEARS? THINK I HAVEN'T SEEN YOU MAKING EYES AT MY WIFE?

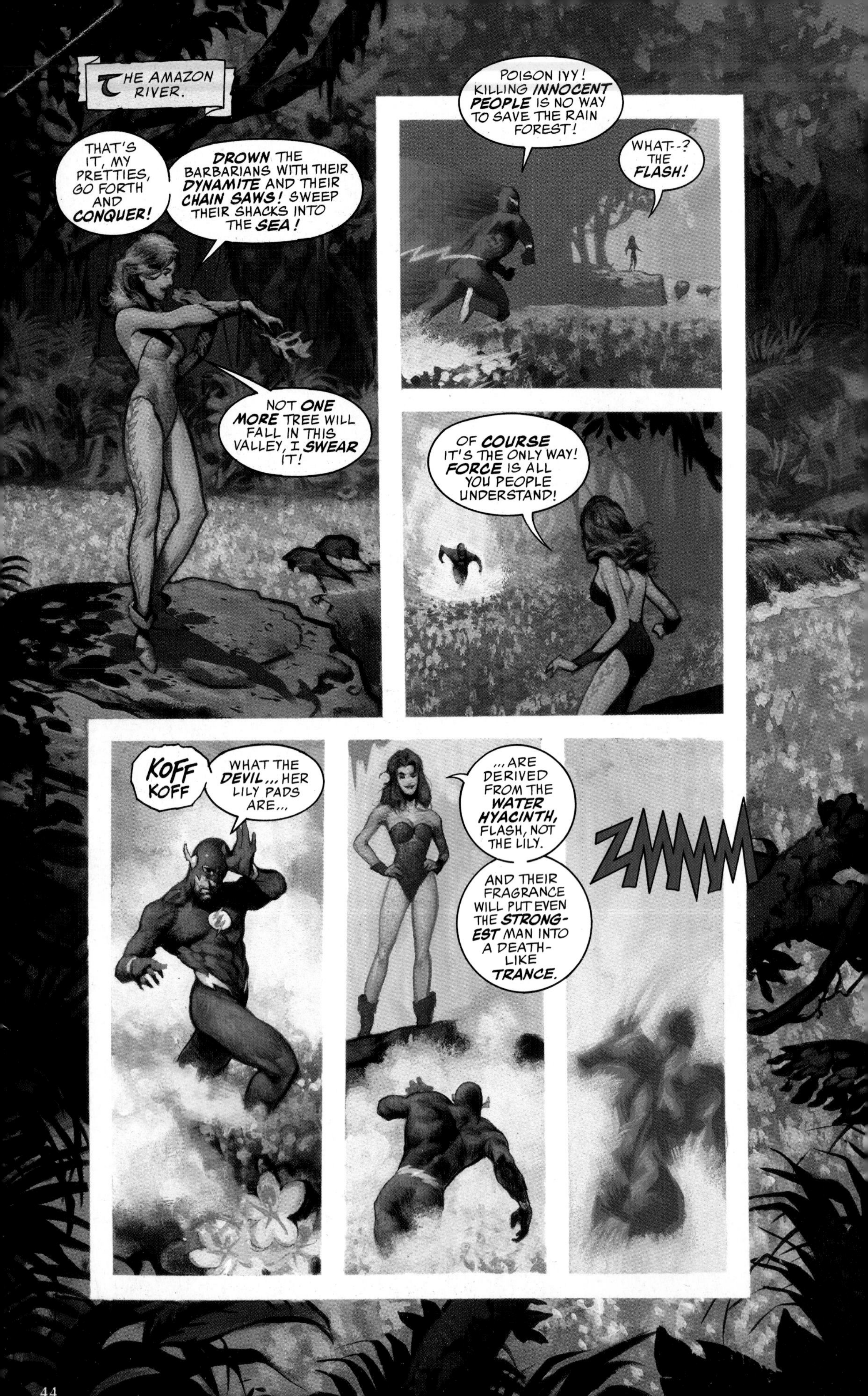
THE AMAZON RIVER.
THAT'S IT, MY PRETTIES, GO FORTH AND CONQUER!
DROWN THE BARBARIANS WITH THEIR DYNAMITE AND THEIR CHAIN SAWS! SWEEP THEIR SHACKS INTO THE SEA!
NOT ONE MORE TREE WILL FALL IN THIS VALLEY, I SWEAR IT!
POISON IVY! KILLING INNOCENT PEOPLE IS NO WAY TO SAVE THE RAIN FOREST!
WHAT--? THE FLASH!
OF COURSE IT'S THE ONLY WAY! FORCE IS ALL YOU PEOPLE UNDERSTAND!
KOFF KOFF
WHAT THE DEVIL... HER LILY PADS ARE...
...ARE DERIVED FROM THE WATER HYACINTH, FLASH, NOT THE LILY.
AND THEIR FRAGRANCE WILL PUT EVEN THE STRONGEST MAN INTO A DEATH-LIKE TRANCE.
ZMMM

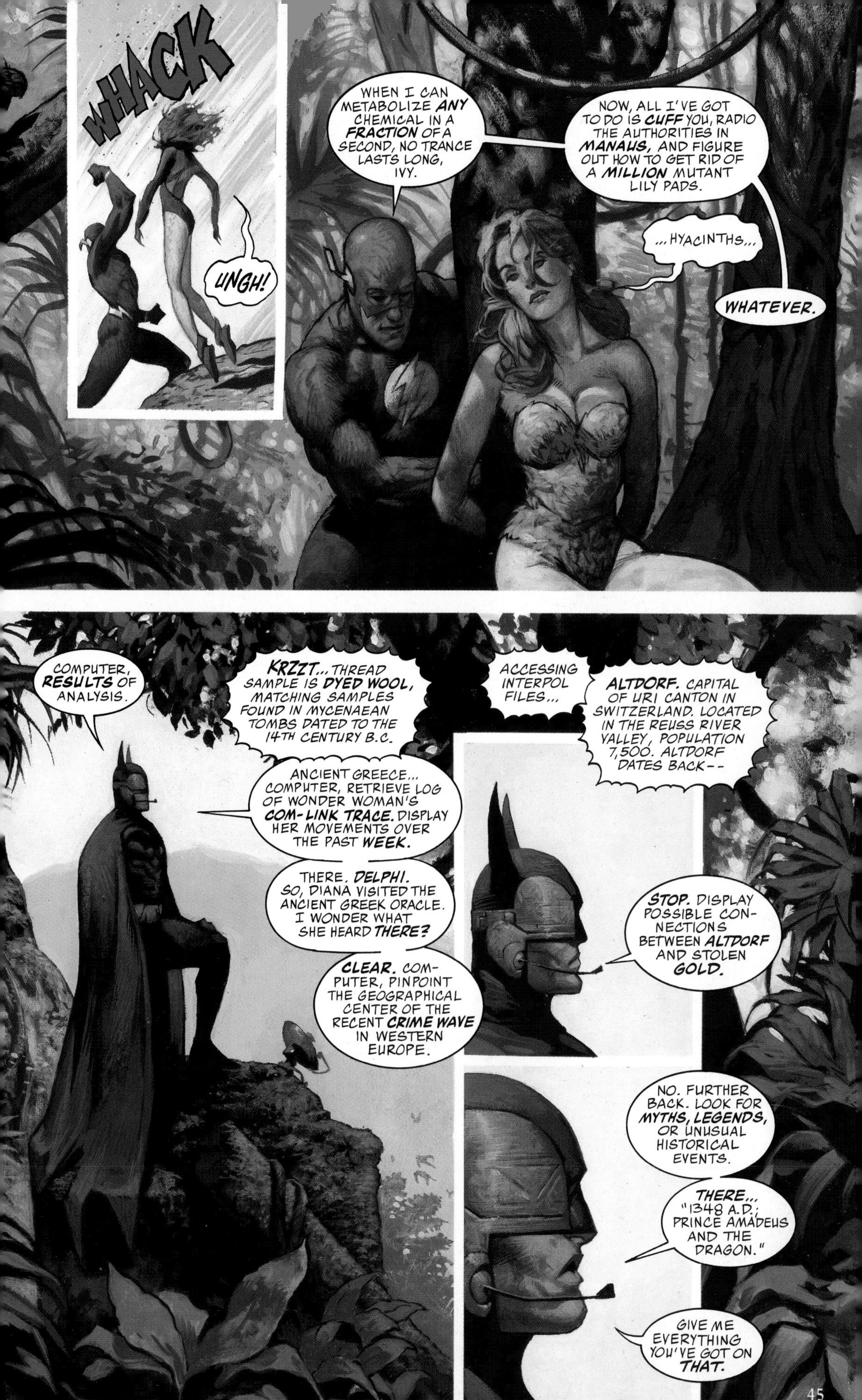
WHACK
UNGH!
WHEN I CAN METABOLIZE ANY CHEMICAL IN A FRACTION OF A SECOND, NO TRANCE LASTS LONG, IVY.
NOW, ALL I'VE GOT TO DO IS CUFF YOU, RADIO THE AUTHORITIES IN MANAUS, AND FIGURE OUT HOW TO GET RID OF A MILLION MUTANT LILY PADS.
...HYACINTHS...
WHATEVER.
COMPUTER, RESULTS OF ANALYSIS.
KRZZT... THREAD SAMPLE IS DYED WOOL, MATCHING SAMPLES FOUND IN MYCENAEAN TOMBS DATED TO THE 14TH CENTURY B.C.
ANCIENT GREECE... COMPUTER, RETRIEVE LOG OF WONDER WOMAN'S COM-LINK TRACE. DISPLAY HER MOVEMENTS OVER THE PAST WEEK.
THERE. DELPHI. SO, DIANA VISITED THE ANCIENT GREEK ORACLE. I WONDER WHAT SHE HEARD THERE?
CLEAR. COMPUTER, PINPOINT THE GEOGRAPHICAL CENTER OF THE RECENT CRIME WAVE IN WESTERN EUROPE.
ACCESSING INTERPOL FILES...
ALTDORF. CAPITAL OF URI CANTON IN SWITZERLAND. LOCATED IN THE REUSS RIVER VALLEY, POPULATION 7,500. ALTDORF DATES BACK--
STOP. DISPLAY POSSIBLE CONNECTIONS BETWEEN ALTDORF AND STOLEN GOLD.
NO. FURTHER BACK. LOOK FOR MYTHS, LEGENDS, OR UNUSUAL HISTORICAL EVENTS.
THERE... "1348 A.D.: PRINCE AMADEUS AND THE DRAGON."
GIVE ME EVERYTHING YOU'VE GOT ON THAT.

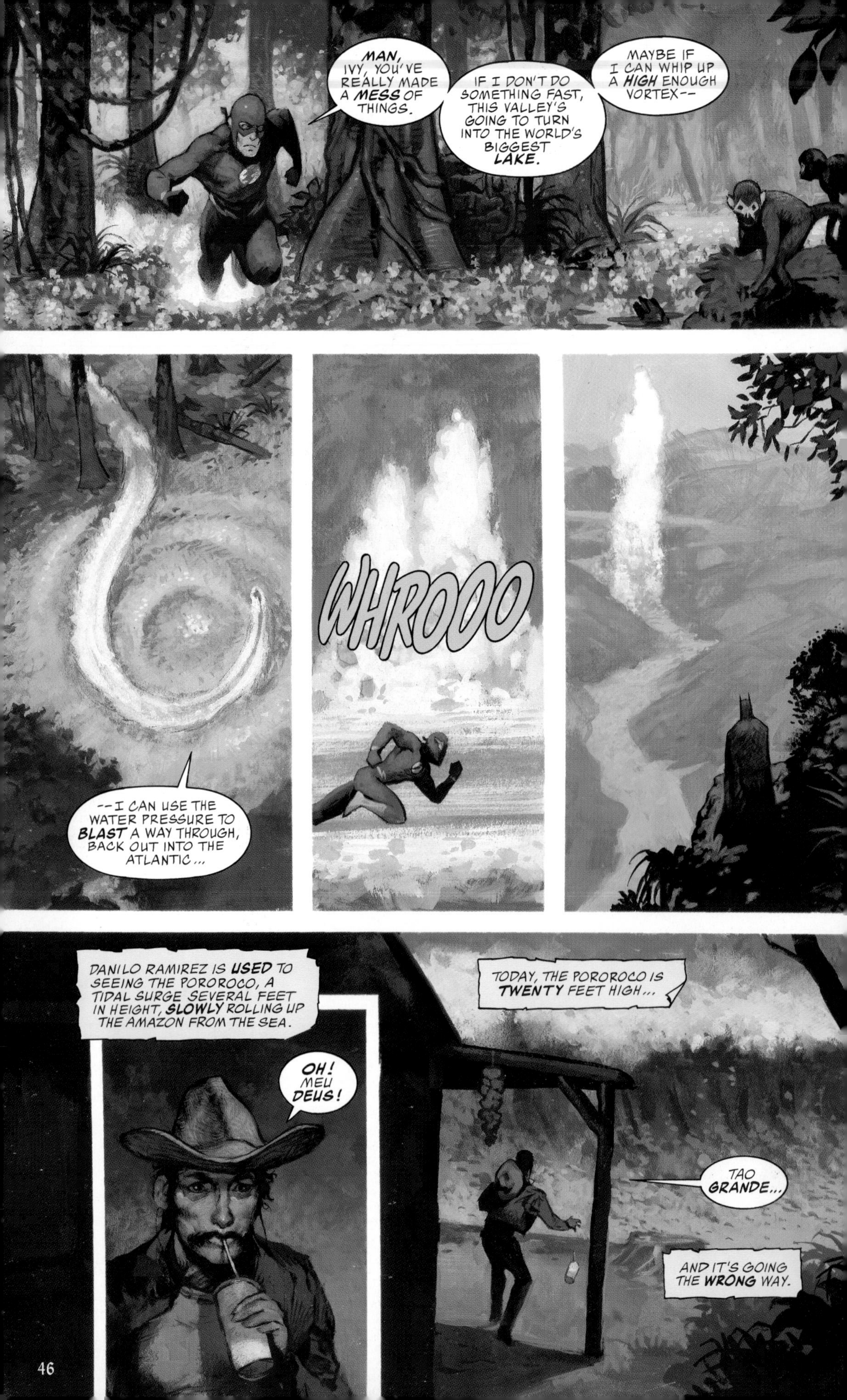
MAN, IVY, YOU'VE REALLY MADE A MESS OF THINGS.
IF I DON'T DO SOMETHING FAST, THIS VALLEY'S GOING TO TURN INTO THE WORLD'S BIGGEST LAKE.
MAYBE IF I CAN WHIP UP A HIGH ENOUGH VORTEX--
--I CAN USE THE WATER PRESSURE TO BLAST A WAY THROUGH, BACK OUT INTO THE ATLANTIC...
WHROOO
DANILO RAMIREZ IS USED TO SEEING THE POROROCO, A TIDAL SURGE SEVERAL FEET IN HEIGHT, SLOWLY ROLLING UP THE AMAZON FROM THE SEA.
OH! MEU DEUS!
TODAY, THE POROROCO IS TWENTY FEET HIGH...
TAO GRANDE...
AND IT'S GOING THE WRONG WAY.

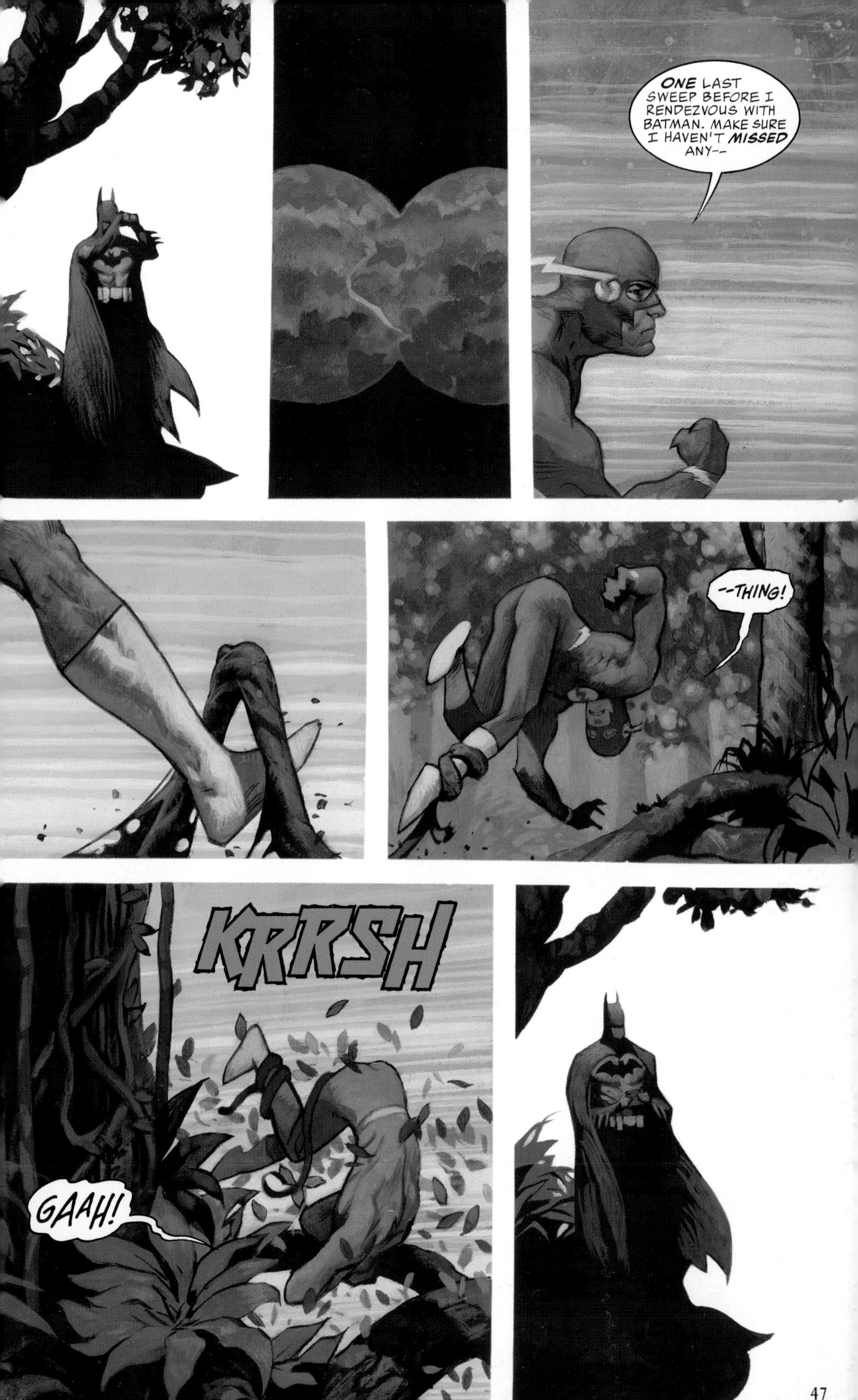
ONE LAST SWEEP BEFORE I RENDEZVOUS WITH BATMAN. MAKE SURE I HAVEN'T MISSED ANY--
--THING!
KRRSH
GAAH!

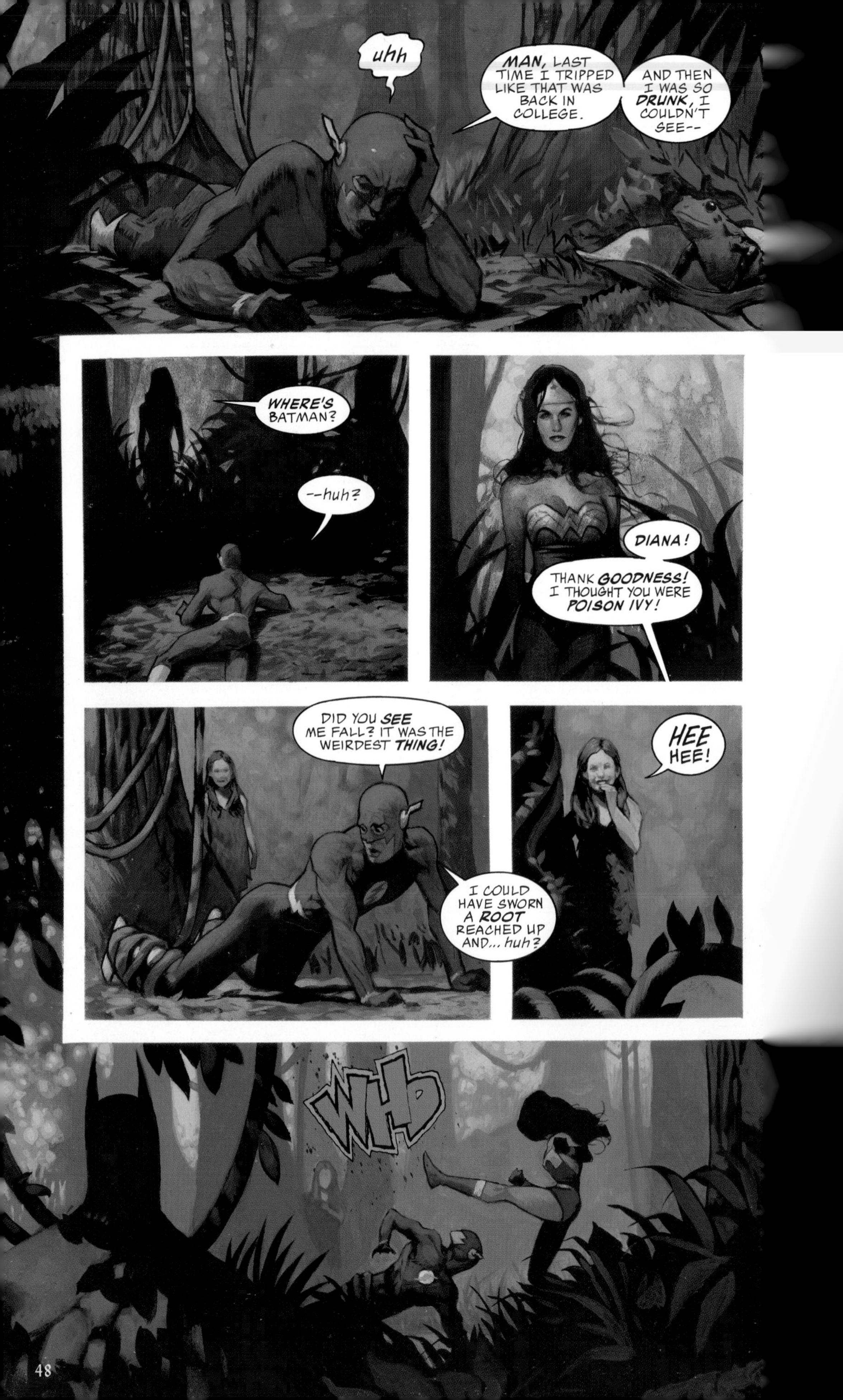
uhh
MAN, LAST TIME I TRIPPED LIKE THAT WAS BACK IN COLLEGE.
AND THEN I WAS SO DRUNK, I COULDN'T SEE--
WHERE'S BATMAN?
--huh?
DIANA!
THANK GOODNESS! I THOUGHT YOU WERE POISON IVY!
DID YOU SEE ME FALL? IT WAS THE WEIRDEST THING!
I COULD HAVE SWORN A ROOT REACHED UP AND... huh?
HEE HEE!
WHD

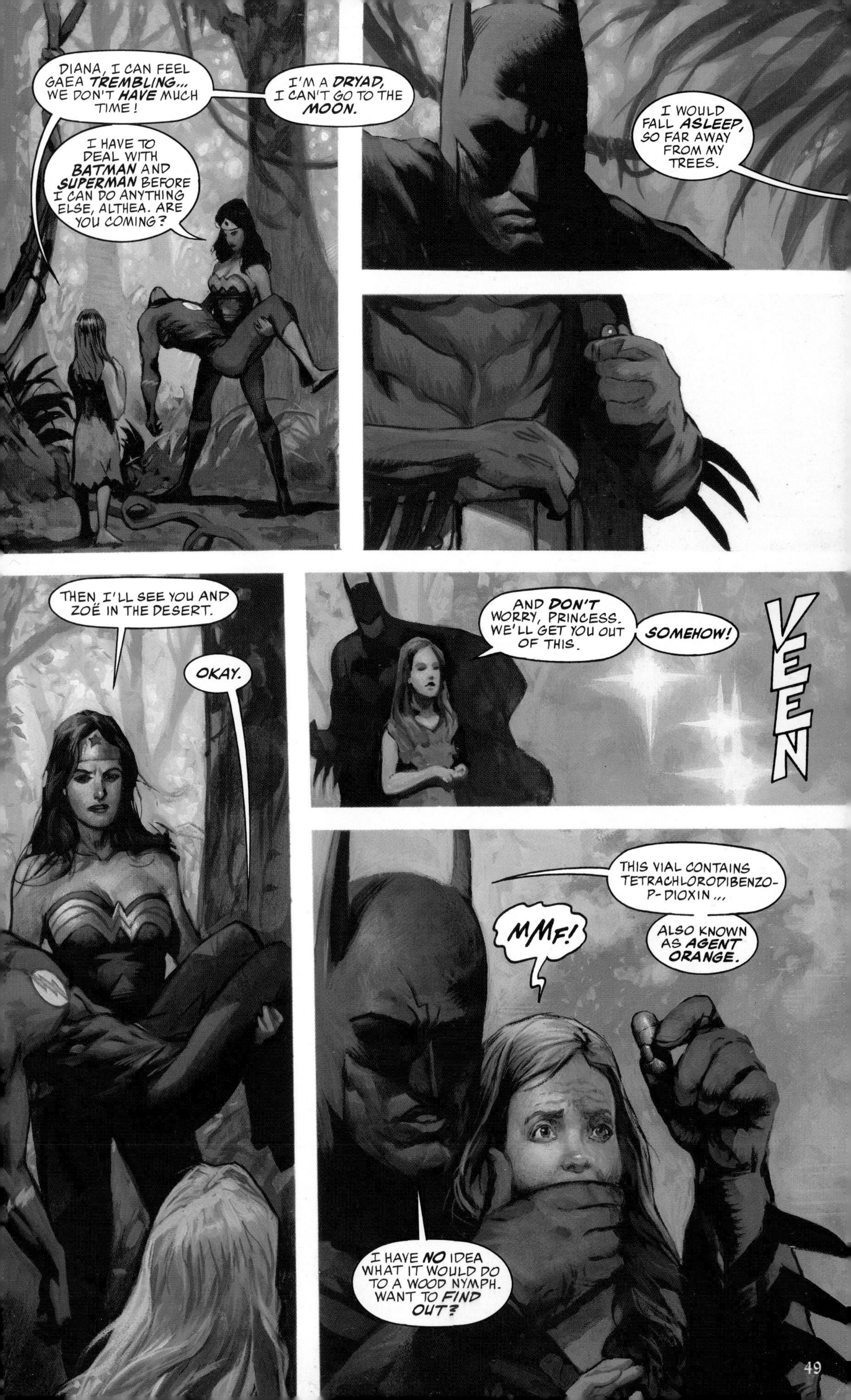

DIANA, I CAN FEEL GAEA TREMBLING... WE DON'T HAVE MUCH TIME!
I'M A DRYAD, I CAN'T GO TO THE MOON.
I HAVE TO DEAL WITH BATMAN AND SUPERMAN BEFORE I CAN DO ANYTHING ELSE, ALTHEA. ARE YOU COMING?
I WOULD FALL ASLEEP, SO FAR AWAY FROM MY TREES.
THEN I'LL SEE YOU AND ZOË IN THE DESERT.
OKAY.
AND DON'T WORRY, PRINCESS. WE'LL GET YOU OUT OF THIS.
SOMEHOW!
VEEN
THIS VIAL CONTAINS TETRACHLORODIBENZO-P-DIOXIN...
MMF!
ALSO KNOWN AS AGENT ORANGE.
I HAVE NO IDEA WHAT IT WOULD DO TO A WOOD NYMPH. WANT TO FIND OUT?

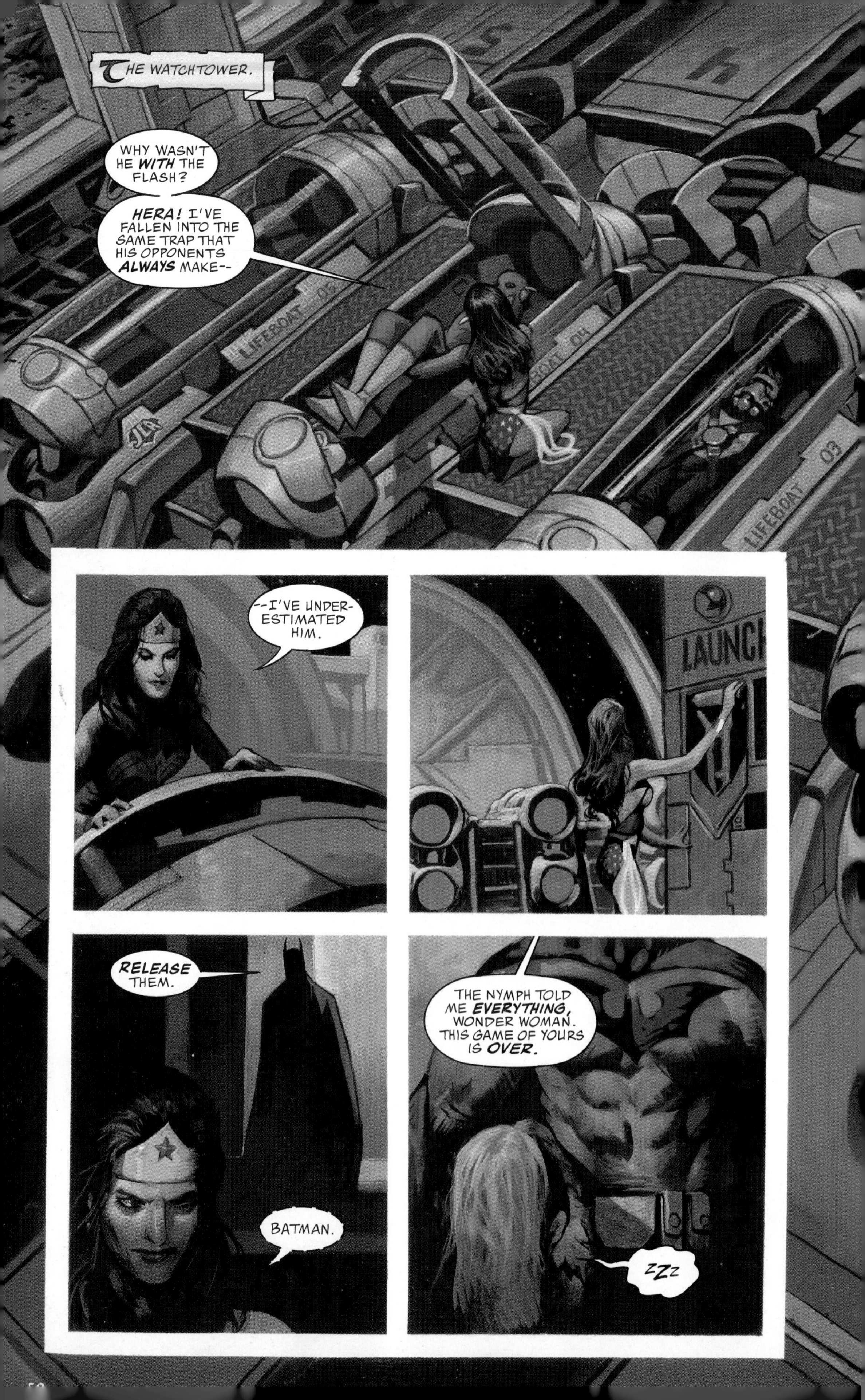
THE WATCHTOWER.
WHY WASN'T HE WITH THE FLASH?
HERA! I'VE FALLEN INTO THE SAME TRAP THAT HIS OPPONENTS ALWAYS MAKE--
LIFEBOAT 05
LIFEBOAT 04
LIFEBOAT 03
--I'VE UNDER-ESTIMATED HIM.
LAUNCH
RELEASE THEM.
BATMAN.
THE NYMPH TOLD ME EVERYTHING, WONDER WOMAN. THIS GAME OF YOURS IS OVER.
ZZZ

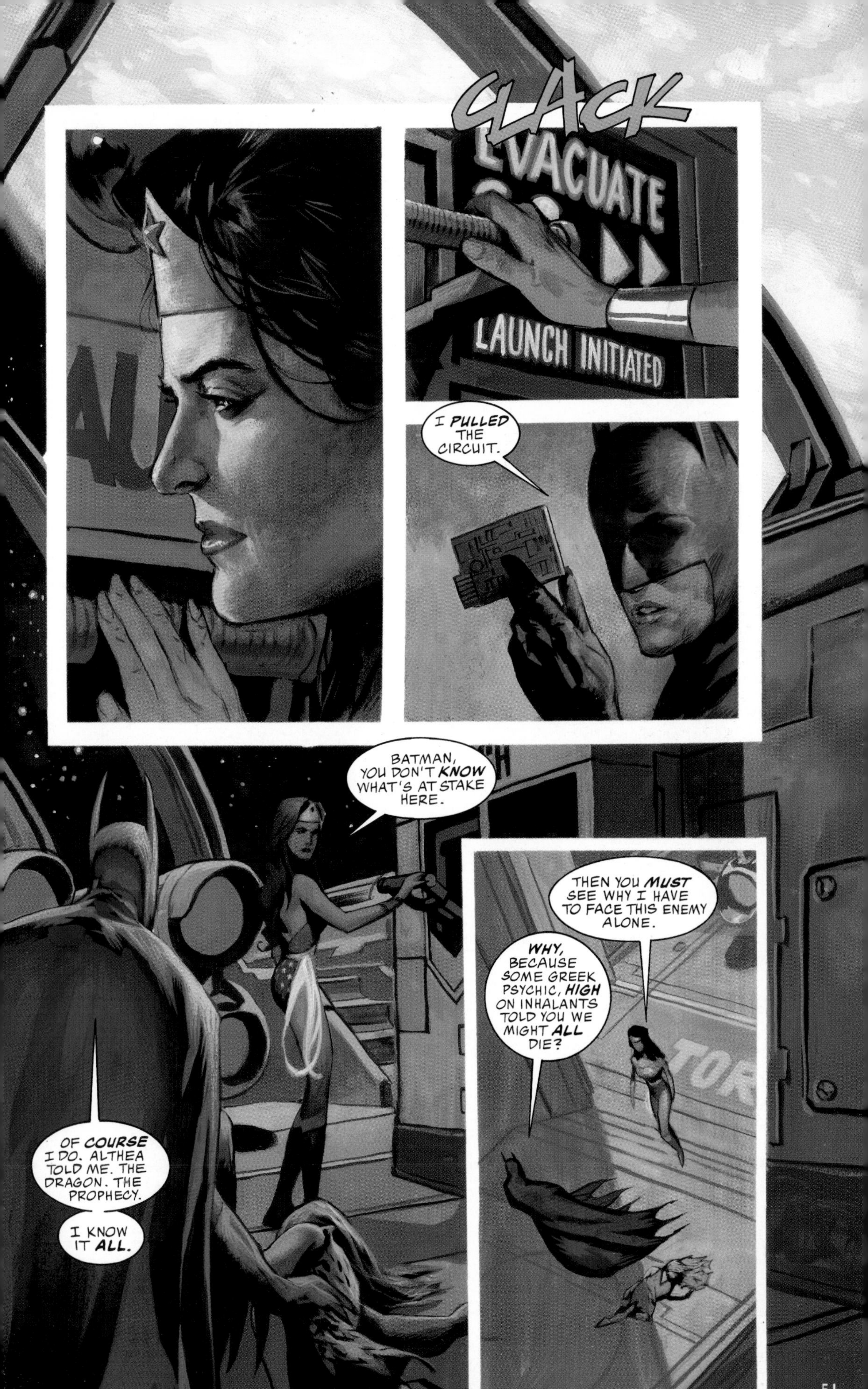
CLACK
EVACUATE
LAUNCH INITIATED
I PULLED THE CIRCUIT.
BATMAN, YOU DON'T KNOW WHAT'S AT STAKE HERE.
OF COURSE I DO. ALTHEA TOLD ME. THE DRAGON. THE PROPHECY.
I KNOW IT ALL.
THEN YOU MUST SEE WHY I HAVE TO FACE THIS ENEMY ALONE.
WHY, BECAUSE SOME GREEK PSYCHIC, HIGH ON INHALANTS TOLD YOU WE MIGHT ALL DIE?

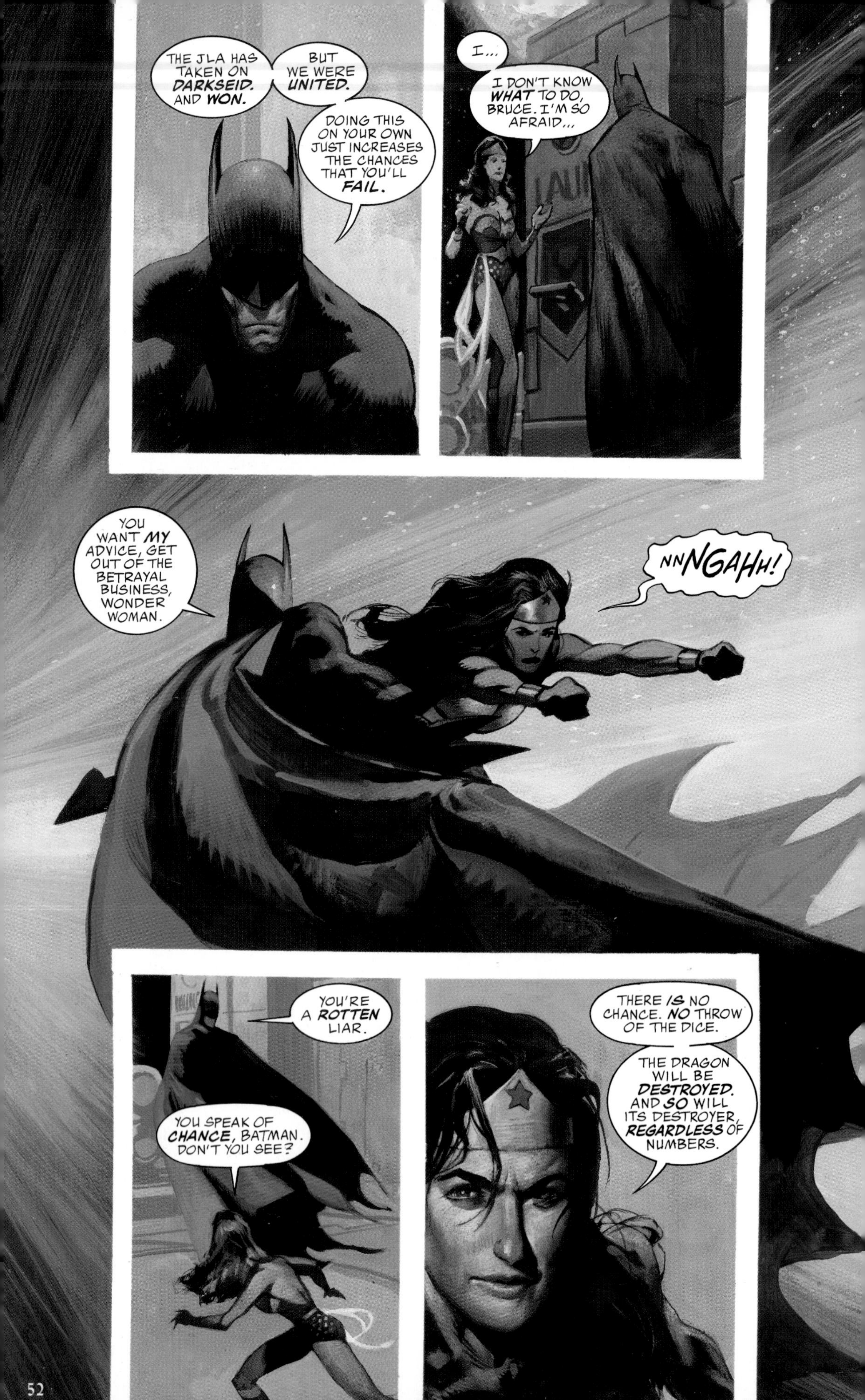
THE JLA HAS TAKEN ON DARKSEID. AND WON.
BUT WE WERE UNITED.
DOING THIS ON YOUR OWN JUST INCREASES THE CHANCES THAT YOU'LL FAIL.
I...
I DON'T KNOW WHAT TO DO, BRUCE. I'M SO AFRAID...
YOU WANT MY ADVICE, GET OUT OF THE BETRAYAL BUSINESS, WONDER WOMAN.
NNNGAHH!
YOU'RE A ROTTEN LIAR.
YOU SPEAK OF CHANCE, BATMAN. DON'T YOU SEE?
THERE IS NO CHANCE. NO THROW OF THE DICE.
THE DRAGON WILL BE DESTROYED. AND SO WILL ITS DESTROYER, REGARDLESS OF NUMBERS.

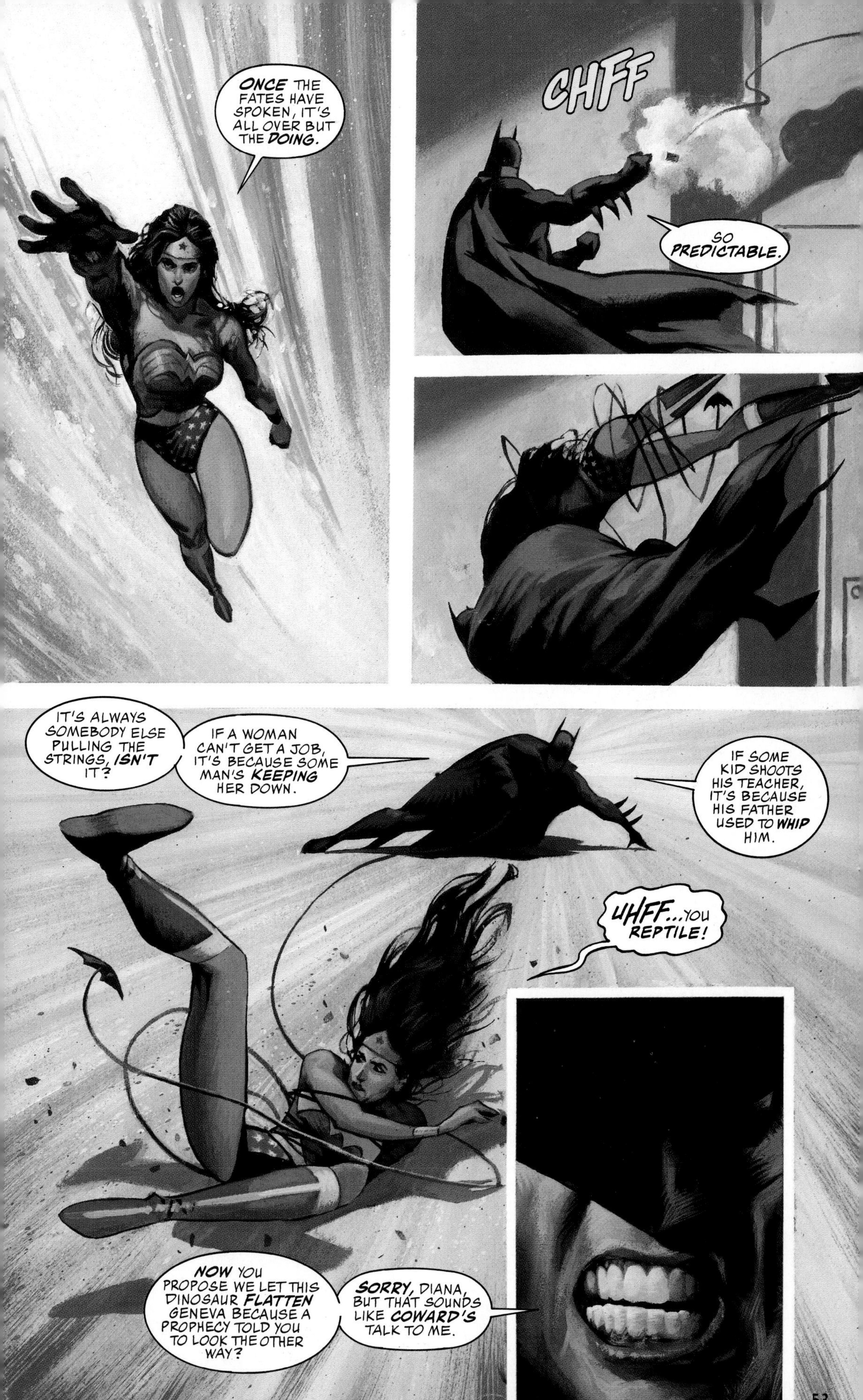
ONCE THE FATES HAVE SPOKEN, IT'S ALL OVER BUT THE DOING.
CHFF
SO PREDICTABLE.
IT'S ALWAYS SOMEBODY ELSE PULLING THE STRINGS, ISN'T IT?
IF A WOMAN CAN'T GET A JOB, IT'S BECAUSE SOME MAN'S KEEPING HER DOWN.
IF SOME KID SHOOTS HIS TEACHER, IT'S BECAUSE HIS FATHER USED TO WHIP HIM.
UHFF... YOU REPTILE!
NOW YOU PROPOSE WE LET THIS DINOSAUR FLATTEN GENEVA BECAUSE A PROPHECY TOLD YOU TO LOOK THE OTHER WAY?
SORRY, DIANA, BUT THAT SOUNDS LIKE COWARD'S TALK TO ME.

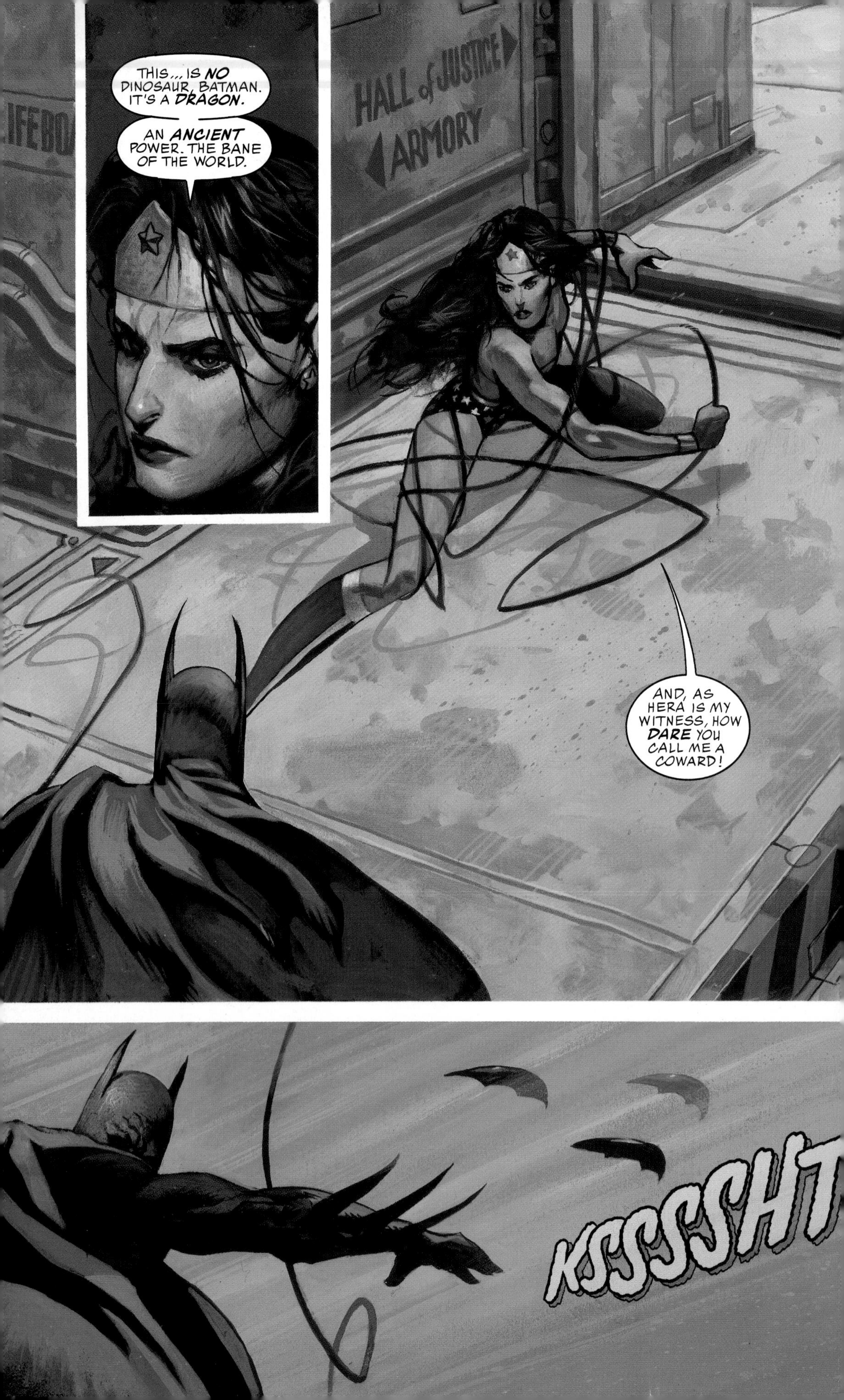

THIS... IS NO DINOSAUR, BATMAN. IT'S A DRAGON.
AN ANCIENT POWER. THE BANE OF THE WORLD.
HALL of JUSTICE
ARMORY
AND, AS HERA IS MY WITNESS, HOW DARE YOU CALL ME A COWARD!
KSSSSHT

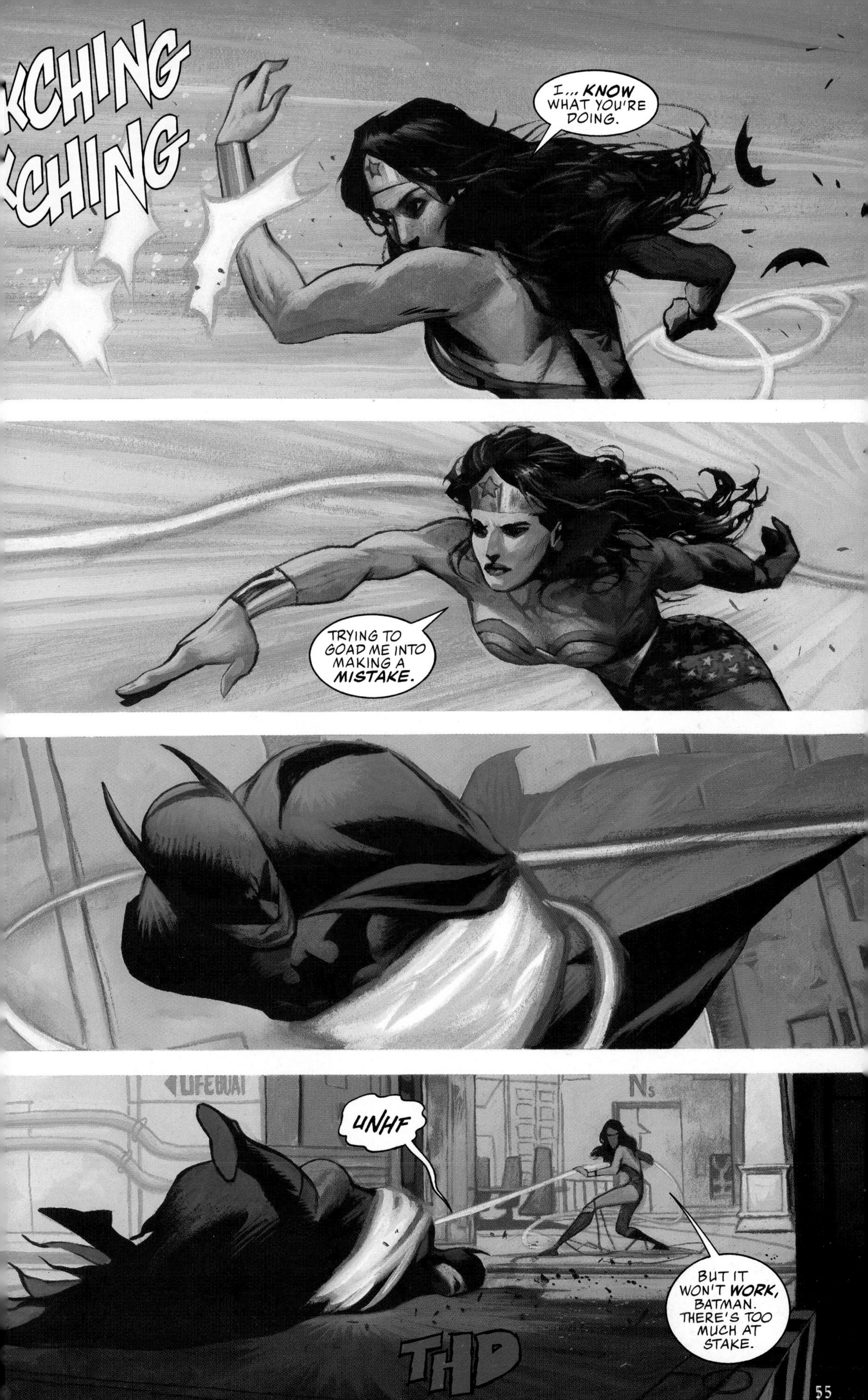
KCHING
CHING
I... KNOW WHAT YOU'RE DOING.
TRYING TO GOAD ME INTO MAKING A MISTAKE.
UNHF
BUT IT WON'T WORK, BATMAN. THERE'S TOO MUCH AT STAKE.
THD

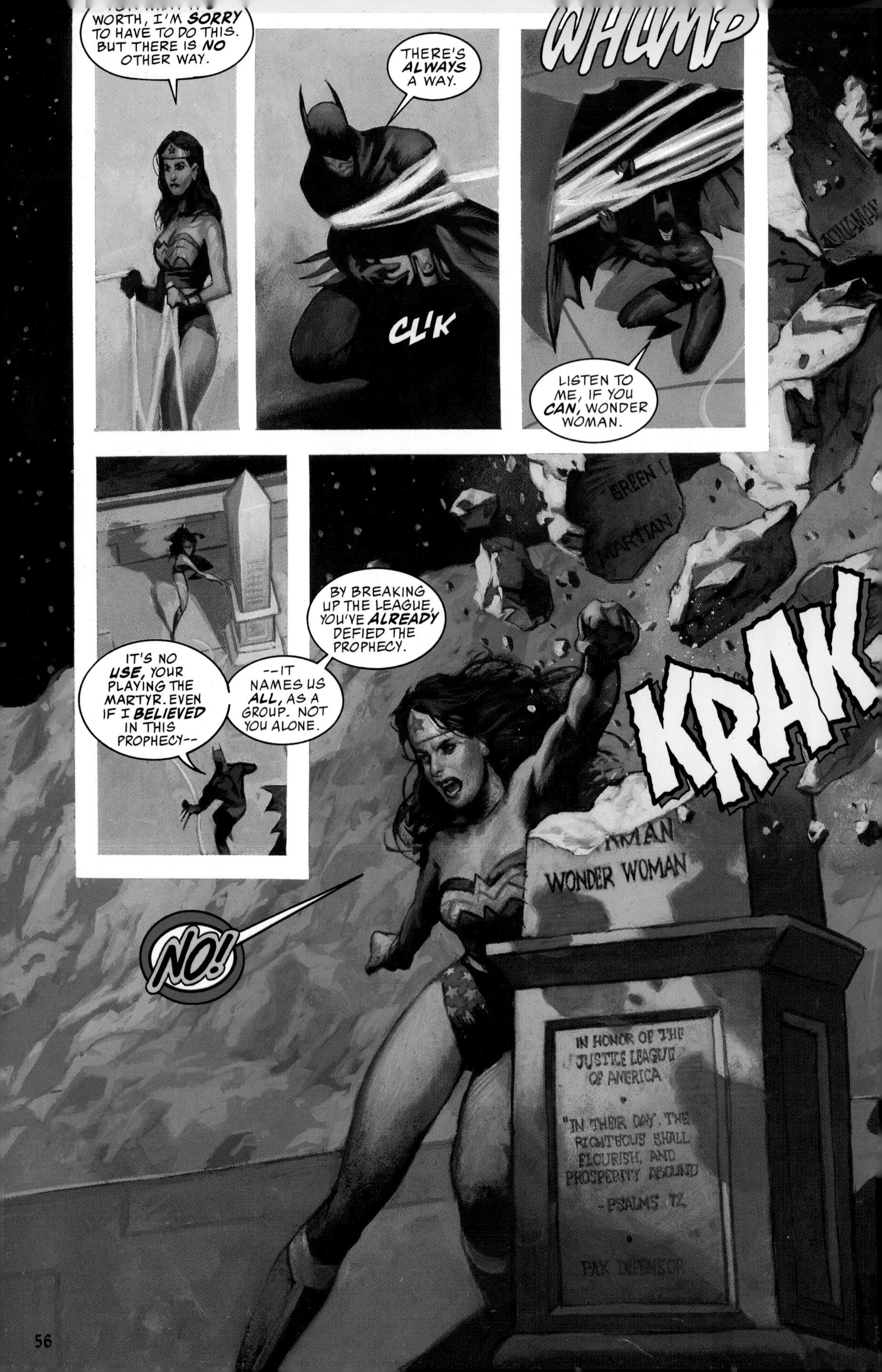
WORTH, I'M SORRY TO HAVE TO DO THIS. BUT THERE IS NO OTHER WAY.
THERE'S ALWAYS A WAY.
CL'K
WHUMP
LISTEN TO ME, IF YOU CAN, WONDER WOMAN.
IT'S NO USE, YOUR PLAYING THE MARTYR. EVEN IF I BELIEVED IN THIS PROPHECY--
--IT NAMES US ALL, AS A GROUP. NOT YOU ALONE.
BY BREAKING UP THE LEAGUE, YOU'VE ALREADY DEFIED THE PROPHECY.
KRAK
NO!
WONDER WOMAN
IN HONOR OF THE JUSTICE LEAGUE OF AMERICA
"IN THEIR DAY, THE RIGHTEOUS SHALL FLOURISH, AND PROSPERITY ABOUND"
-PSALMS 72

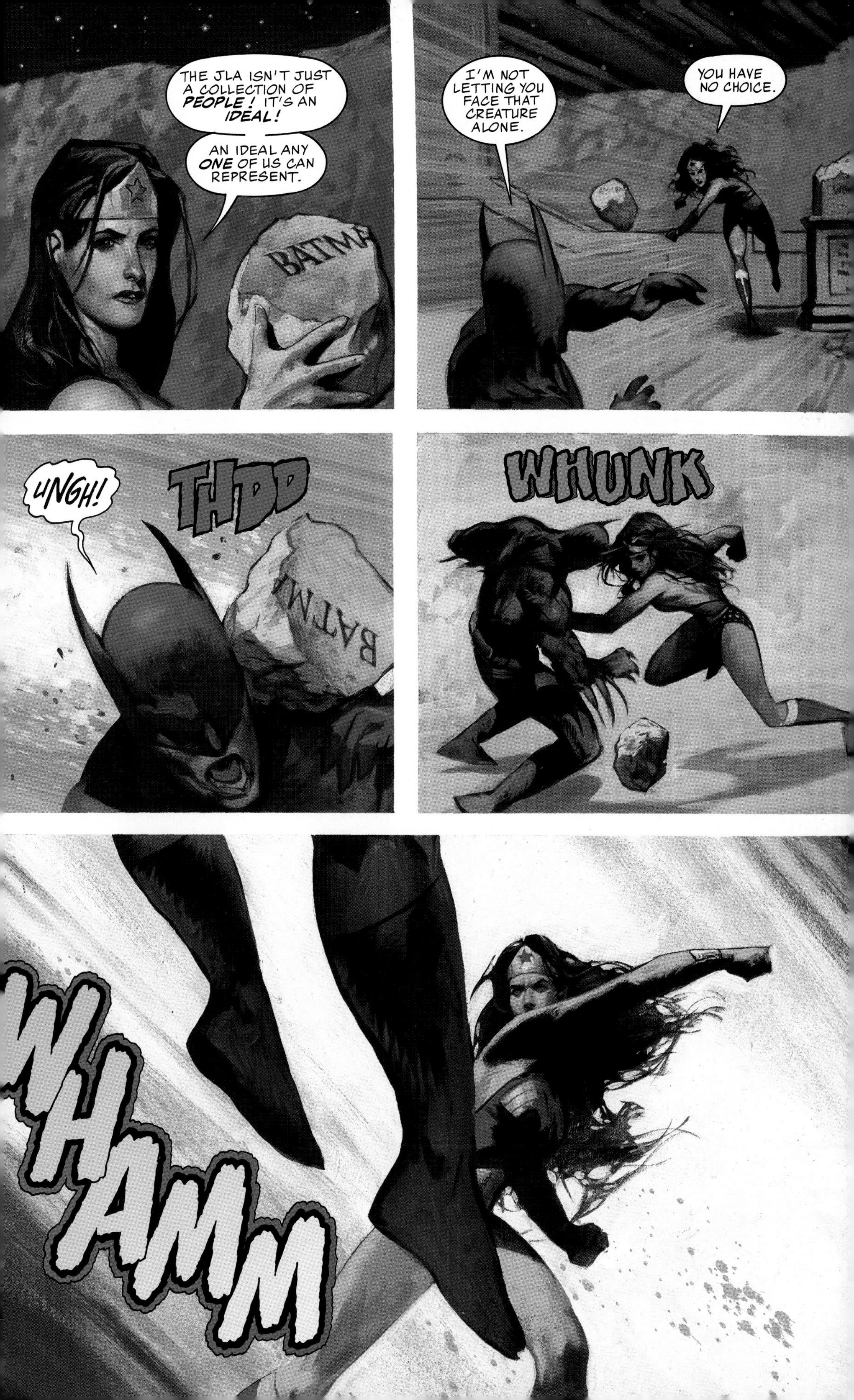
THE JLA ISN'T JUST A COLLECTION OF PEOPLE! IT'S AN IDEAL!
AN IDEAL ANY ONE OF US CAN REPRESENT.
BATMA
I'M NOT LETTING YOU FACE THAT CREATURE ALONE.
YOU HAVE NO CHOICE.
UNGH!
THDD
BATMA
WHUNK
WHAMM

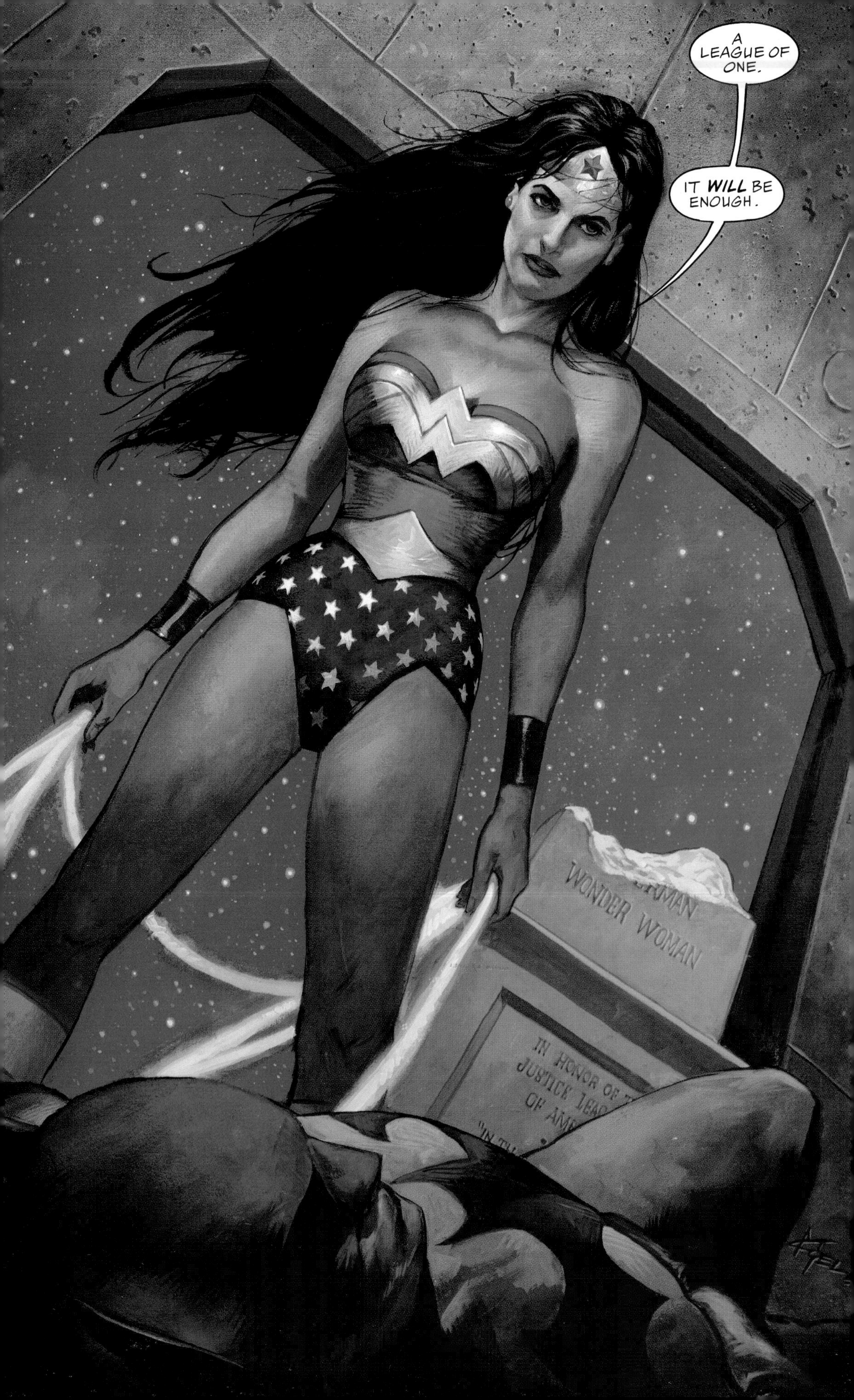
A LEAGUE OF ONE.
IT **WILL** BE ENOUGH.
WONDER WOMAN

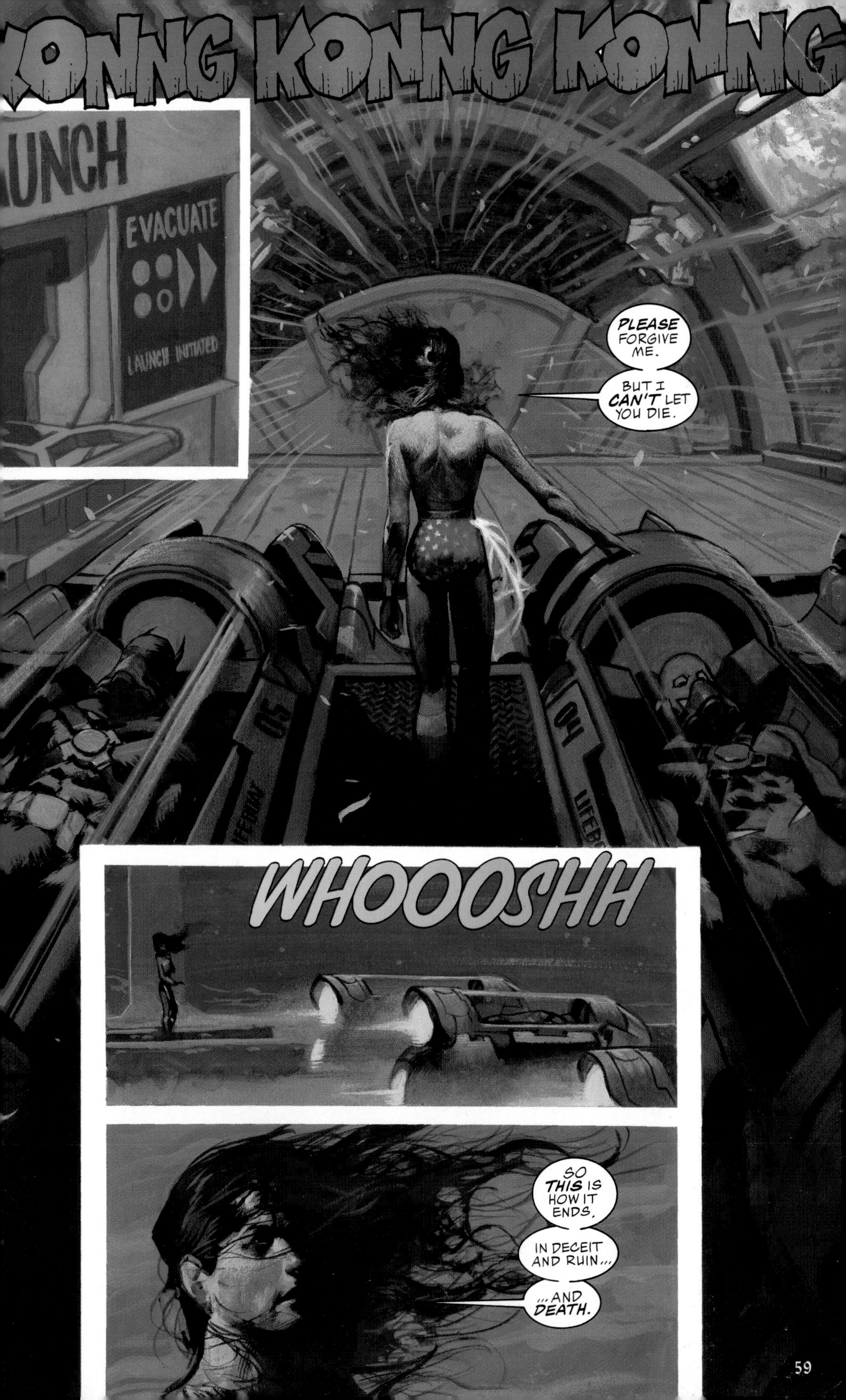
KONNG KONNG KONNG
UNCH
EVACUATE
LAUNCH INITIATED
PLEASE FORGIVE ME.
BUT I CAN'T LET YOU DIE.
05
04
WHOOOSHH
SO THIS IS HOW IT ENDS.
IN DECEIT AND RUIN...
...AND DEATH.

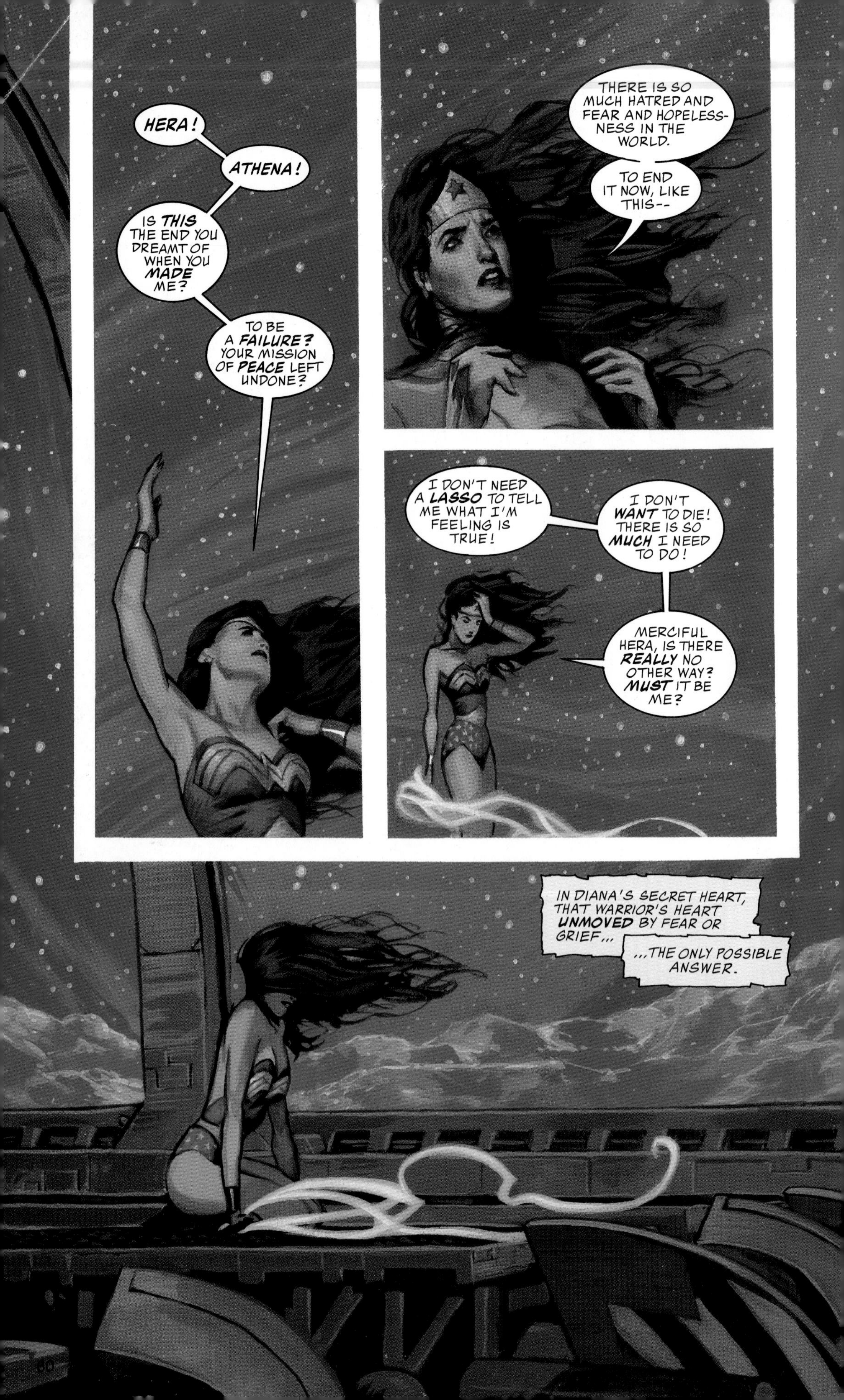
HERA!
ATHENA!
IS THIS THE END YOU DREAMT OF WHEN YOU MADE ME?
TO BE A FAILURE? YOUR MISSION OF PEACE LEFT UNDONE?
THERE IS SO MUCH HATRED AND FEAR AND HOPELESS-NESS IN THE WORLD.
TO END IT NOW, LIKE THIS--
I DON'T NEED A LASSO TO TELL ME WHAT I'M FEELING IS TRUE!
I DON'T WANT TO DIE! THERE IS SO MUCH I NEED TO DO!
MERCIFUL HERA, IS THERE REALLY NO OTHER WAY? MUST IT BE ME?
IN DIANA'S SECRET HEART, THAT WARRIOR'S HEART UNMOVED BY FEAR OR GRIEF...
...THE ONLY POSSIBLE ANSWER.

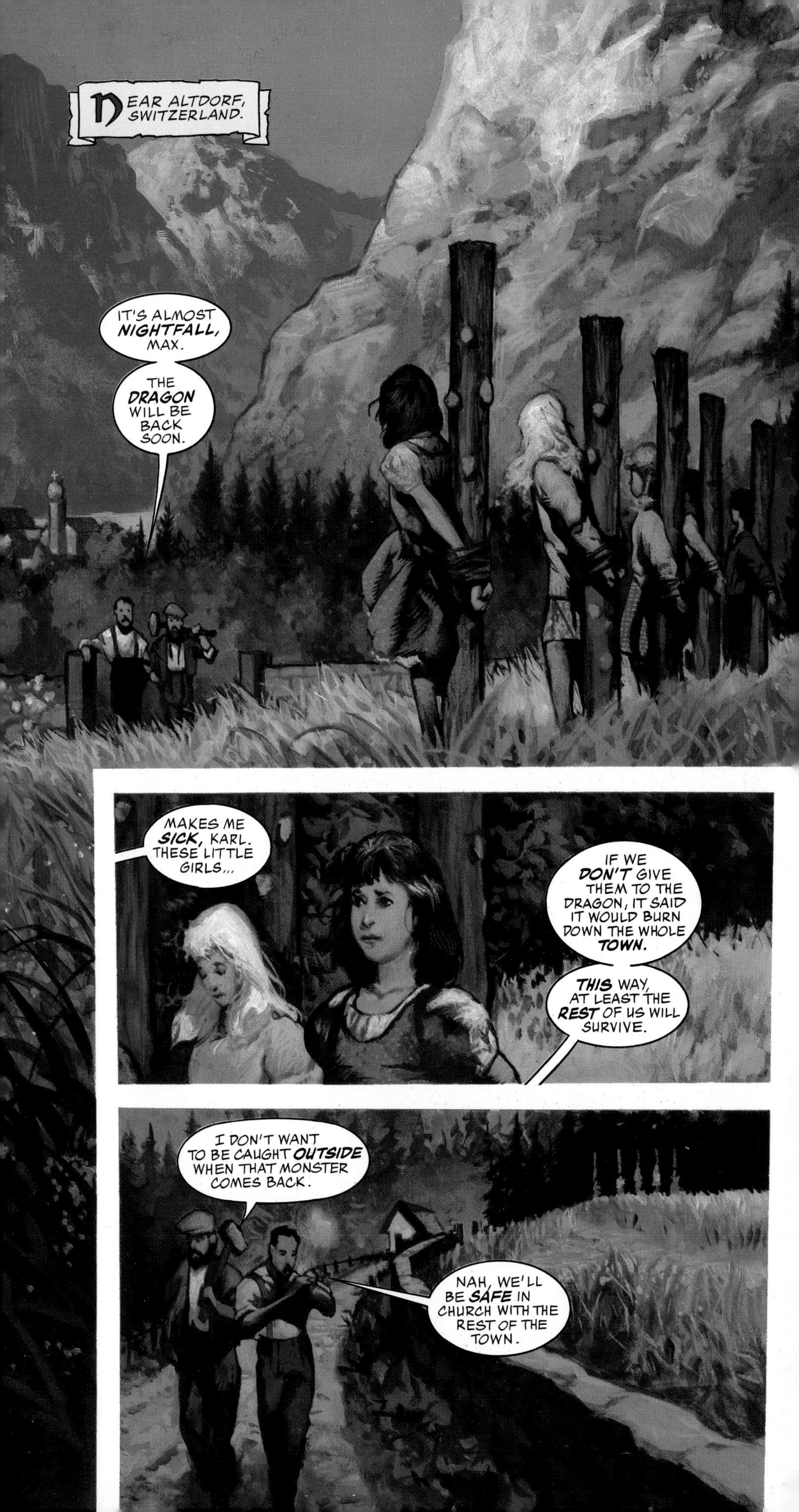
NEAR ALTDORF, SWITZERLAND.
IT'S ALMOST NIGHTFALL, MAX.
THE DRAGON WILL BE BACK SOON.
MAKES ME SICK, KARL. THESE LITTLE GIRLS...
IF WE DON'T GIVE THEM TO THE DRAGON, IT SAID IT WOULD BURN DOWN THE WHOLE TOWN.
THIS WAY, AT LEAST THE REST OF US WILL SURVIVE.
I DON'T WANT TO BE CAUGHT OUTSIDE WHEN THAT MONSTER COMES BACK.
NAH, WE'LL BE SAFE IN CHURCH WITH THE REST OF THE TOWN.

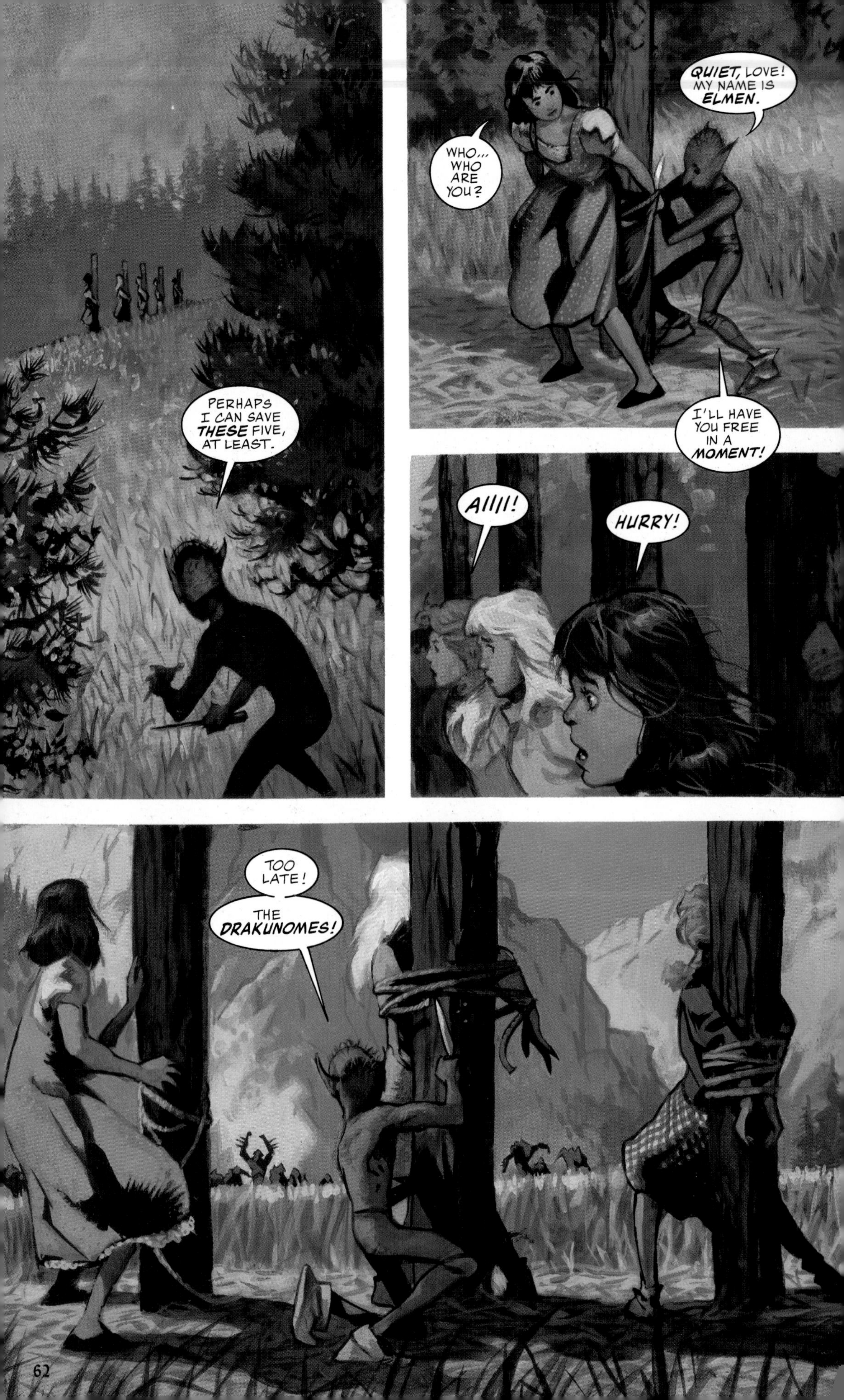
PERHAPS I CAN SAVE ***THESE*** FIVE, AT LEAST.
WHO... WHO ARE YOU?
QUIET, LOVE! MY NAME IS ***ELMEN.***
I'LL HAVE YOU FREE IN A ***MOMENT!***
AIIII!
HURRY!
TOO LATE!
THE ***DRAKUNOMES!***

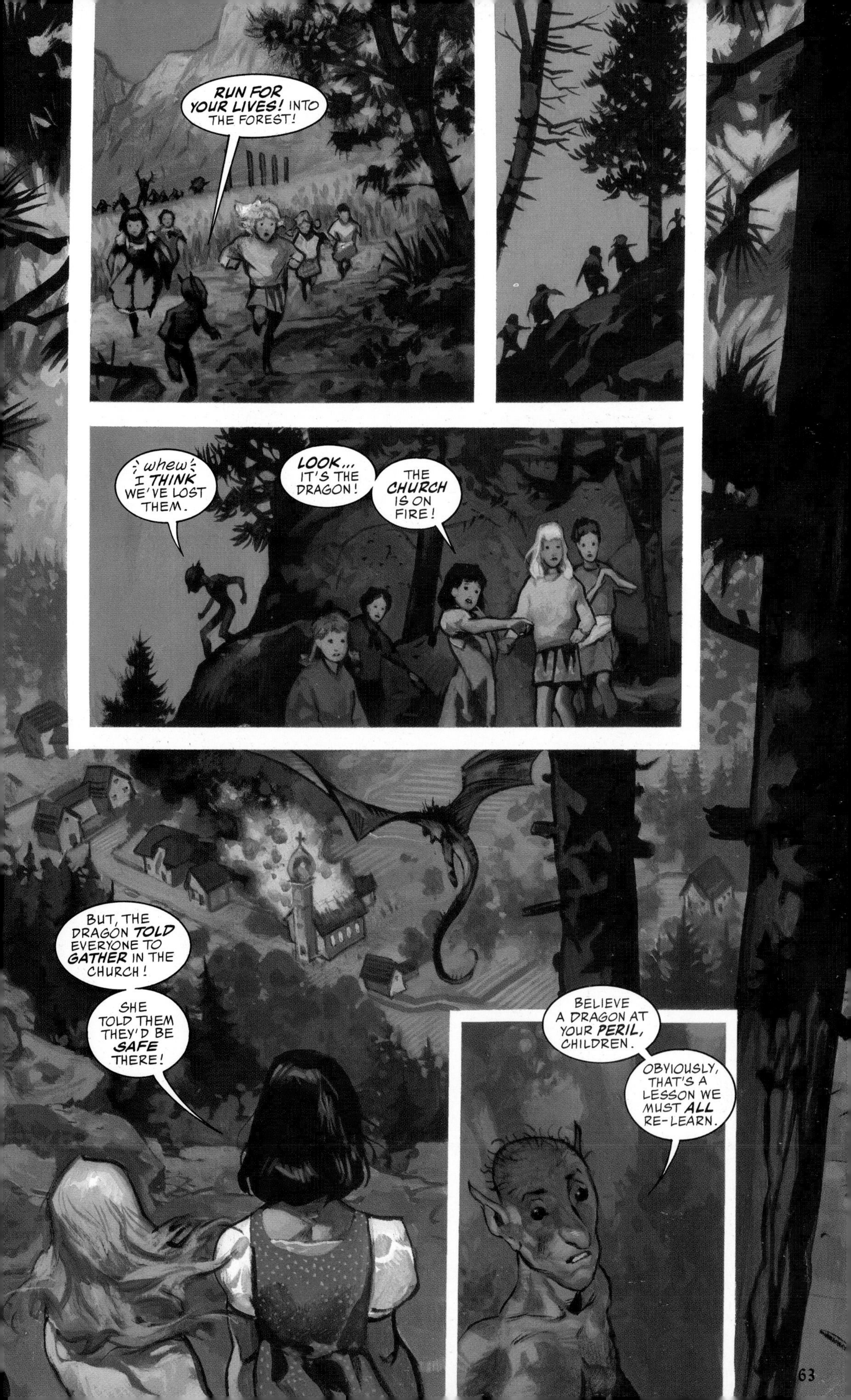
RUN FOR YOUR LIVES! INTO THE FOREST!
whew I THINK WE'VE LOST THEM.
LOOK... IT'S THE DRAGON!
THE CHURCH IS ON FIRE!
BUT, THE DRAGON TOLD EVERYONE TO GATHER IN THE CHURCH!
SHE TOLD THEM THEY'D BE SAFE THERE!
BELIEVE A DRAGON AT YOUR PERIL, CHILDREN.
OBVIOUSLY, THAT'S A LESSON WE MUST ALL RE-LEARN.

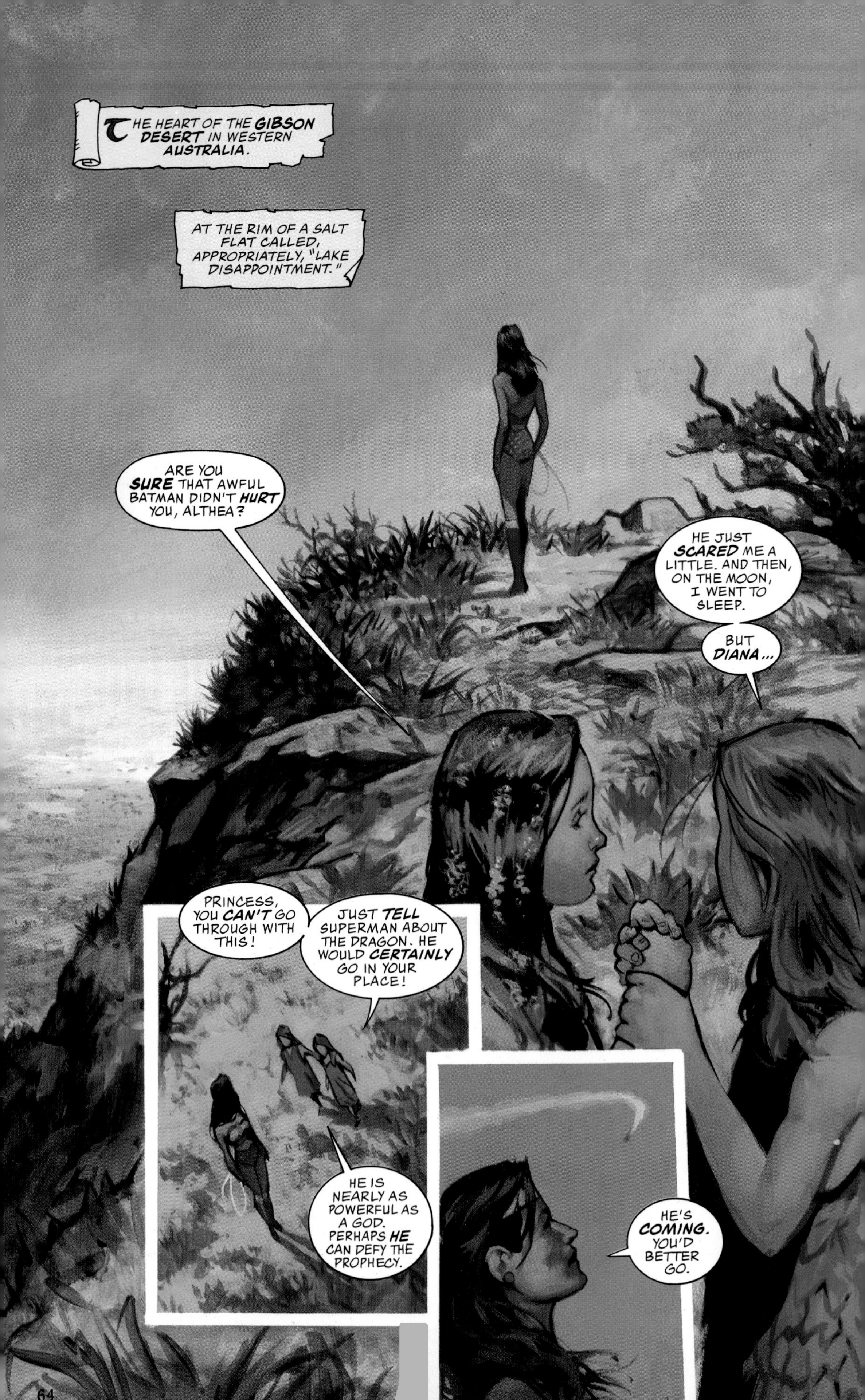
THE HEART OF THE GIBSON DESERT IN WESTERN AUSTRALIA.
AT THE RIM OF A SALT FLAT CALLED, APPROPRIATELY, "LAKE DISAPPOINTMENT."
ARE YOU SURE THAT AWFUL BATMAN DIDN'T HURT YOU, ALTHEA?
HE JUST SCARED ME A LITTLE. AND THEN, ON THE MOON, I WENT TO SLEEP.
BUT DIANA...
PRINCESS, YOU CAN'T GO THROUGH WITH THIS!
JUST TELL SUPERMAN ABOUT THE DRAGON. HE WOULD CERTAINLY GO IN YOUR PLACE!
HE IS NEARLY AS POWERFUL AS A GOD. PERHAPS HE CAN DEFY THE PROPHECY.
HE'S COMING. YOU'D BETTER GO.

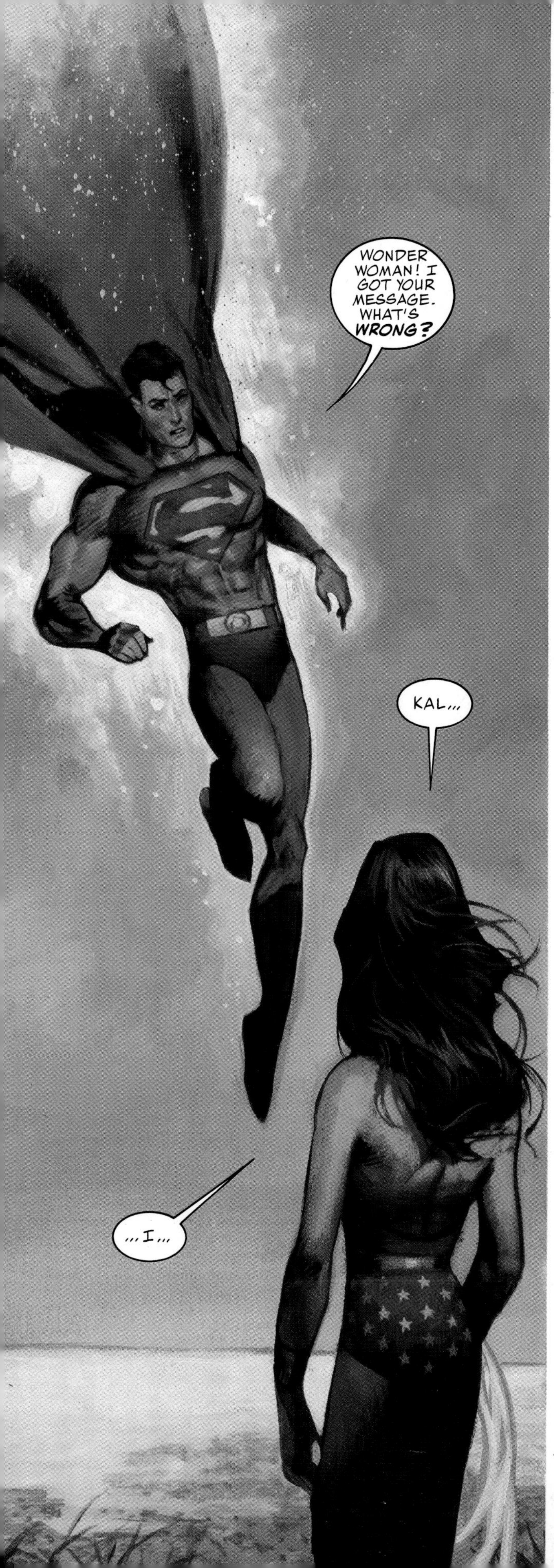
WONDER WOMAN! I GOT YOUR MESSAGE. WHAT'S **WRONG?**
KAL...
...I...

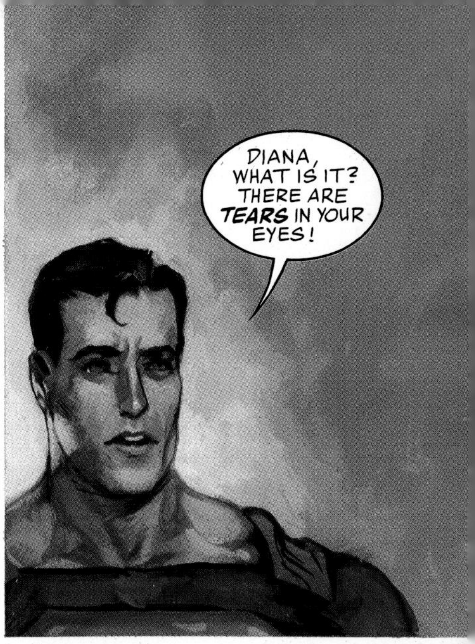
DIANA, WHAT IS IT? THERE ARE **TEARS** IN YOUR EYES!

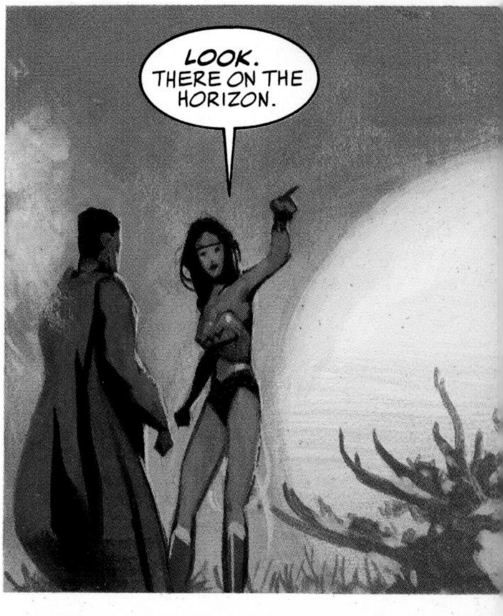
LOOK. THERE ON THE HORIZON.

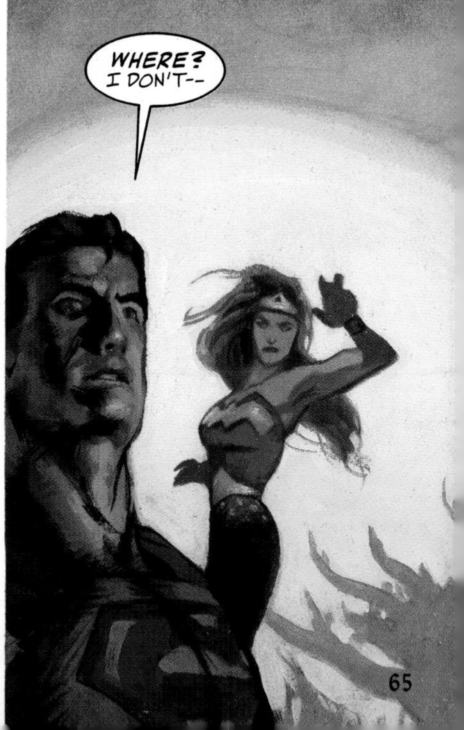
WHERE? I DON'T--

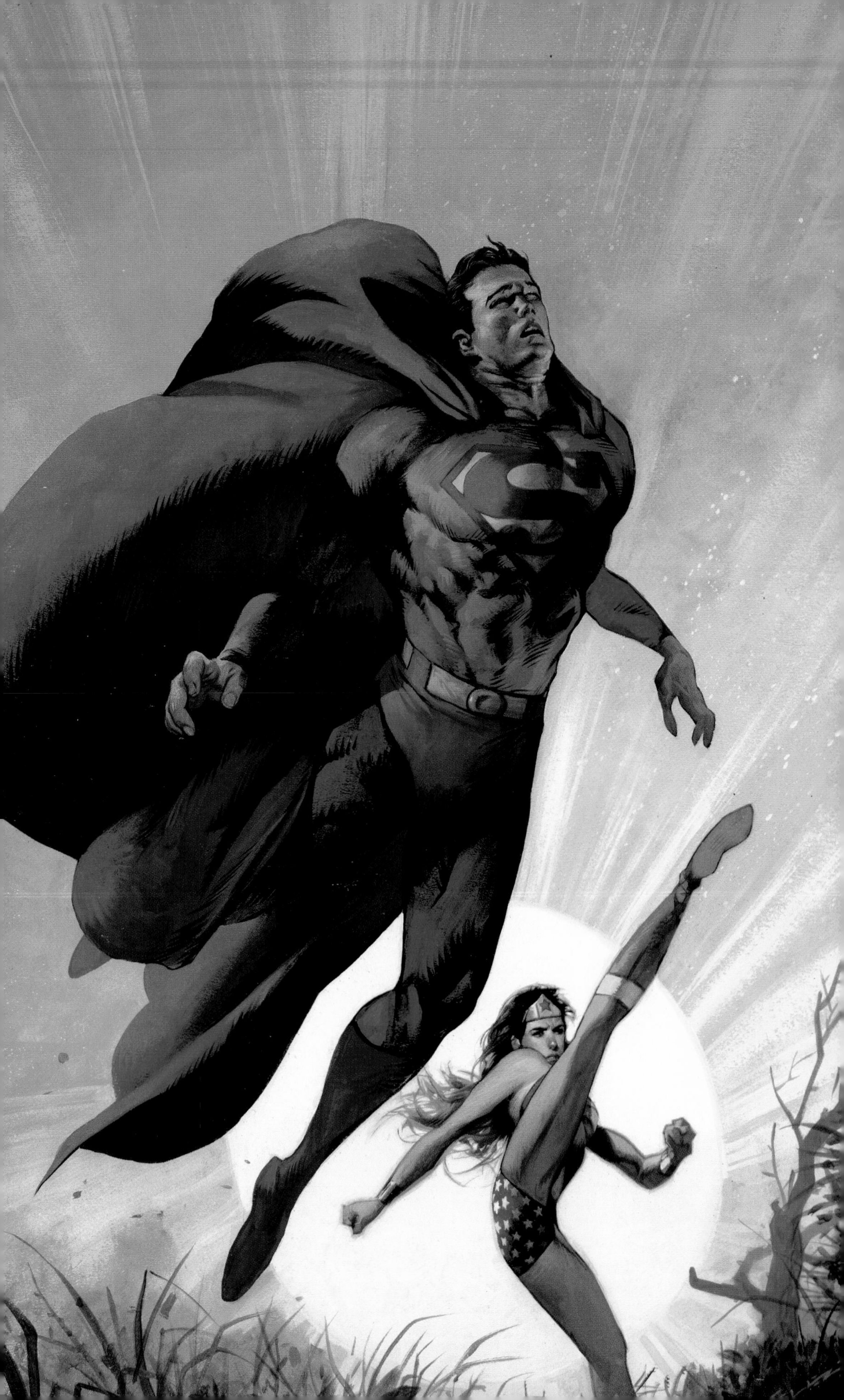

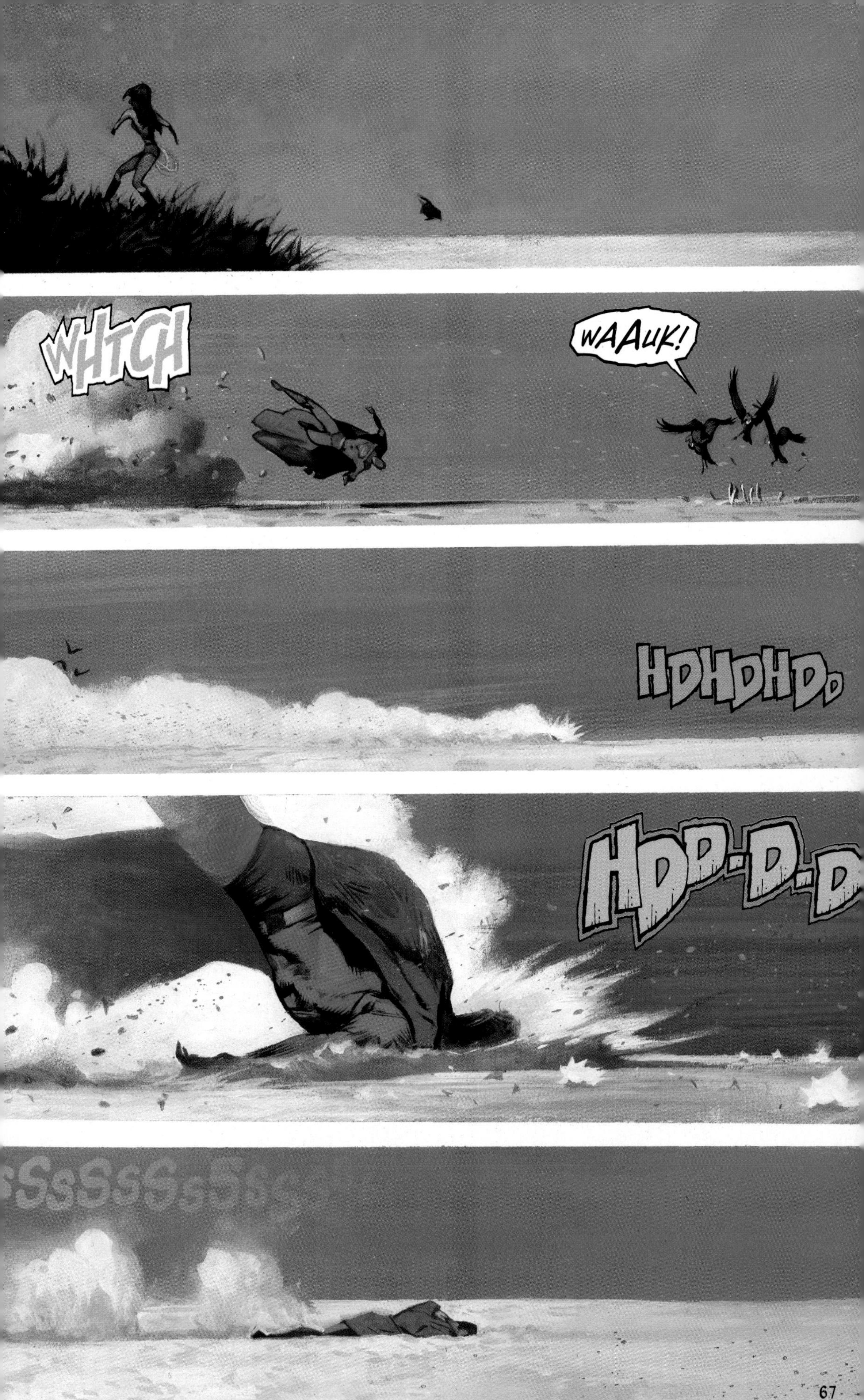
WHTCH
WAAUK!
HDHDHDD
HDD-D-D

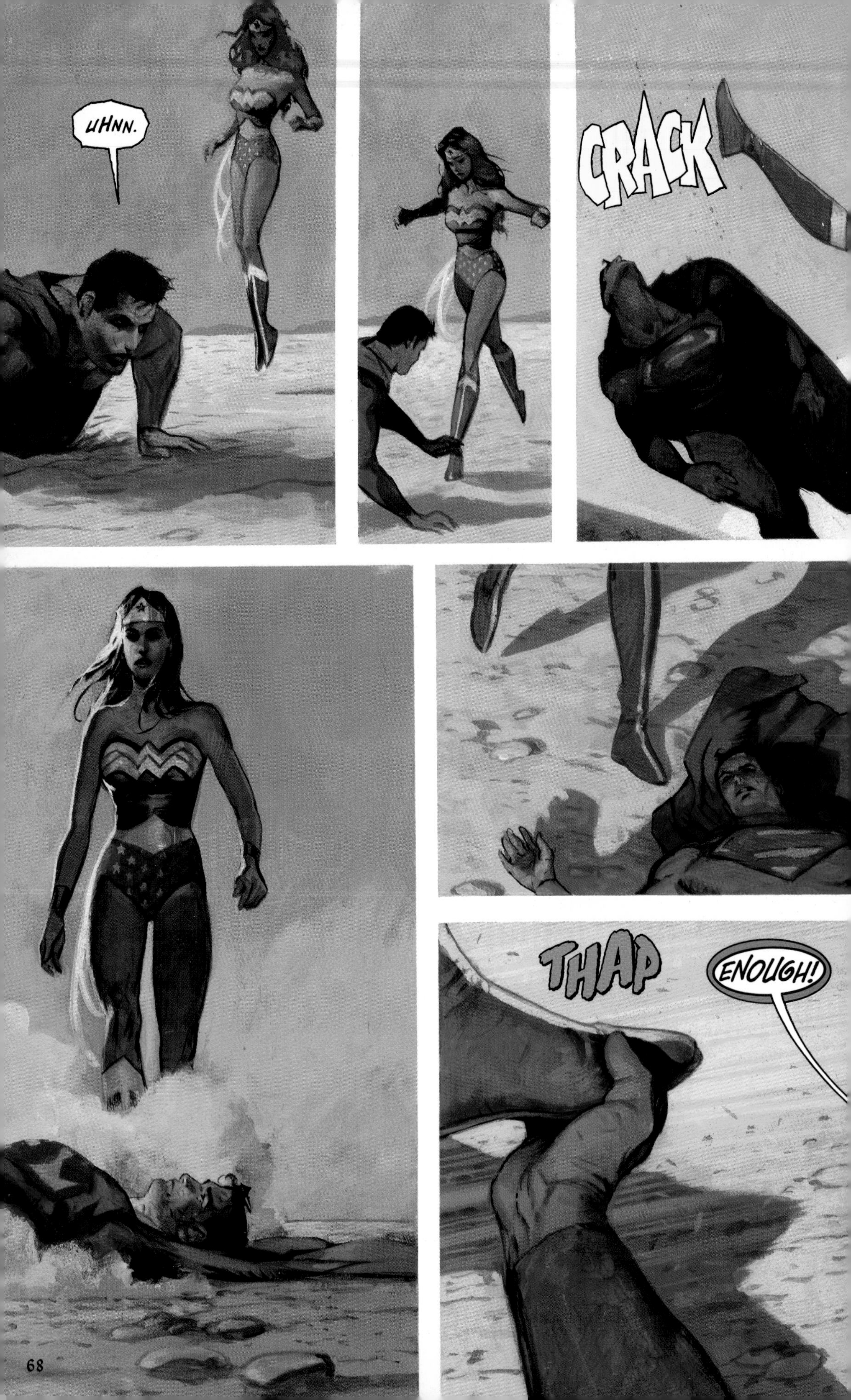
UHNN.
CRACK
THAP
ENOUGH!

WHAT *IS* THIS?

WHUF!

SOME KIND OF *TEST?*

TAP

ALL RIGHT, IF THAT'S HOW YOU *WANT* IT...

WHAM

HD HD HD HD

HD HD HD

HD HD HD HD HD

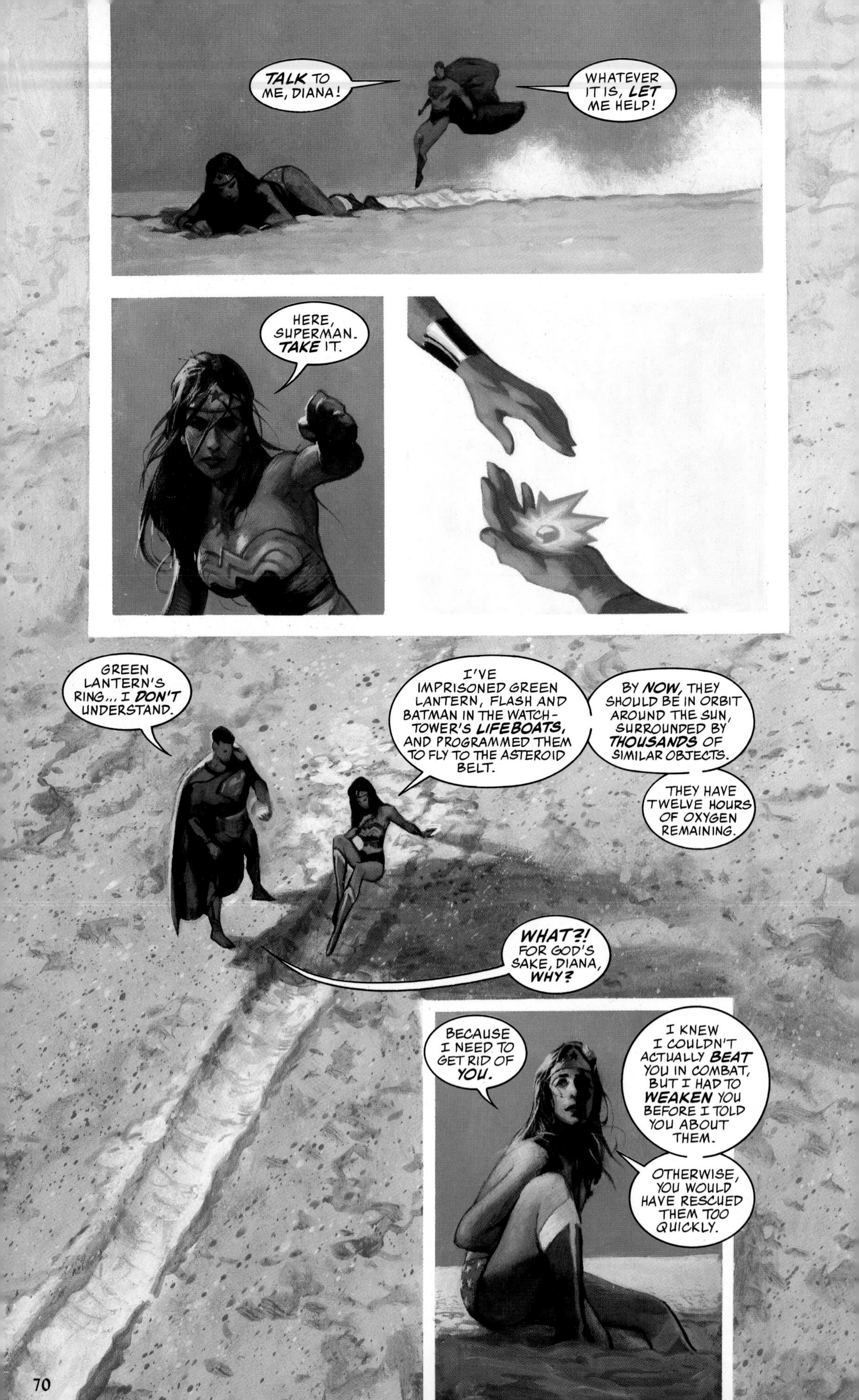

TALK TO ME, DIANA!
WHATEVER IT IS, LET ME HELP!
HERE, SUPERMAN. TAKE IT.
GREEN LANTERN'S RING... I DON'T UNDERSTAND.
I'VE IMPRISONED GREEN LANTERN, FLASH AND BATMAN IN THE WATCH-TOWER'S LIFEBOATS, AND PROGRAMMED THEM TO FLY TO THE ASTEROID BELT.
BY NOW, THEY SHOULD BE IN ORBIT AROUND THE SUN, SURROUNDED BY THOUSANDS OF SIMILAR OBJECTS.
THEY HAVE TWELVE HOURS OF OXYGEN REMAINING.
WHAT?! FOR GOD'S SAKE, DIANA, WHY?
BECAUSE I NEED TO GET RID OF YOU.
I KNEW I COULDN'T ACTUALLY BEAT YOU IN COMBAT, BUT I HAD TO WEAKEN YOU BEFORE I TOLD YOU ABOUT THEM.
OTHERWISE, YOU WOULD HAVE RESCUED THEM TOO QUICKLY.

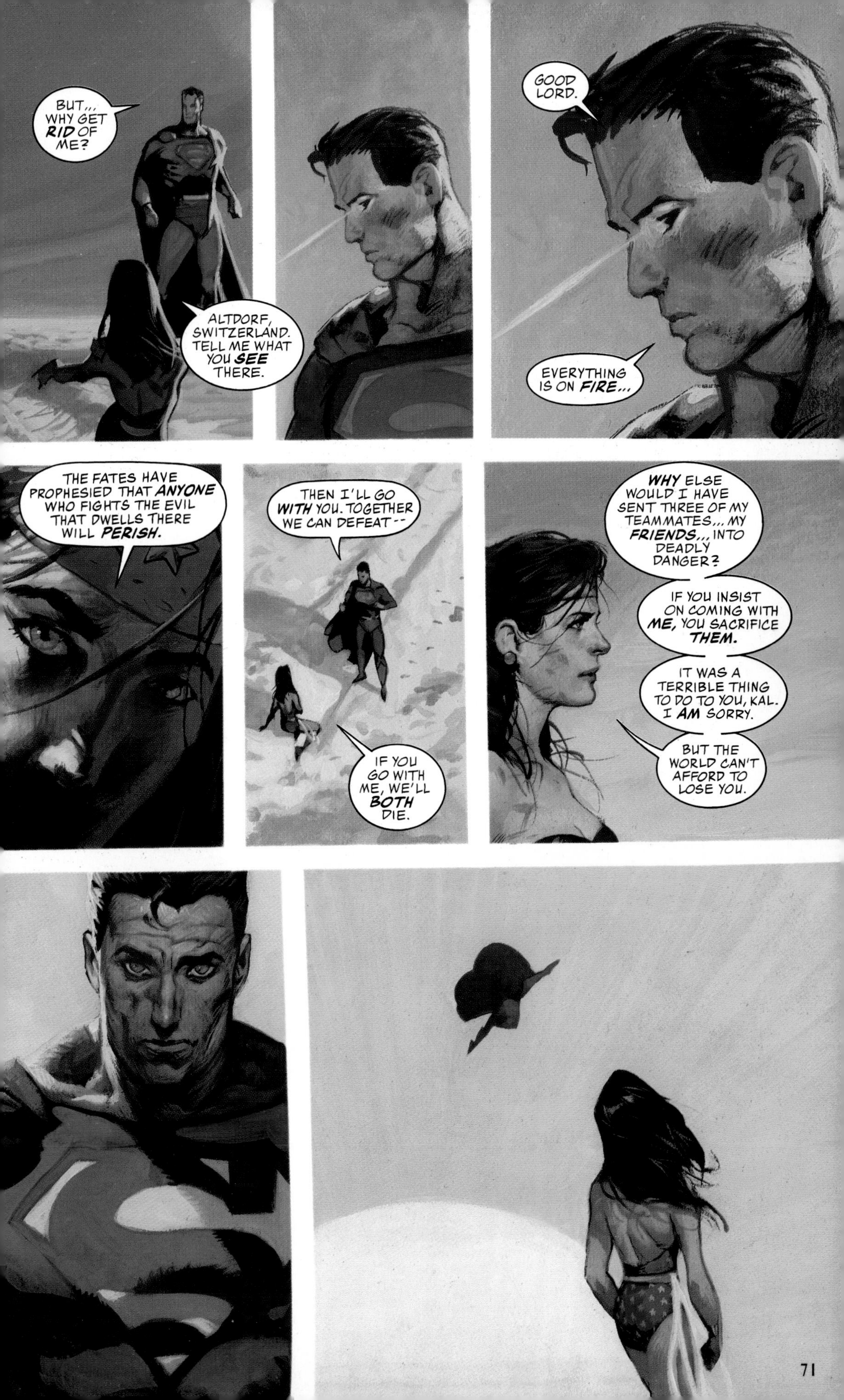
BUT... WHY GET RID OF ME?
ALTDORF, SWITZERLAND. TELL ME WHAT YOU SEE THERE.
GOOD LORD.
EVERYTHING IS ON FIRE...
THE FATES HAVE PROPHESIED THAT ANYONE WHO FIGHTS THE EVIL THAT DWELLS THERE WILL PERISH.
THEN I'LL GO WITH YOU. TOGETHER WE CAN DEFEAT--
IF YOU GO WITH ME, WE'LL BOTH DIE.
WHY ELSE WOULD I HAVE SENT THREE OF MY TEAMMATES... MY FRIENDS... INTO DEADLY DANGER?
IF YOU INSIST ON COMING WITH ME, YOU SACRIFICE THEM.
IT WAS A TERRIBLE THING TO DO TO YOU, KAL. I AM SORRY.
BUT THE WORLD CAN'T AFFORD TO LOSE YOU.

THE REUSS RIVER VALLEY, NEAR ALTDORF.
THE ENTIRE VALLEY IS ABLAZE. BARN, FIELD AND FOREST.
AND YET, BLACKER THAN THE SMOKE THAT DARKENS THE SKY HANGS A TERROR OF ANCIENT EVIL COME RAGING OUT OF THE PAST.
LOOK, MISTRESS! A HERD OF FAT CATTLE!
FLAME-BROIL THEM!
TURN THEM INTO DRACUCOWS!

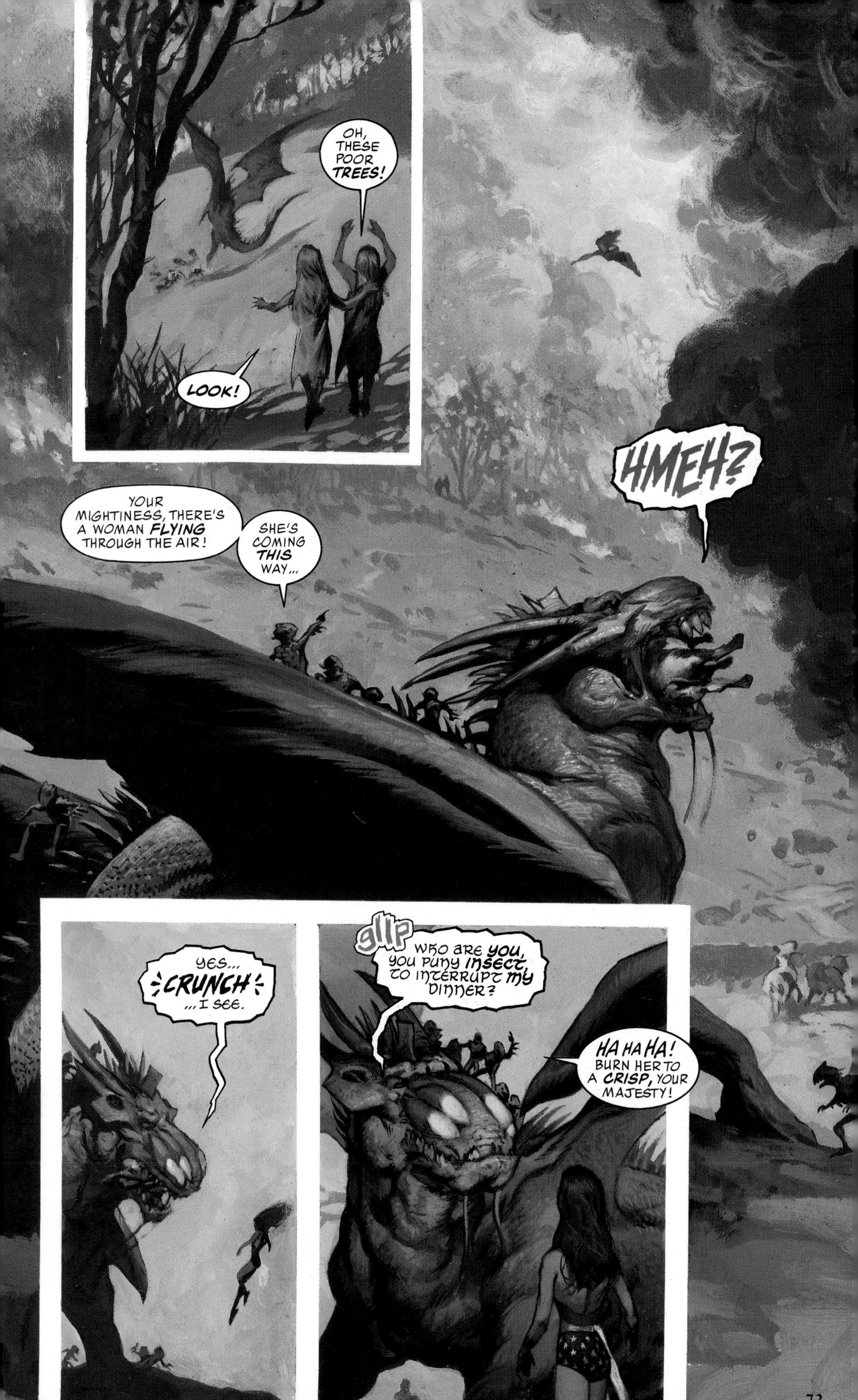

OH, THESE POOR TREES!
LOOK!
YOUR MIGHTINESS, THERE'S A WOMAN FLYING THROUGH THE AIR!
SHE'S COMING THIS WAY...
HMEH?
YES... CRUNCH ...I SEE.
gllp
WHO ARE YOU, YOU PUNY INSECT, TO INTERRUPT MY DINNER?
HA HA HA! BURN HER TO A CRISP, YOUR MAJESTY!

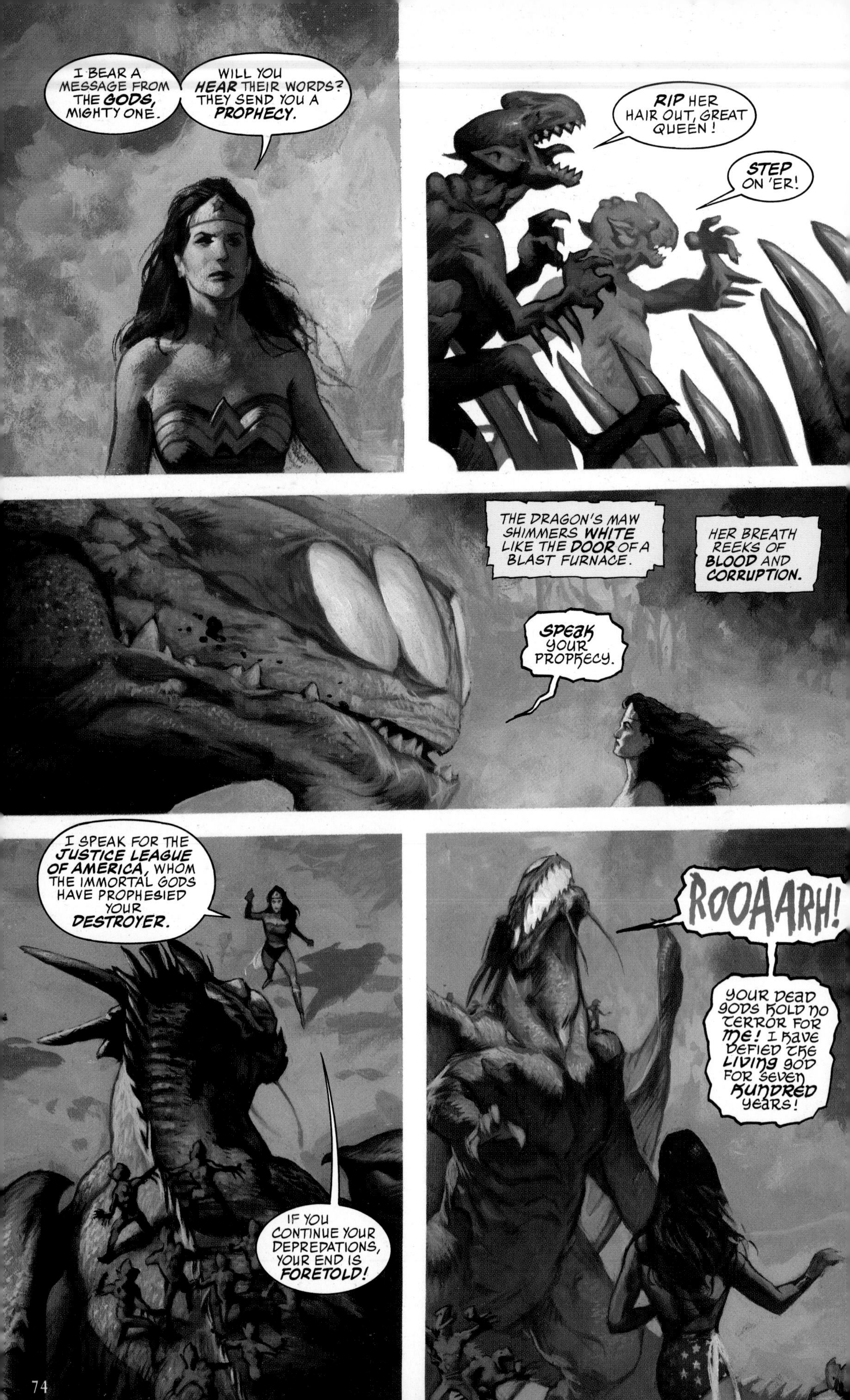
I BEAR A MESSAGE FROM THE **GODS,** MIGHTY ONE.
WILL YOU **HEAR** THEIR WORDS? THEY SEND YOU A **PROPHECY.**
RIP HER HAIR OUT, GREAT QUEEN!
STEP ON 'ER!
THE DRAGON'S MAW SHIMMERS **WHITE** LIKE THE **DOOR** OF A BLAST FURNACE.
HER BREATH REEKS OF **BLOOD** AND **CORRUPTION.**
SPEAK YOUR PROPHECY.
I SPEAK FOR THE **JUSTICE LEAGUE OF AMERICA,** WHOM THE IMMORTAL GODS HAVE PROPHESIED YOUR **DESTROYER.**
IF YOU CONTINUE YOUR DEPREDATIONS, YOUR END IS **FORETOLD!**
ROOAARH!
YOUR DEAD GODS HOLD NO TERROR FOR **ME!** I HAVE DEFIED THE **LIVING** GOD FOR SEVEN **HUNDRED** YEARS!

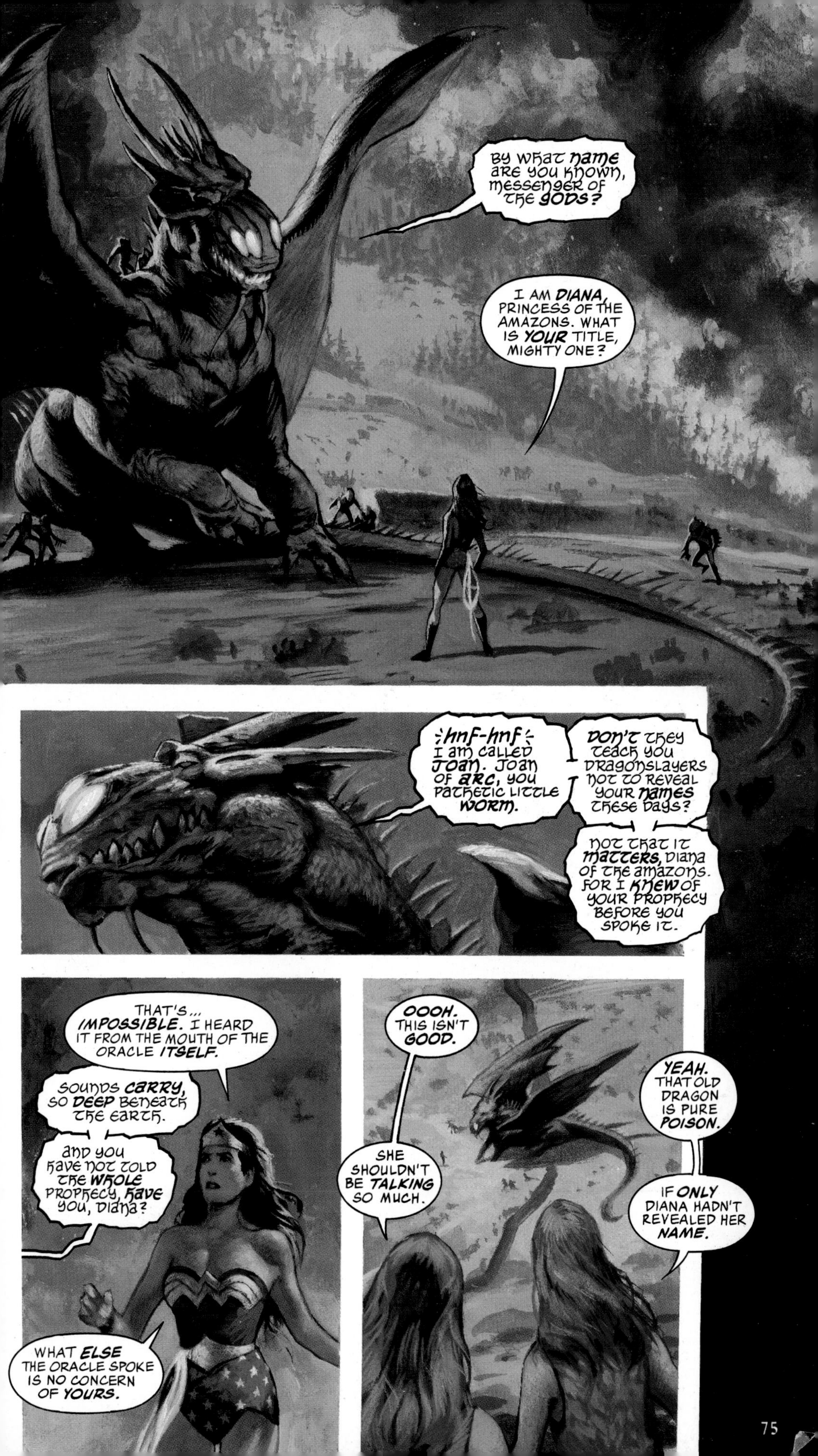
BY WHAT NAME ARE YOU KNOWN, MESSENGER OF THE GODS?
I AM DIANA, PRINCESS OF THE AMAZONS. WHAT IS YOUR TITLE, MIGHTY ONE?
-HNF-HNF- I AM CALLED JOAN. JOAN OF ARC, YOU PATHETIC LITTLE WORM.
DON'T THEY TEACH YOU DRAGONSLAYERS NOT TO REVEAL YOUR NAMES THESE DAYS?
NOT THAT IT MATTERS, DIANA OF THE AMAZONS. FOR I KNEW OF YOUR PROPHECY BEFORE YOU SPOKE IT.
THAT'S... IMPOSSIBLE. I HEARD IT FROM THE MOUTH OF THE ORACLE ITSELF.
SOUNDS CARRY, SO DEEP BENEATH THE EARTH.
AND YOU HAVE NOT TOLD THE WHOLE PROPHECY, HAVE YOU, DIANA?
WHAT ELSE THE ORACLE SPOKE IS NO CONCERN OF YOURS.
OOOH. THIS ISN'T GOOD.
SHE SHOULDN'T BE TALKING SO MUCH.
YEAH. THAT OLD DRAGON IS PURE POISON.
IF ONLY DIANA HADN'T REVEALED HER NAME.

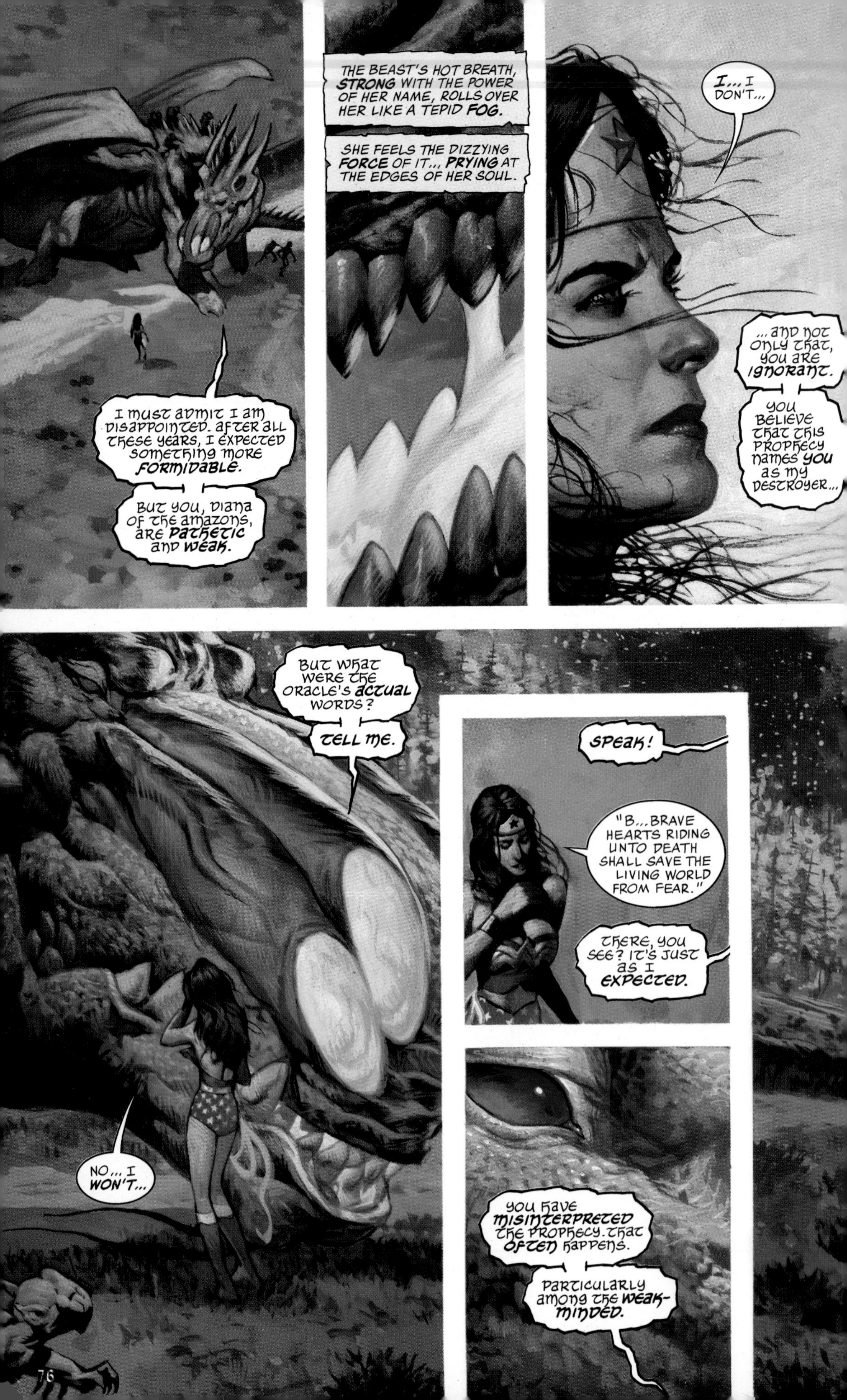
I MUST ADMIT I AM DISAPPOINTED. AFTER ALL THESE YEARS, I EXPECTED SOMETHING MORE FORMIDABLE.
BUT YOU, DIANA OF THE AMAZONS, ARE PATHETIC AND WEAK.
THE BEAST'S HOT BREATH, STRONG WITH THE POWER OF HER NAME, ROLLS OVER HER LIKE A TEPID FOG.
SHE FEELS THE DIZZYING FORCE OF IT... PRYING AT THE EDGES OF HER SOUL.
I... I DON'T...
...AND NOT ONLY THAT, YOU ARE IGNORANT.
YOU BELIEVE THAT THIS PROPHECY NAMES YOU AS MY DESTROYER...
BUT WHAT WERE THE ORACLE'S ACTUAL WORDS?
TELL ME.
NO... I WON'T...
SPEAK!
"B... BRAVE HEARTS RIDING UNTO DEATH SHALL SAVE THE LIVING WORLD FROM FEAR."
THERE, YOU SEE? IT'S JUST AS I EXPECTED.
YOU HAVE MISINTERPRETED THE PROPHECY. THAT OFTEN HAPPENS.
PARTICULARLY AMONG THE WEAK-MINDED.

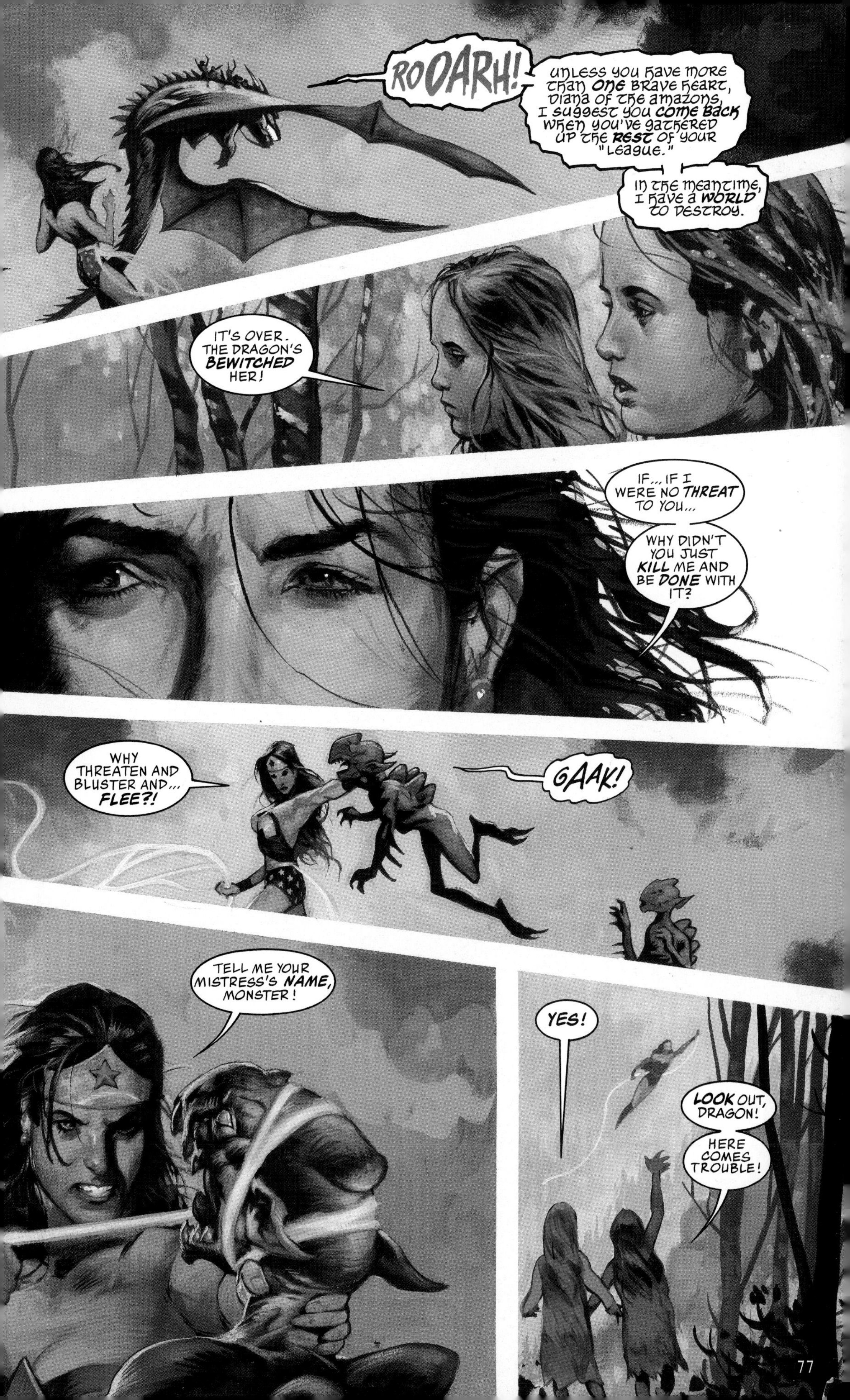

ROOARH!
UNLESS YOU HAVE MORE THAN ONE BRAVE HEART, DIANA OF THE AMAZONS, I SUGGEST YOU COME BACK WHEN YOU'VE GATHERED UP THE REST OF YOUR "LEAGUE."
IN THE MEANTIME, I HAVE A WORLD TO DESTROY.
IT'S OVER. THE DRAGON'S BEWITCHED HER!
IF... IF I WERE NO THREAT TO YOU...
WHY DIDN'T YOU JUST KILL ME AND BE DONE WITH IT?
WHY THREATEN AND BLUSTER AND... FLEE?!
GAAK!
TELL ME YOUR MISTRESS'S NAME, MONSTER!
YES!
LOOK OUT, DRAGON!
HERE COMES TROUBLE!

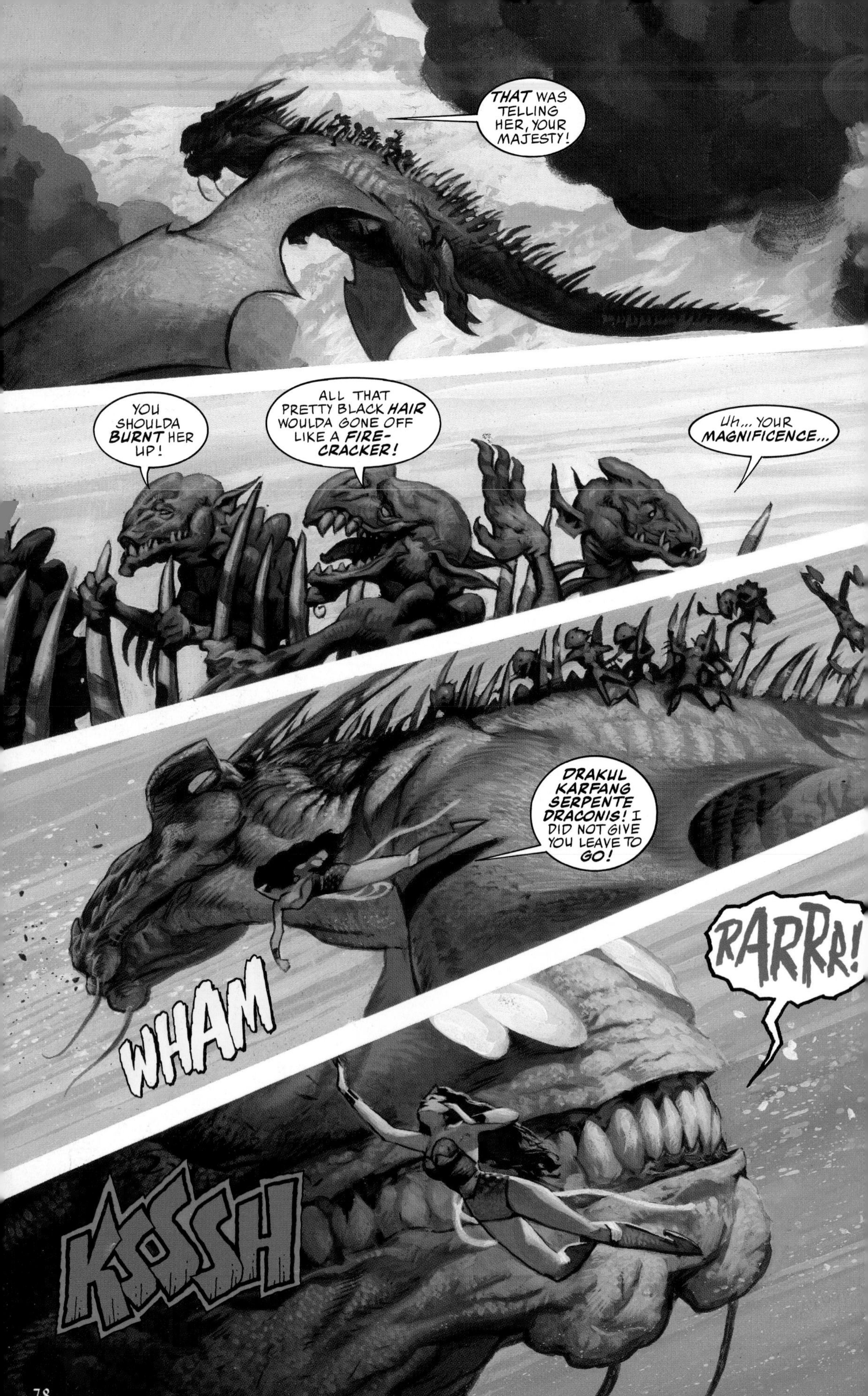
THAT WAS TELLING HER, YOUR MAJESTY!
YOU SHOULDA BURNT HER UP!
ALL THAT PRETTY BLACK HAIR WOULDA GONE OFF LIKE A FIRE-CRACKER!
UH... YOUR MAGNIFICENCE...
DRAKUL KARFANG SERPENTE DRACONIS! I DID NOT GIVE YOU LEAVE TO GO!
WHAM
RARRR!
KSSH

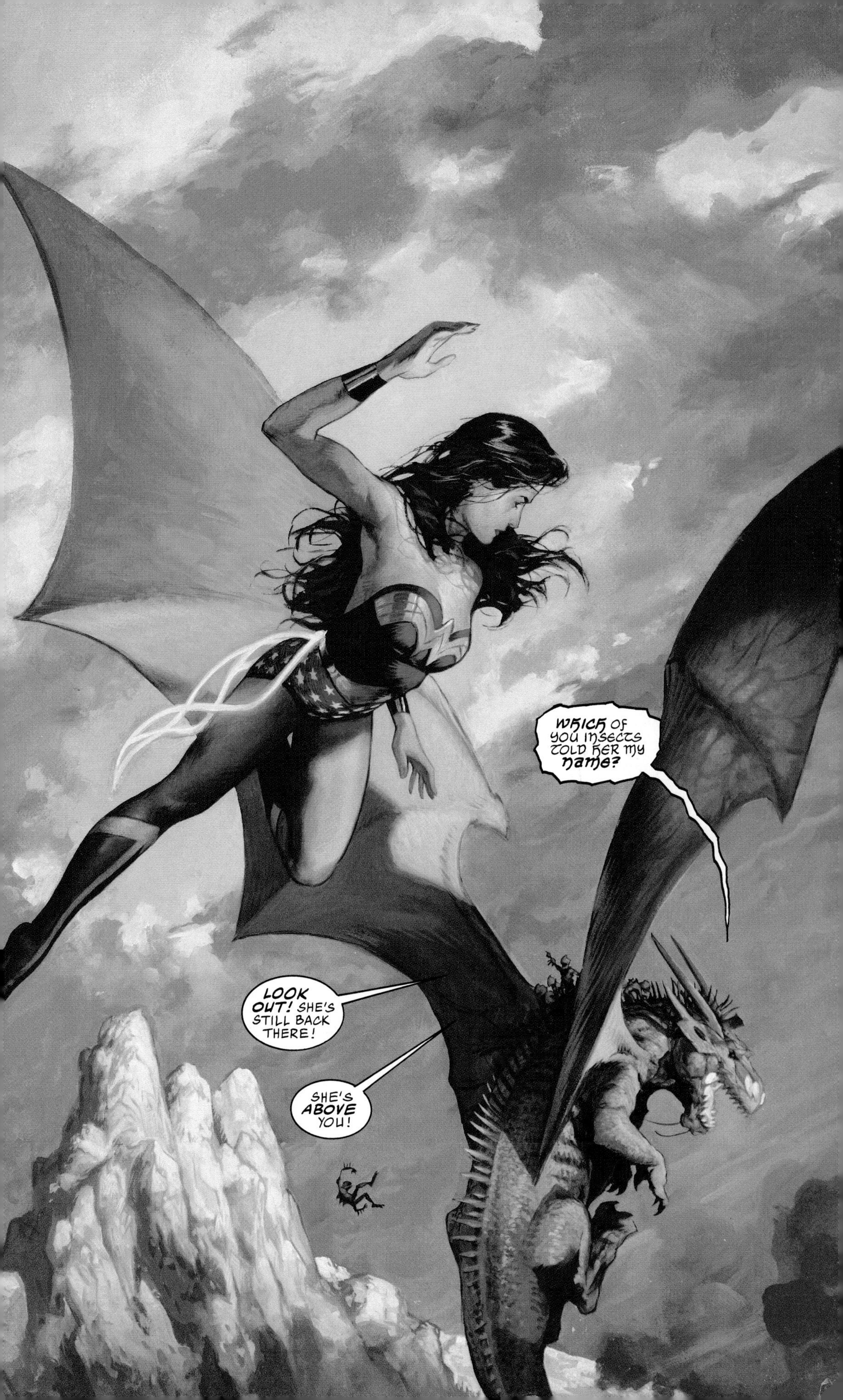
WHICH OF YOU INSECTS TOLD HER MY NAME?
LOOK OUT! SHE'S STILL BACK THERE!
SHE'S ABOVE YOU!

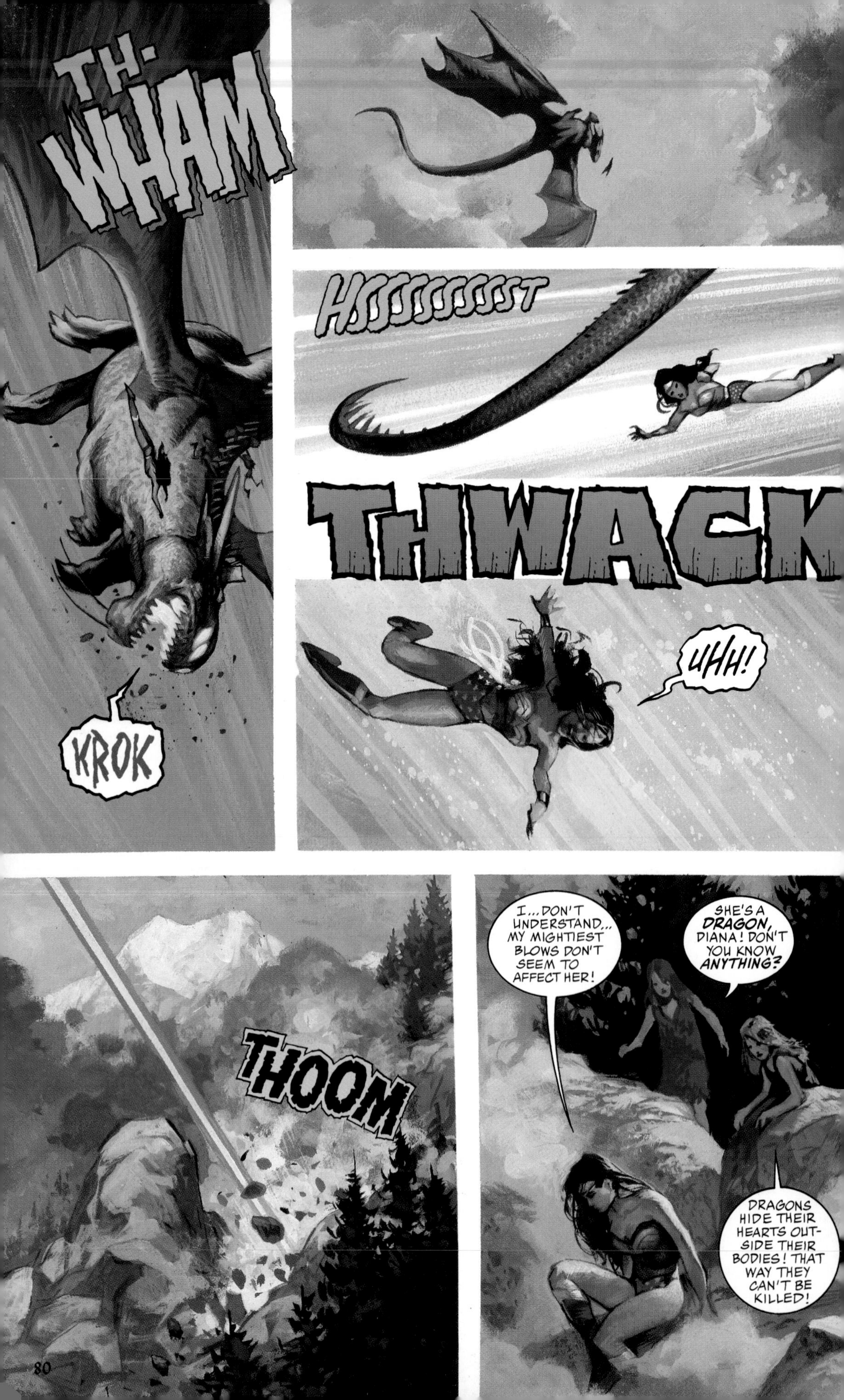
TH-WHAM
KROK
HSSSSSSSST
THWACK
UHH!
THOOM
I... DON'T UNDERSTAND... MY MIGHTIEST BLOWS DON'T SEEM TO AFFECT HER!
SHE'S A *DRAGON*, DIANA! DON'T YOU KNOW *ANYTHING?*
DRAGONS HIDE THEIR HEARTS OUT-SIDE THEIR BODIES! THAT WAY THEY CAN'T BE KILLED!

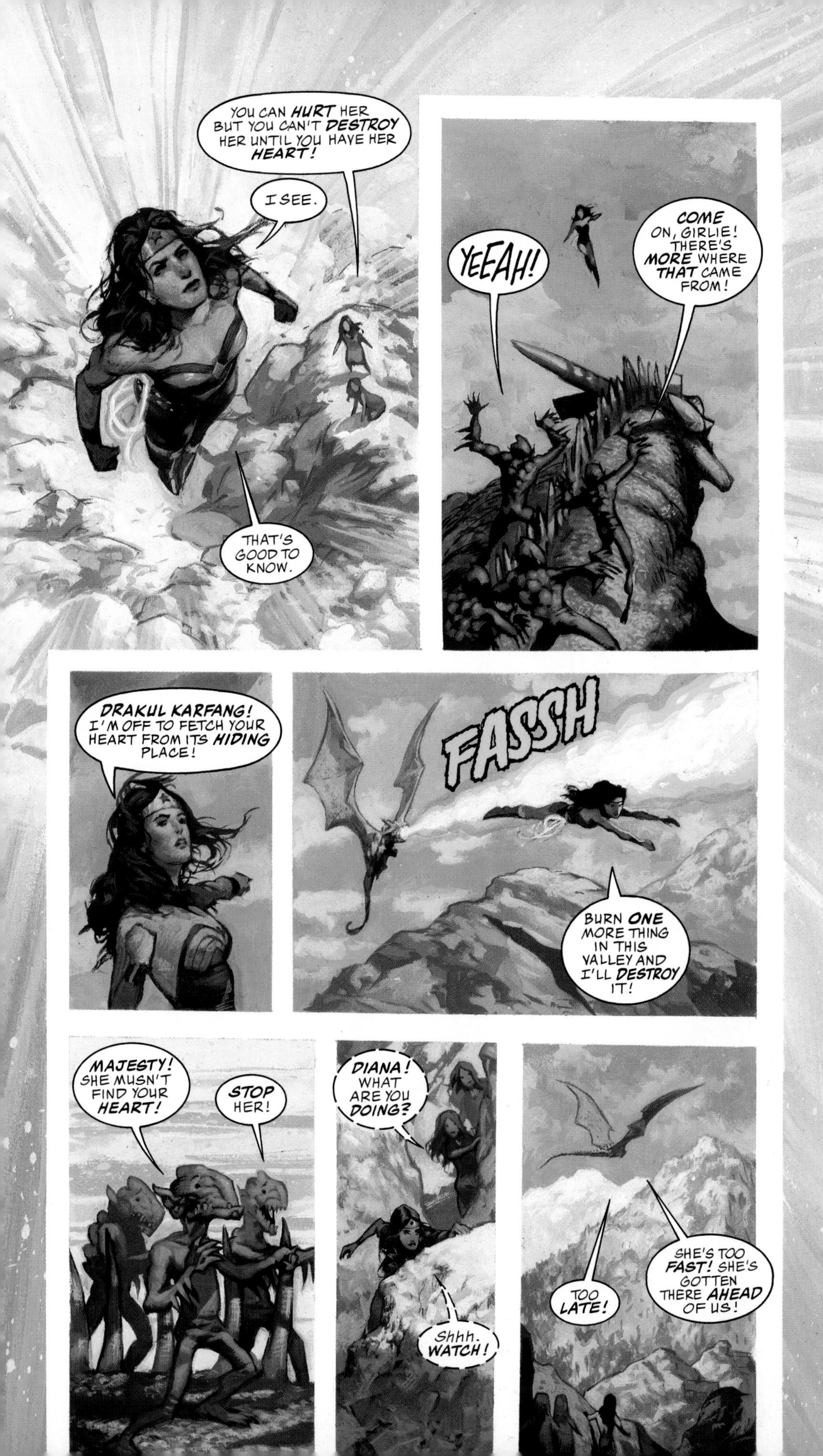
YOU CAN HURT HER BUT YOU CAN'T DESTROY HER UNTIL YOU HAVE HER HEART!
I SEE.
THAT'S GOOD TO KNOW.
YEEAH!
COME ON, GIRLIE! THERE'S MORE WHERE THAT CAME FROM!
DRAKUL KARFANG! I'M OFF TO FETCH YOUR HEART FROM ITS HIDING PLACE!
FASSH
BURN ONE MORE THING IN THIS VALLEY AND I'LL DESTROY IT!
MAJESTY! SHE MUSN'T FIND YOUR HEART!
STOP HER!
DIANA! WHAT ARE YOU DOING?
Shhh. WATCH!
SHE'S TOO FAST! SHE'S GOTTEN THERE AHEAD OF US!
TOO LATE!

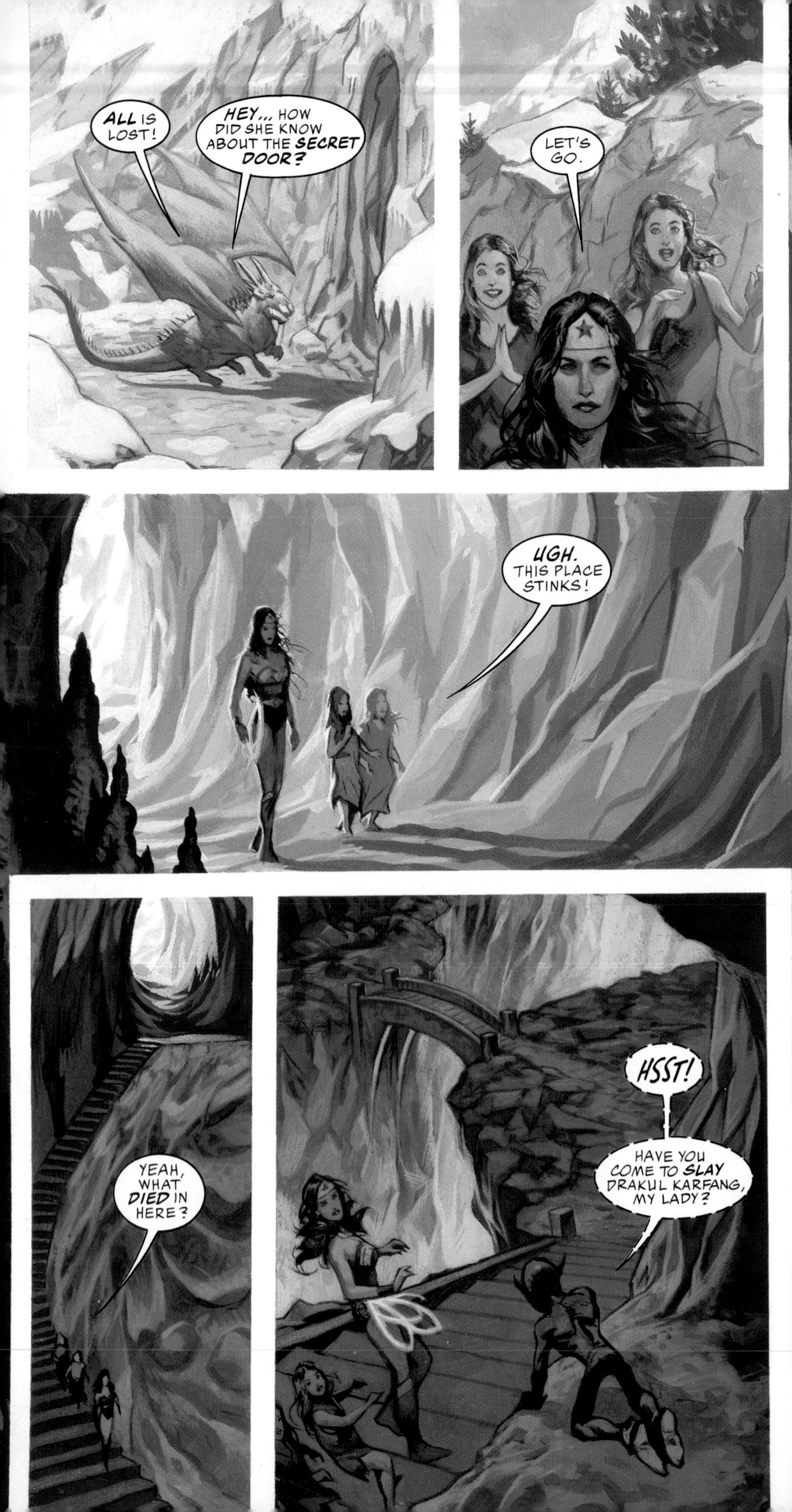
ALL IS LOST!
HEY... HOW DID SHE KNOW ABOUT THE SECRET DOOR?
LET'S GO.
UGH. THIS PLACE STINKS!
YEAH, WHAT DIED IN HERE?
HSST!
HAVE YOU COME TO SLAY DRAKUL KARFANG, MY LADY?

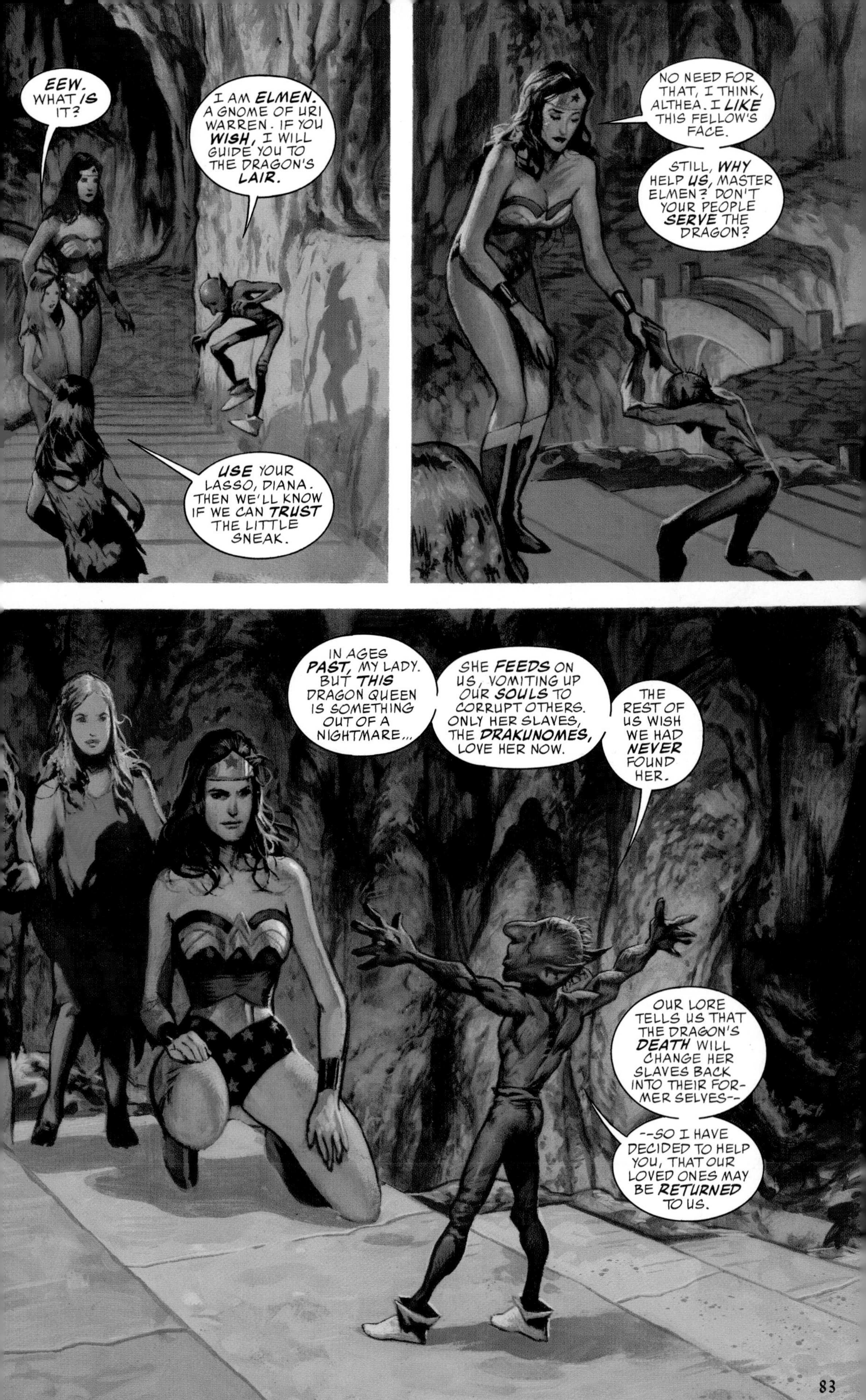
EEW. WHAT IS IT?
I AM ELMEN. A GNOME OF URI WARREN. IF YOU WISH, I WILL GUIDE YOU TO THE DRAGON'S LAIR.
USE YOUR LASSO, DIANA. THEN WE'LL KNOW IF WE CAN TRUST THE LITTLE SNEAK.
NO NEED FOR THAT, I THINK, ALTHEA. I LIKE THIS FELLOW'S FACE.
STILL, WHY HELP US, MASTER ELMEN? DON'T YOUR PEOPLE SERVE THE DRAGON?
IN AGES PAST, MY LADY. BUT THIS DRAGON QUEEN IS SOMETHING OUT OF A NIGHTMARE...
SHE FEEDS ON US, VOMITING UP OUR SOULS TO CORRUPT OTHERS. ONLY HER SLAVES, THE DRAKUNOMES, LOVE HER NOW.
THE REST OF US WISH WE HAD NEVER FOUND HER.
OUR LORE TELLS US THAT THE DRAGON'S DEATH WILL CHANGE HER SLAVES BACK INTO THEIR FOR-MER SELVES--
--SO I HAVE DECIDED TO HELP YOU, THAT OUR LOVED ONES MAY BE RETURNED TO US.

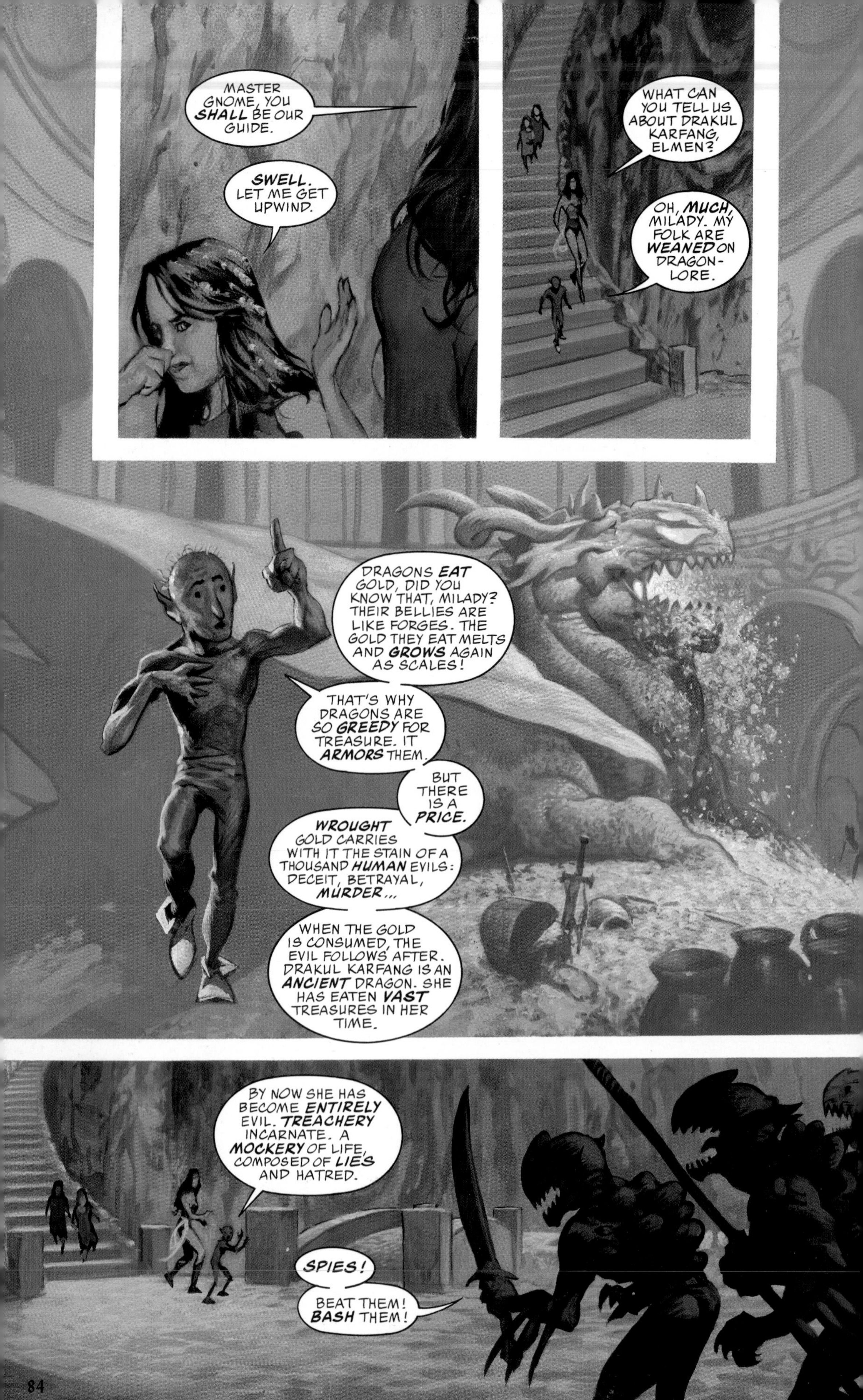
MASTER GNOME, YOU SHALL BE OUR GUIDE.
SWELL. LET ME GET UPWIND.
WHAT CAN YOU TELL US ABOUT DRAKUL KARFANG, ELMEN?
OH, MUCH, MILADY. MY FOLK ARE WEANED ON DRAGON-LORE.
DRAGONS EAT GOLD, DID YOU KNOW THAT, MILADY? THEIR BELLIES ARE LIKE FORGES. THE GOLD THEY EAT MELTS AND GROWS AGAIN AS SCALES!
THAT'S WHY DRAGONS ARE SO GREEDY FOR TREASURE. IT ARMORS THEM.
BUT THERE IS A PRICE.
WROUGHT GOLD CARRIES WITH IT THE STAIN OF A THOUSAND HUMAN EVILS: DECEIT, BETRAYAL, MURDER...
WHEN THE GOLD IS CONSUMED, THE EVIL FOLLOWS AFTER. DRAKUL KARFANG IS AN ANCIENT DRAGON. SHE HAS EATEN VAST TREASURES IN HER TIME.
BY NOW SHE HAS BECOME ENTIRELY EVIL. TREACHERY INCARNATE. A MOCKERY OF LIFE, COMPOSED OF LIES AND HATRED.
SPIES!
BEAT THEM! BASH THEM!

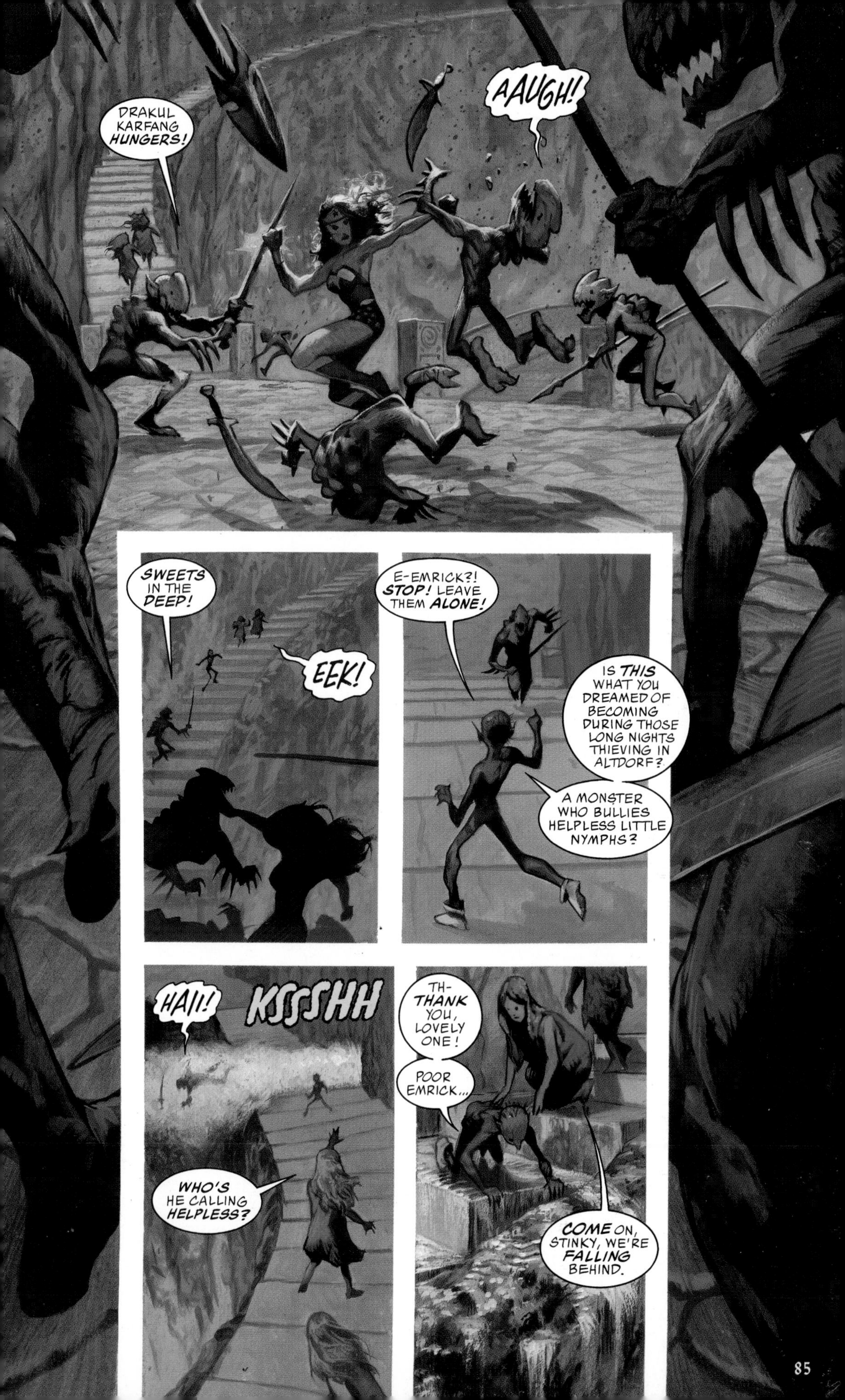
DRAKUL KARFANG HUNGERS!
AAUGH!
SWEETS IN THE DEEP!
EEK!
E-EMRICK?! STOP! LEAVE THEM ALONE!
IS THIS WHAT YOU DREAMED OF BECOMING DURING THOSE LONG NIGHTS THIEVING IN ALTDORF?
A MONSTER WHO BULLIES HELPLESS LITTLE NYMPHS?
HAI!!
KSSSHH
WHO'S HE CALLING HELPLESS?
TH-THANK YOU, LOVELY ONE!
POOR EMRICK...
COME ON, STINKY, WE'RE FALLING BEHIND.

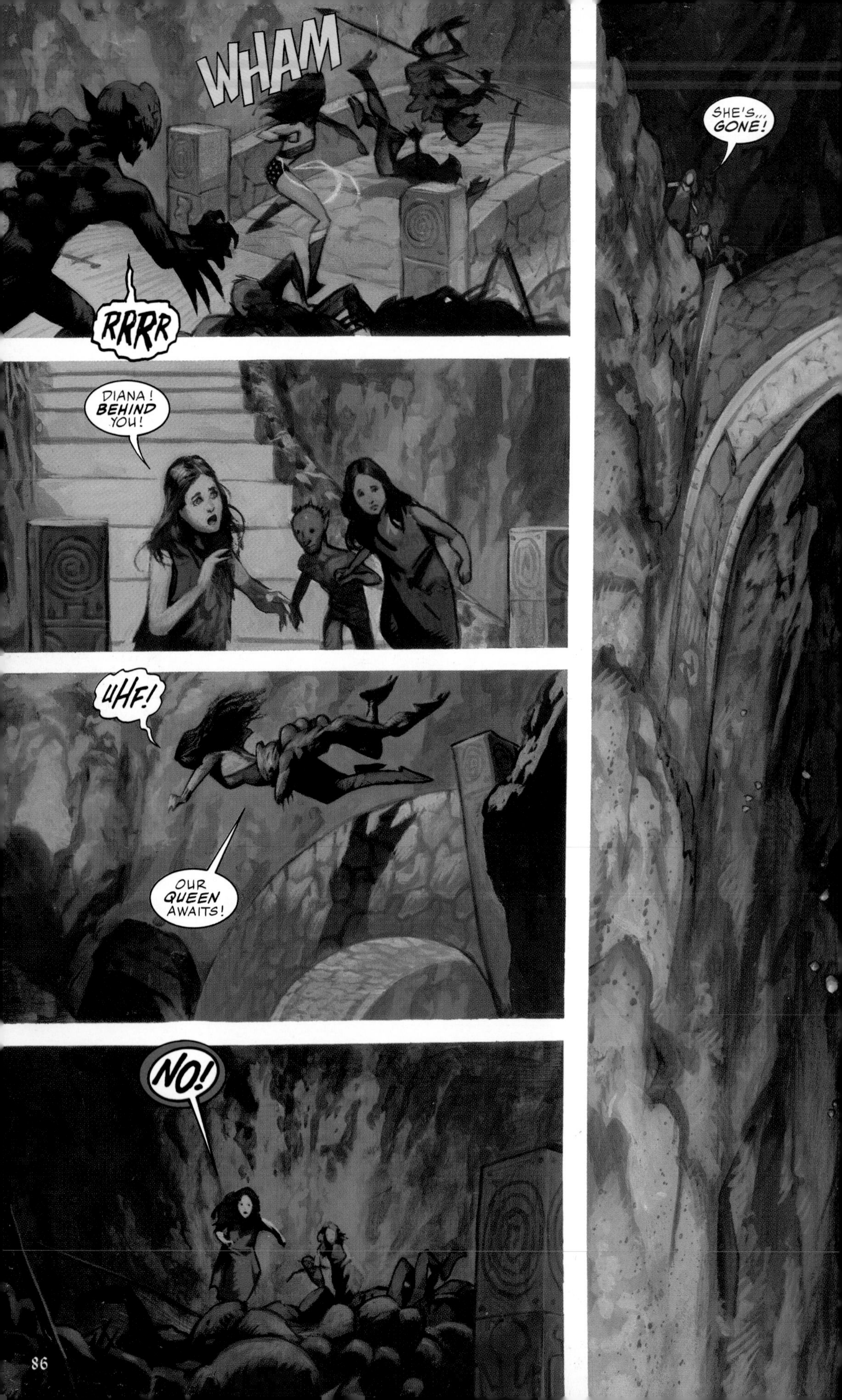
WHAM
RRRR
DIANA! BEHIND YOU!
UHF!
OUR QUEEN AWAITS!
NO!
SHE'S... GONE!

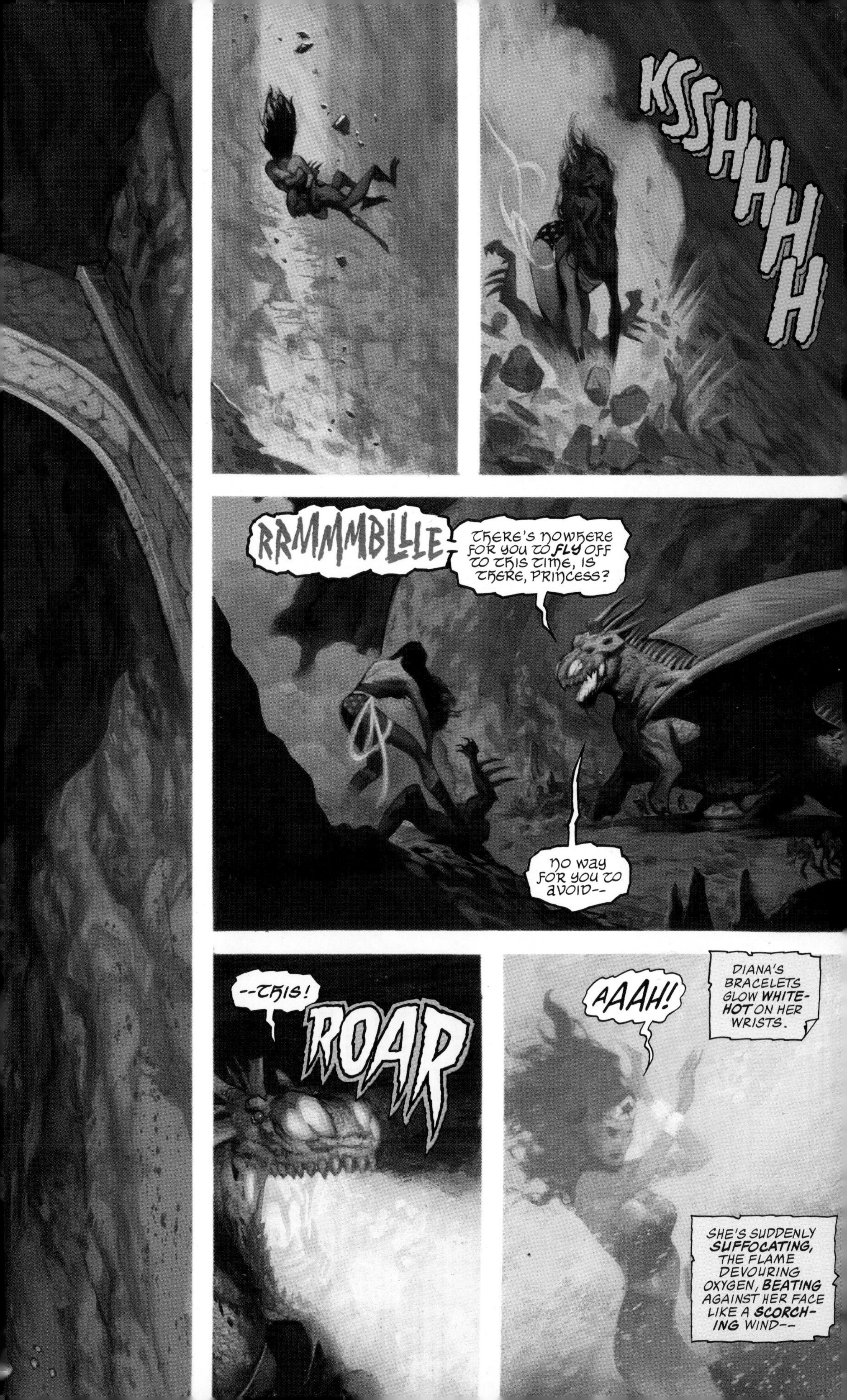
KSSHHHHH
RRMMMBLLLE
THERE'S NOWHERE FOR YOU TO FLY OFF TO THIS TIME, IS THERE, PRINCESS?
NO WAY FOR YOU TO AVOID--
--THIS!
ROAR
AAAH!
DIANA'S BRACELETS GLOW WHITE-HOT ON HER WRISTS.
SHE'S SUDDENLY SUFFOCATING, THE FLAME DEVOURING OXYGEN, BEATING AGAINST HER FACE LIKE A SCORCHING WIND--

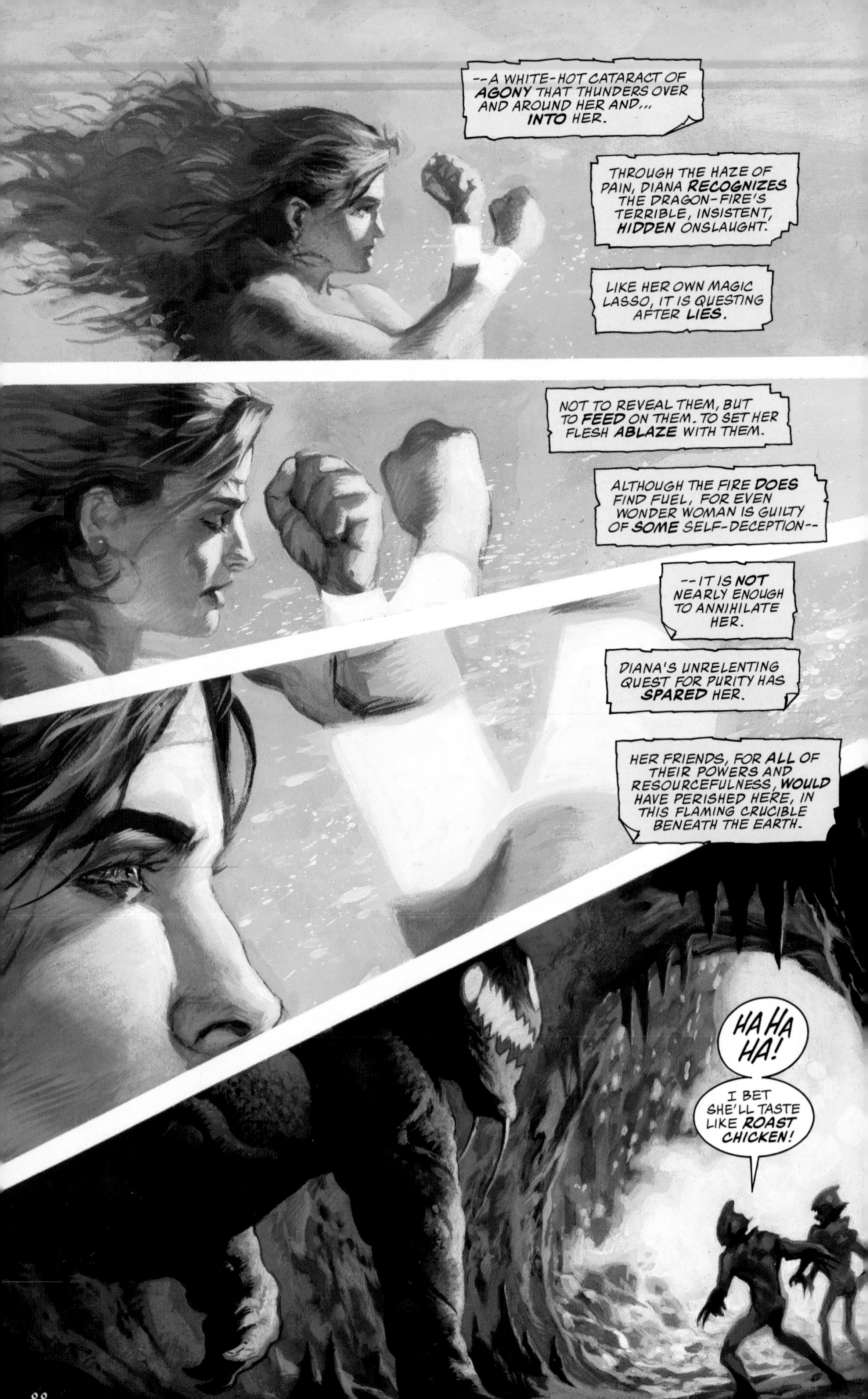
--A WHITE-HOT CATARACT OF AGONY THAT THUNDERS OVER AND AROUND HER AND... INTO HER.
THROUGH THE HAZE OF PAIN, DIANA RECOGNIZES THE DRAGON-FIRE'S TERRIBLE, INSISTENT, HIDDEN ONSLAUGHT.
LIKE HER OWN MAGIC LASSO, IT IS QUESTING AFTER LIES.
NOT TO REVEAL THEM, BUT TO FEED ON THEM. TO SET HER FLESH ABLAZE WITH THEM.
ALTHOUGH THE FIRE DOES FIND FUEL, FOR EVEN WONDER WOMAN IS GUILTY OF SOME SELF-DECEPTION--
--IT IS NOT NEARLY ENOUGH TO ANNIHILATE HER.
DIANA'S UNRELENTING QUEST FOR PURITY HAS SPARED HER.
HER FRIENDS, FOR ALL OF THEIR POWERS AND RESOURCEFULNESS, WOULD HAVE PERISHED HERE, IN THIS FLAMING CRUCIBLE BENEATH THE EARTH.
HA HA HA!
I BET SHE'LL TASTE LIKE ROAST CHICKEN!

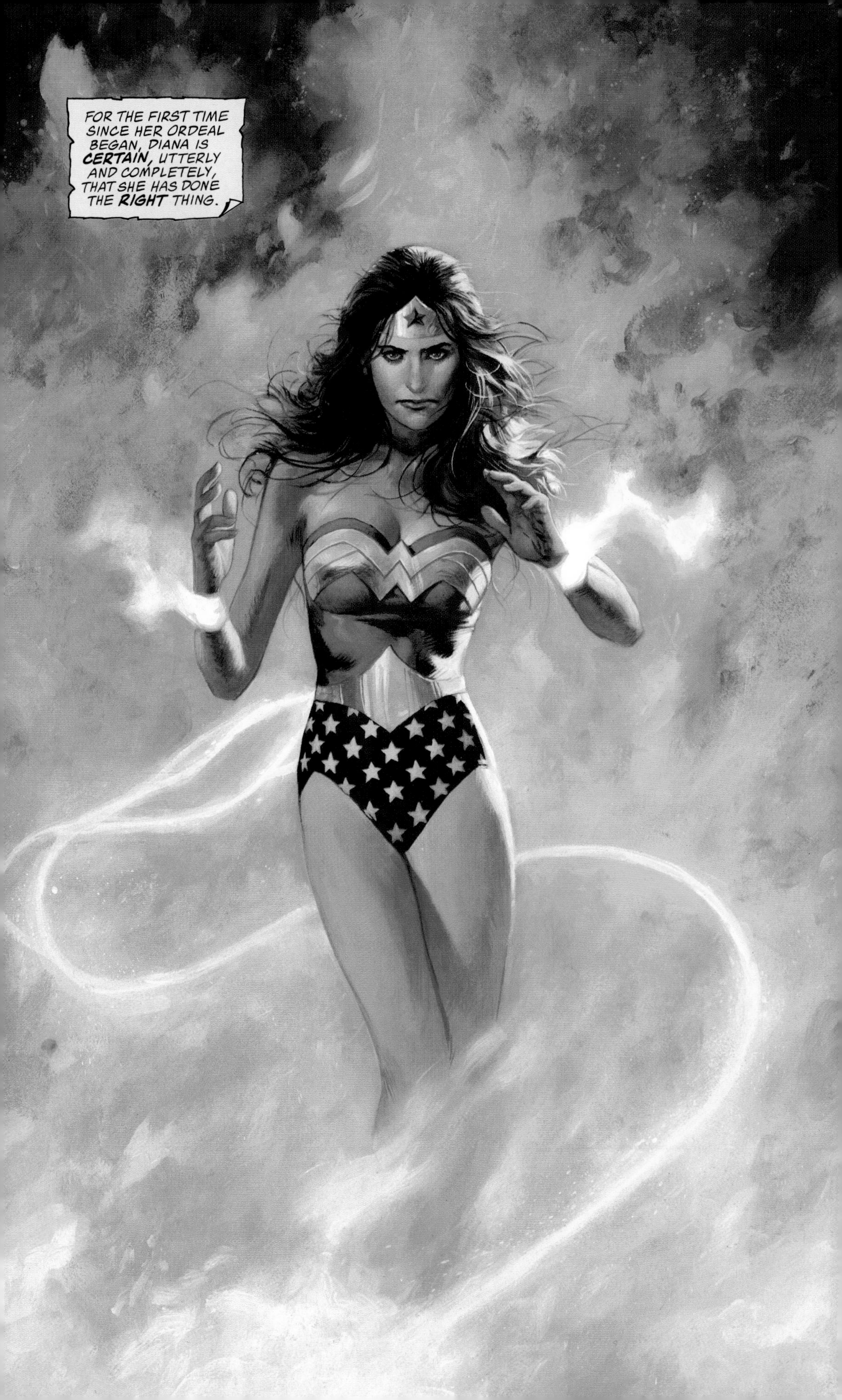
FOR THE FIRST TIME SINCE HER ORDEAL BEGAN, DIANA IS CERTAIN, UTTERLY AND COMPLETELY, THAT SHE HAS DONE THE RIGHT THING.

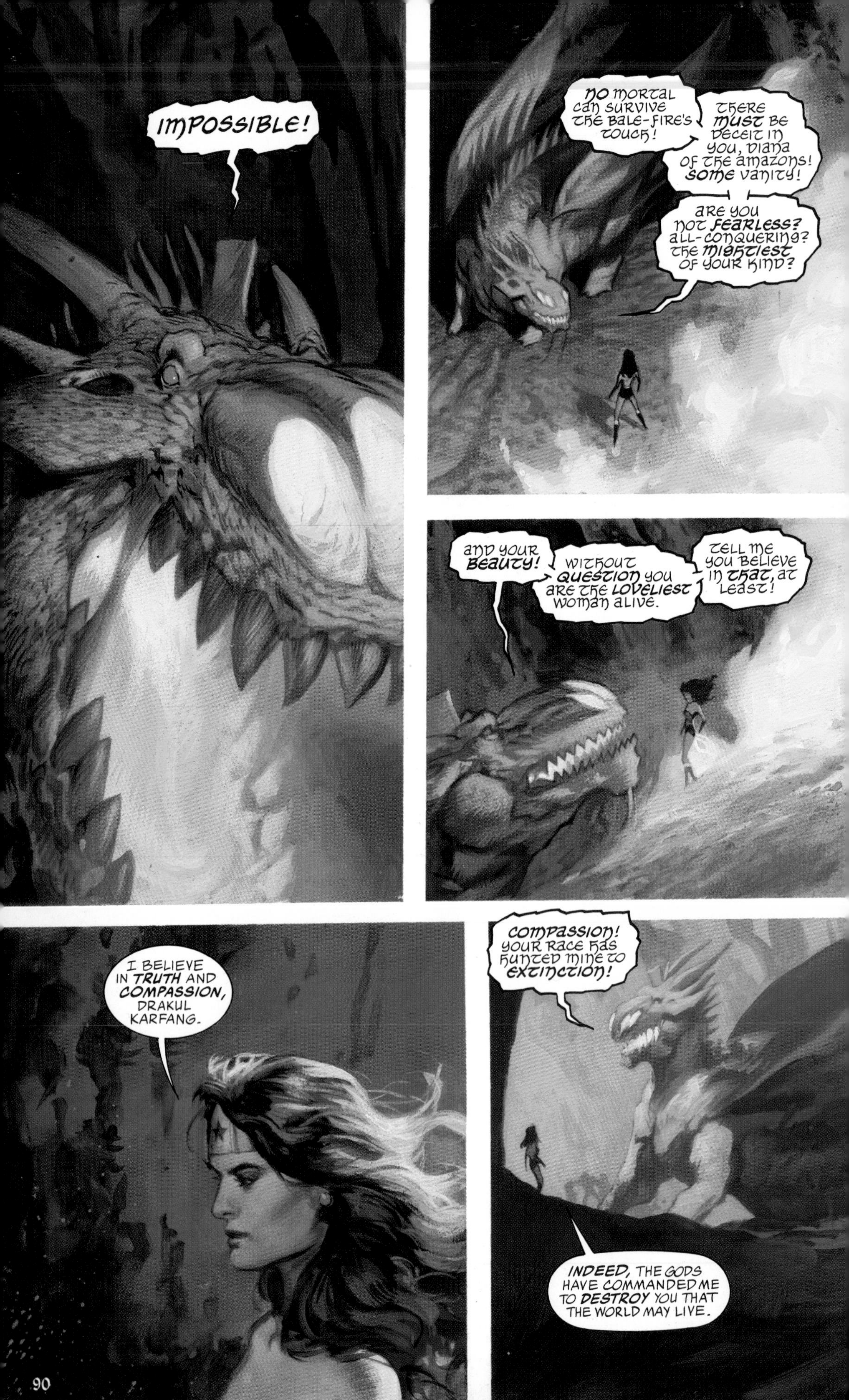
IMPOSSIBLE!
NO MORTAL CAN SURVIVE THE BALE-FIRE'S TOUCH!
THERE MUST BE DECEIT IN YOU, DIANA OF THE AMAZONS! SOME VANITY!
ARE YOU NOT FEARLESS? ALL-CONQUERING? THE MIGHTIEST OF YOUR KIND?
AND YOUR BEAUTY!
WITHOUT QUESTION YOU ARE THE LOVELIEST WOMAN ALIVE.
TELL ME YOU BELIEVE IN THAT, AT LEAST!
I BELIEVE IN TRUTH AND COMPASSION, DRAKUL KARFANG.
COMPASSION! YOUR RACE HAS HUNTED MINE TO EXTINCTION!
INDEED, THE GODS HAVE COMMANDED ME TO DESTROY YOU THAT THE WORLD MAY LIVE.

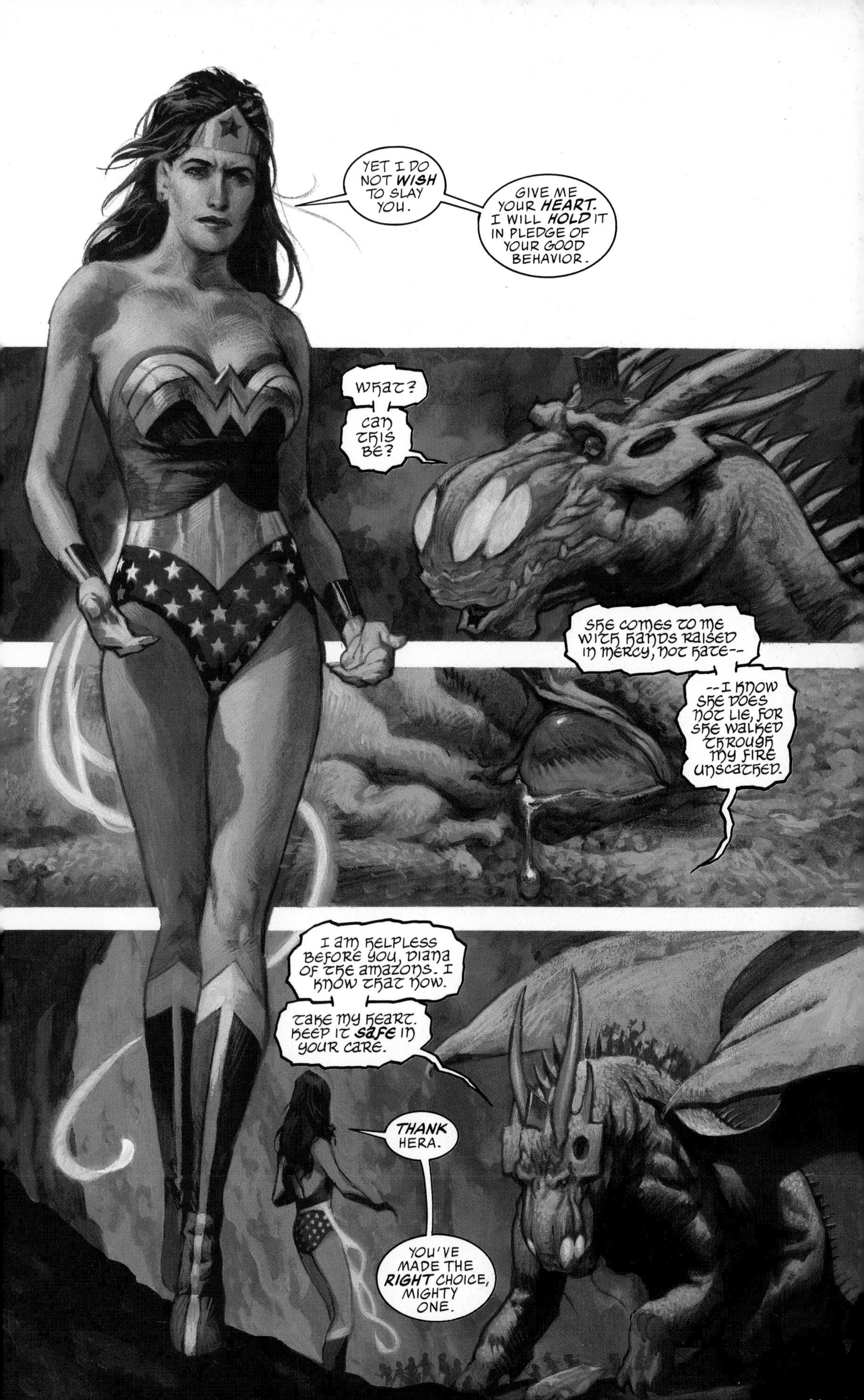
YET I DO NOT WISH TO SLAY YOU.
GIVE ME YOUR HEART. I WILL HOLD IT IN PLEDGE OF YOUR GOOD BEHAVIOR.
WHAT?
CAN THIS BE?
SHE COMES TO ME WITH HANDS RAISED IN MERCY, NOT HATE--
--I KNOW SHE DOES NOT LIE, FOR SHE WALKED THROUGH MY FIRE UNSCATHED.
I AM HELPLESS BEFORE YOU, DIANA OF THE AMAZONS. I KNOW THAT NOW.
TAKE MY HEART. KEEP IT SAFE IN YOUR CARE.
THANK HERA.
YOU'VE MADE THE RIGHT CHOICE, MIGHTY ONE.

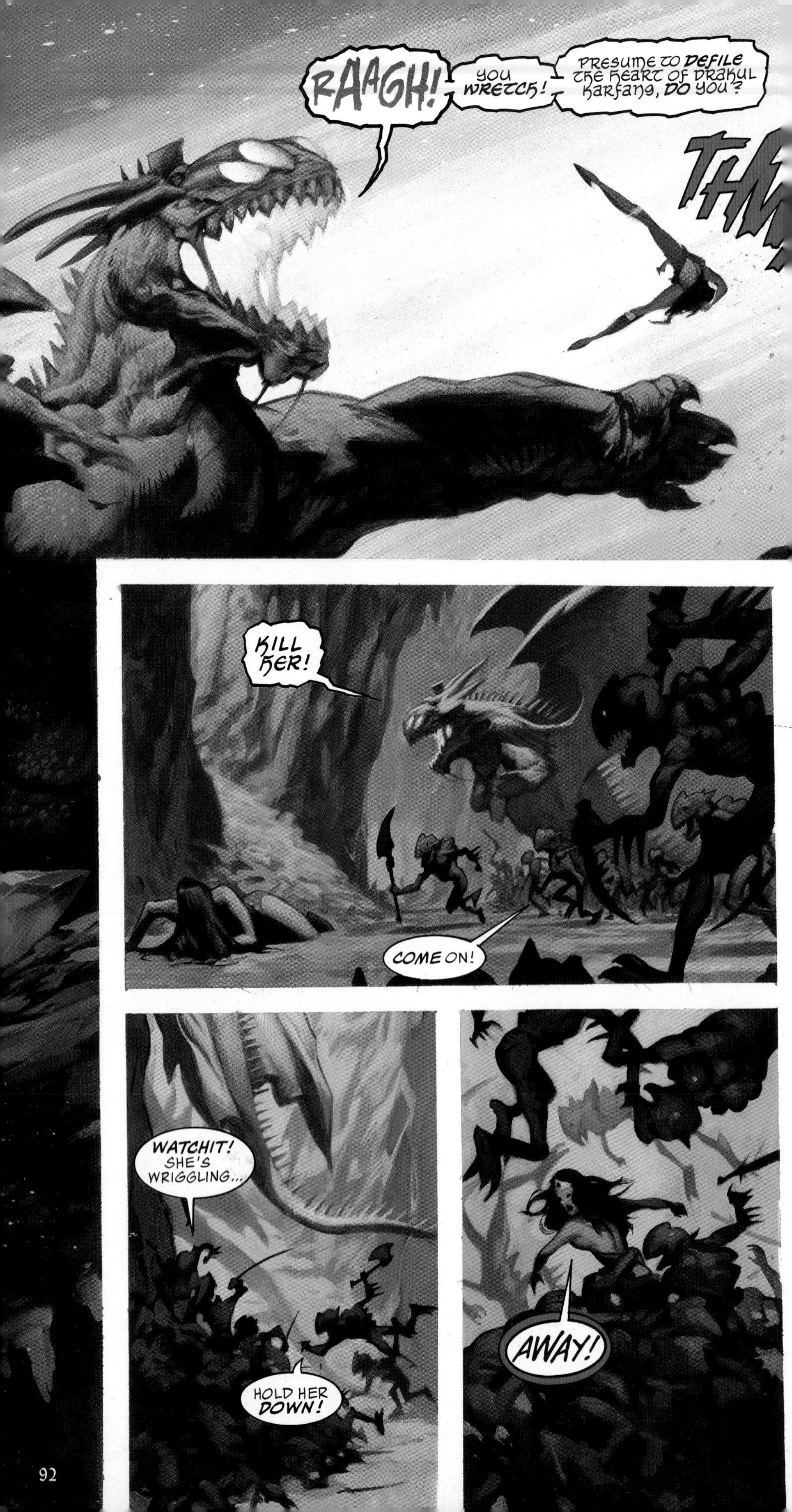
RAAGH!
YOU WRETCH!
PRESUME TO DEFILE THE HEART OF DRAKUL KARFANG, DO YOU?
KILL HER!
COME ON!
WATCHIT! SHE'S WRIGGLING...
HOLD HER DOWN!
AWAY!

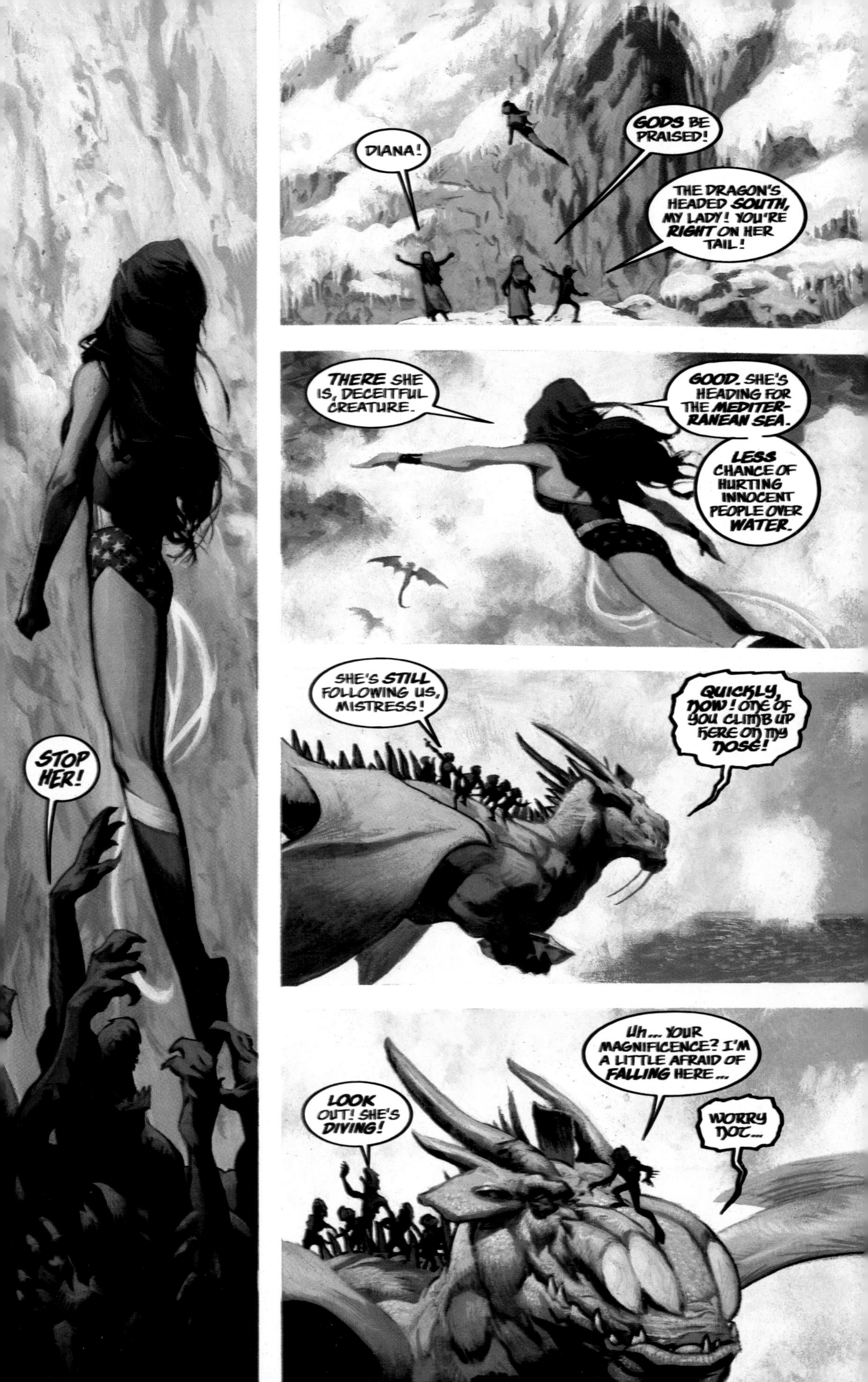
STOP HER!
DIANA!
GODS BE PRAISED!
THE DRAGON'S HEADED SOUTH, MY LADY! YOU'RE RIGHT ON HER TAIL!
THERE SHE IS, DECEITFUL CREATURE.
GOOD. SHE'S HEADING FOR THE MEDITER-RANEAN SEA.
LESS CHANCE OF HURTING INNOCENT PEOPLE OVER WATER.
SHE'S STILL FOLLOWING US, MISTRESS!
QUICKLY, NOW! ONE OF YOU CLIMB UP HERE ON MY NOSE!
LOOK OUT! SHE'S DIVING!
UH... YOUR MAGNIFICENCE? I'M A LITTLE AFRAID OF FALLING HERE...
WORRY NOT...

EEK!

CRUNCH

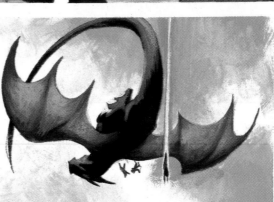

YOUR FIRE FEEDS ON LIES—

—MY GOLDEN LASSO CONQUERS LIES.

BAORAAP

FEED ON THIS!

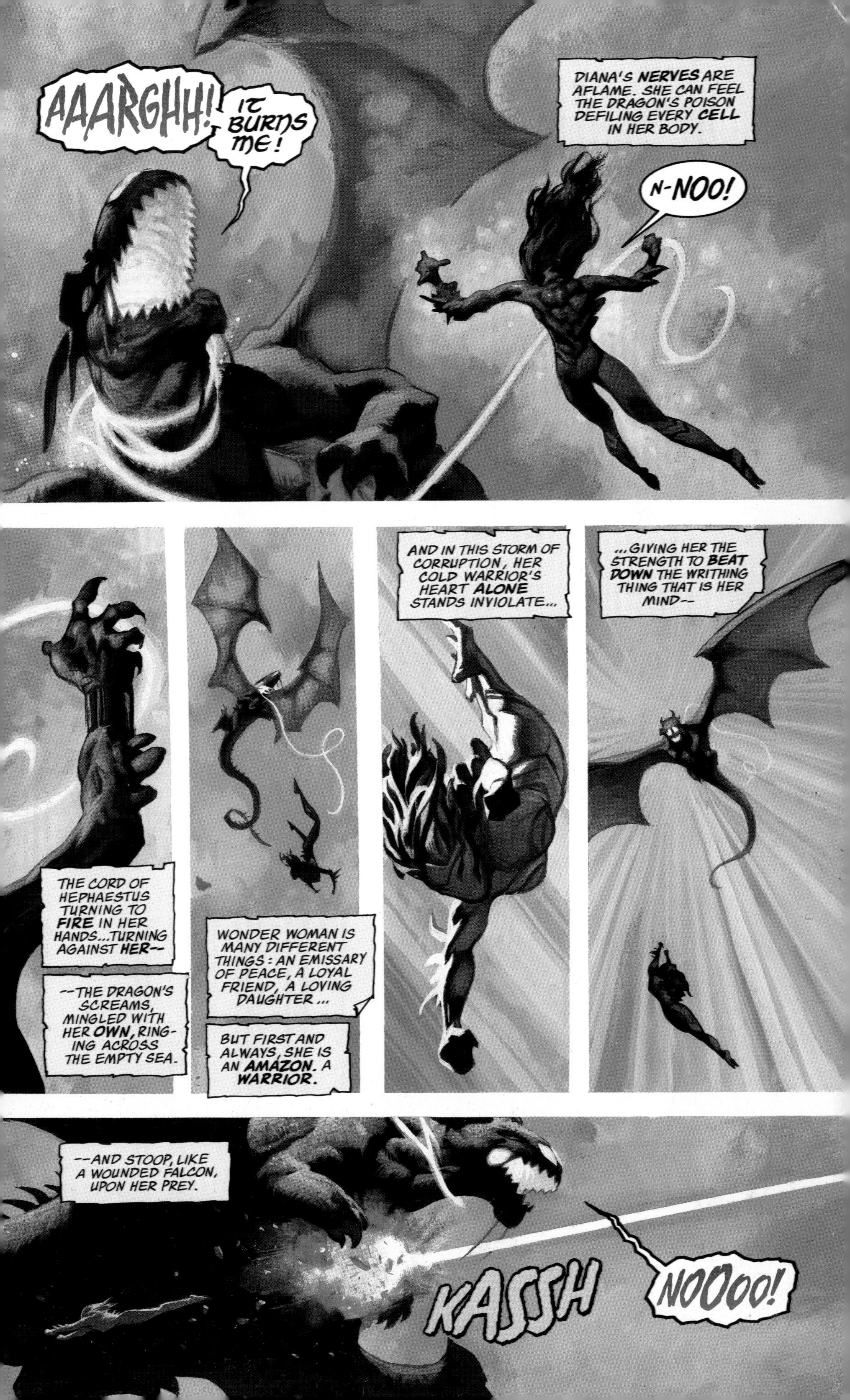
AAARGHH!
IT BURNS ME!
DIANA'S NERVES ARE AFLAME. SHE CAN FEEL THE DRAGON'S POISON DEFILING EVERY CELL IN HER BODY.
N-NOO!
THE CORD OF HEPHAESTUS TURNING TO FIRE IN HER HANDS...TURNING AGAINST HER--
--THE DRAGON'S SCREAMS, MINGLED WITH HER OWN, RINGING ACROSS THE EMPTY SEA.
WONDER WOMAN IS MANY DIFFERENT THINGS: AN EMISSARY OF PEACE, A LOYAL FRIEND, A LOVING DAUGHTER...
BUT FIRST AND ALWAYS, SHE IS AN AMAZON. A WARRIOR.
AND IN THIS STORM OF CORRUPTION, HER COLD WARRIOR'S HEART ALONE STANDS INVIOLATE...
...GIVING HER THE STRENGTH TO BEAT DOWN THE WRITHING THING THAT IS HER MIND--
--AND STOOP, LIKE A WOUNDED FALCON, UPON HER PREY.
KASSH
NOOOO!

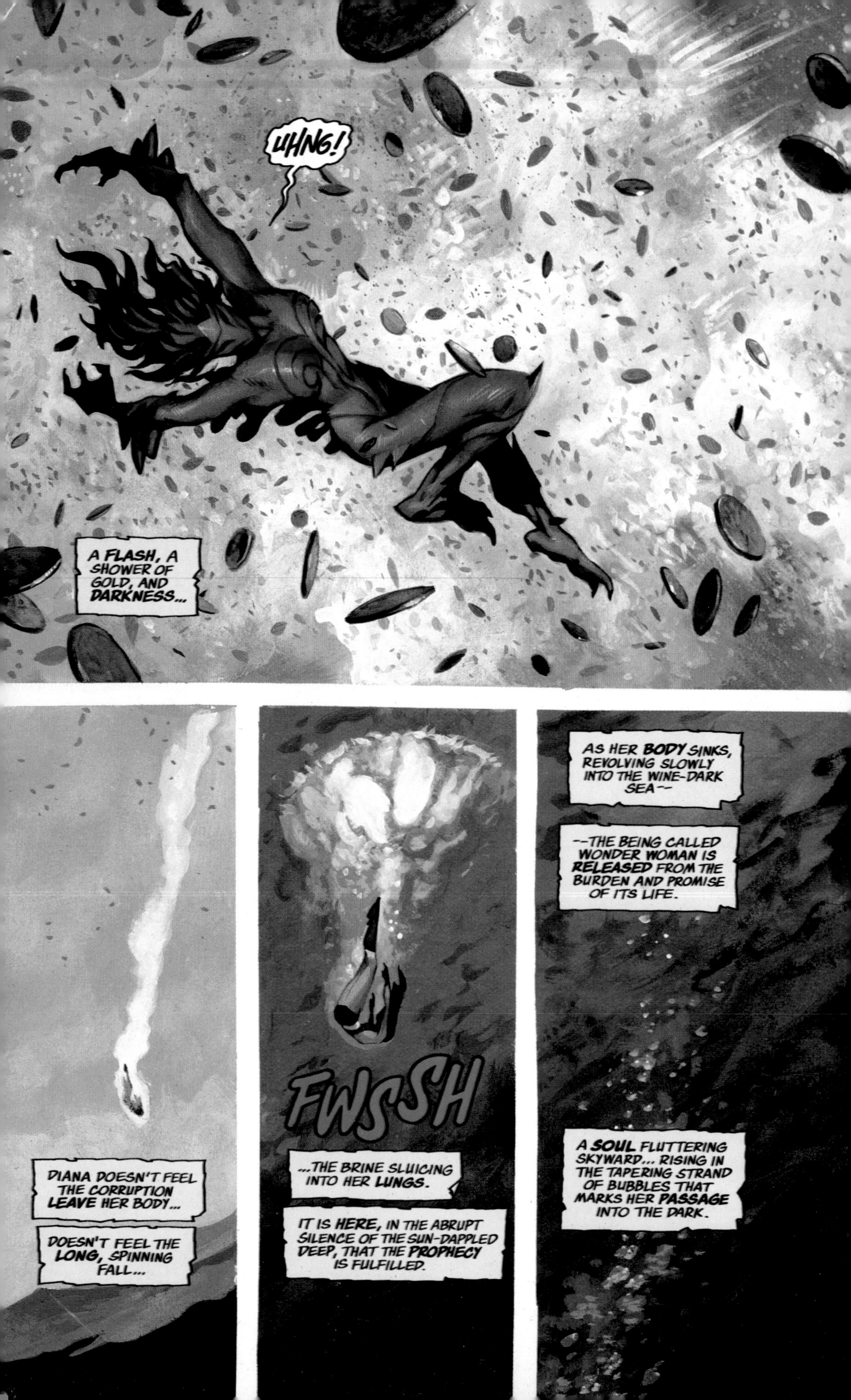
UHNG!
A FLASH, A SHOWER OF GOLD, AND DARKNESS...
DIANA DOESN'T FEEL THE CORRUPTION LEAVE HER BODY...
DOESN'T FEEL THE LONG, SPINNING FALL...
FWSSH
...THE BRINE SLUICING INTO HER LUNGS.
IT IS HERE, IN THE ABRUPT SILENCE OF THE SUN-DAPPLED DEEP, THAT THE PROPHECY IS FULFILLED.
AS HER BODY SINKS, REVOLVING SLOWLY INTO THE WINE-DARK SEA--
--THE BEING CALLED WONDER WOMAN IS RELEASED FROM THE BURDEN AND PROMISE OF ITS LIFE.
A SOUL FLUTTERING SKYWARD... RISING IN THE TAPERING STRAND OF BUBBLES THAT MARKS HER PASSAGE INTO THE DARK.

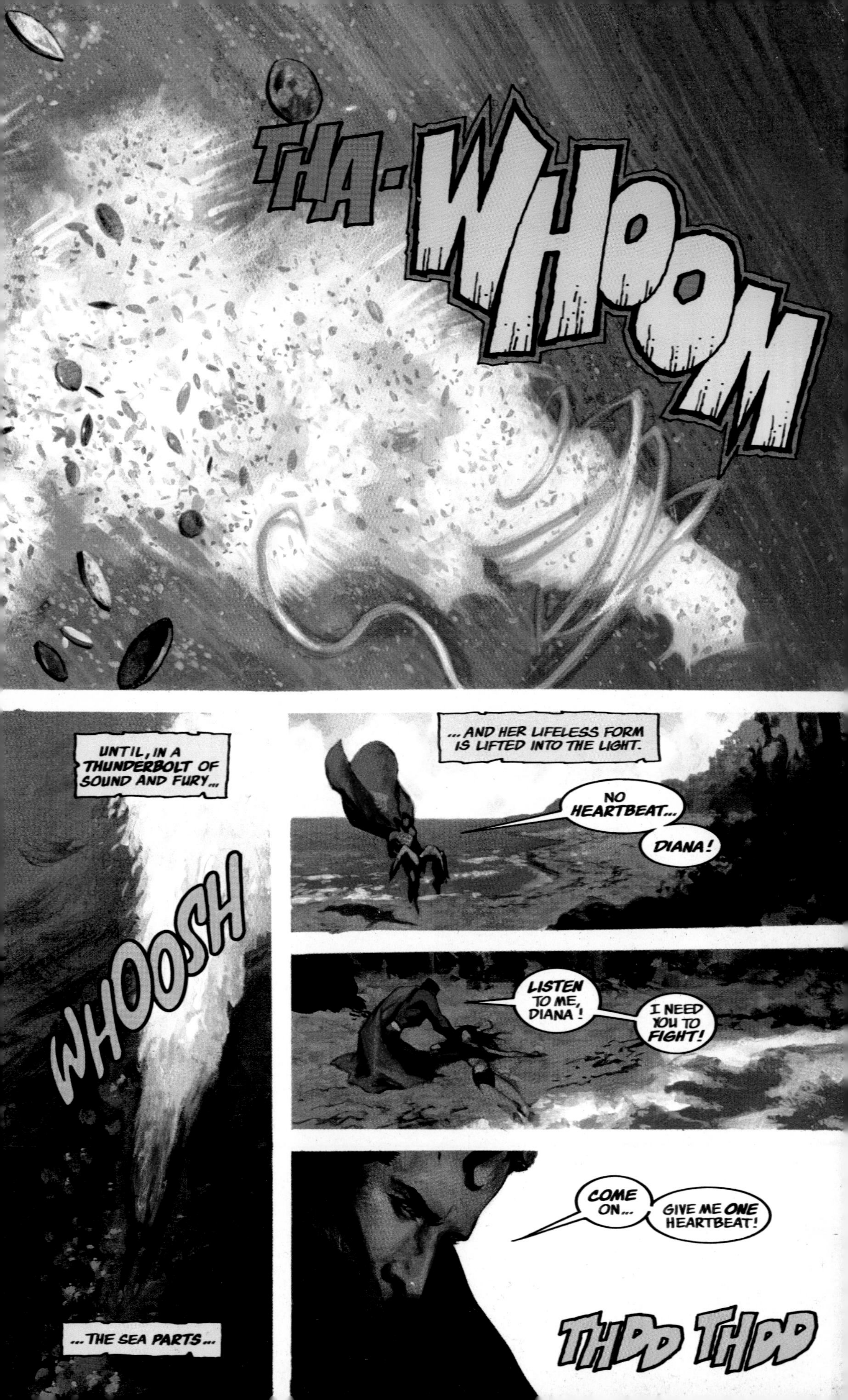
THA-WHOOOM
UNTIL, IN A THUNDERBOLT OF SOUND AND FURY...
WHOOSH
...THE SEA PARTS...
...AND HER LIFELESS FORM IS LIFTED INTO THE LIGHT.
NO HEARTBEAT...
DIANA!
LISTEN TO ME, DIANA!
I NEED YOU TO FIGHT!
COME ON...
GIVE ME ONE HEARTBEAT!
THDD THDD

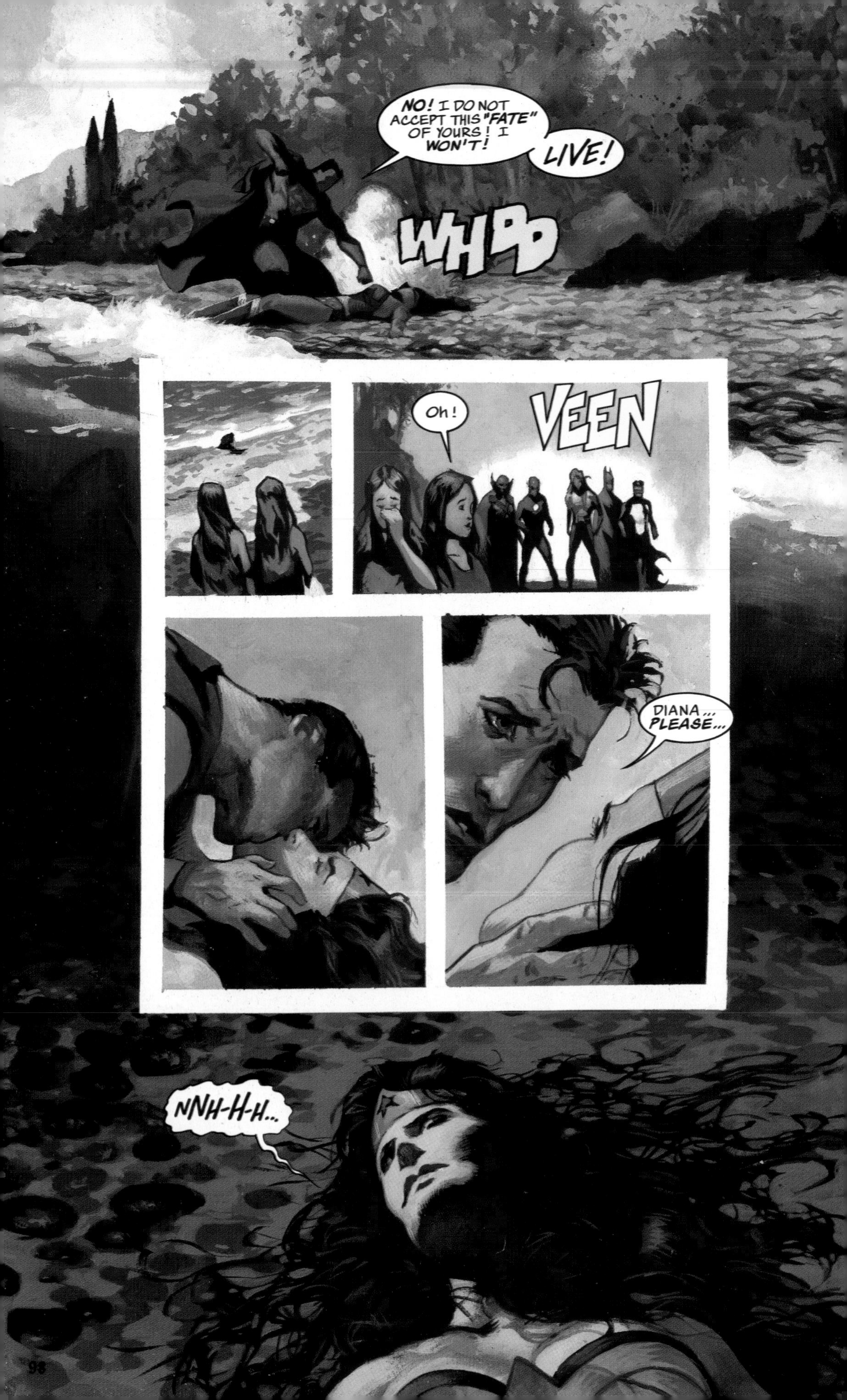

NO! I DO NOT ACCEPT THIS "FATE" OF YOURS! I WON'T!
LIVE!
WHDD
Oh!
VEEN
DIANA... PLEASE...
NNH-H-H...

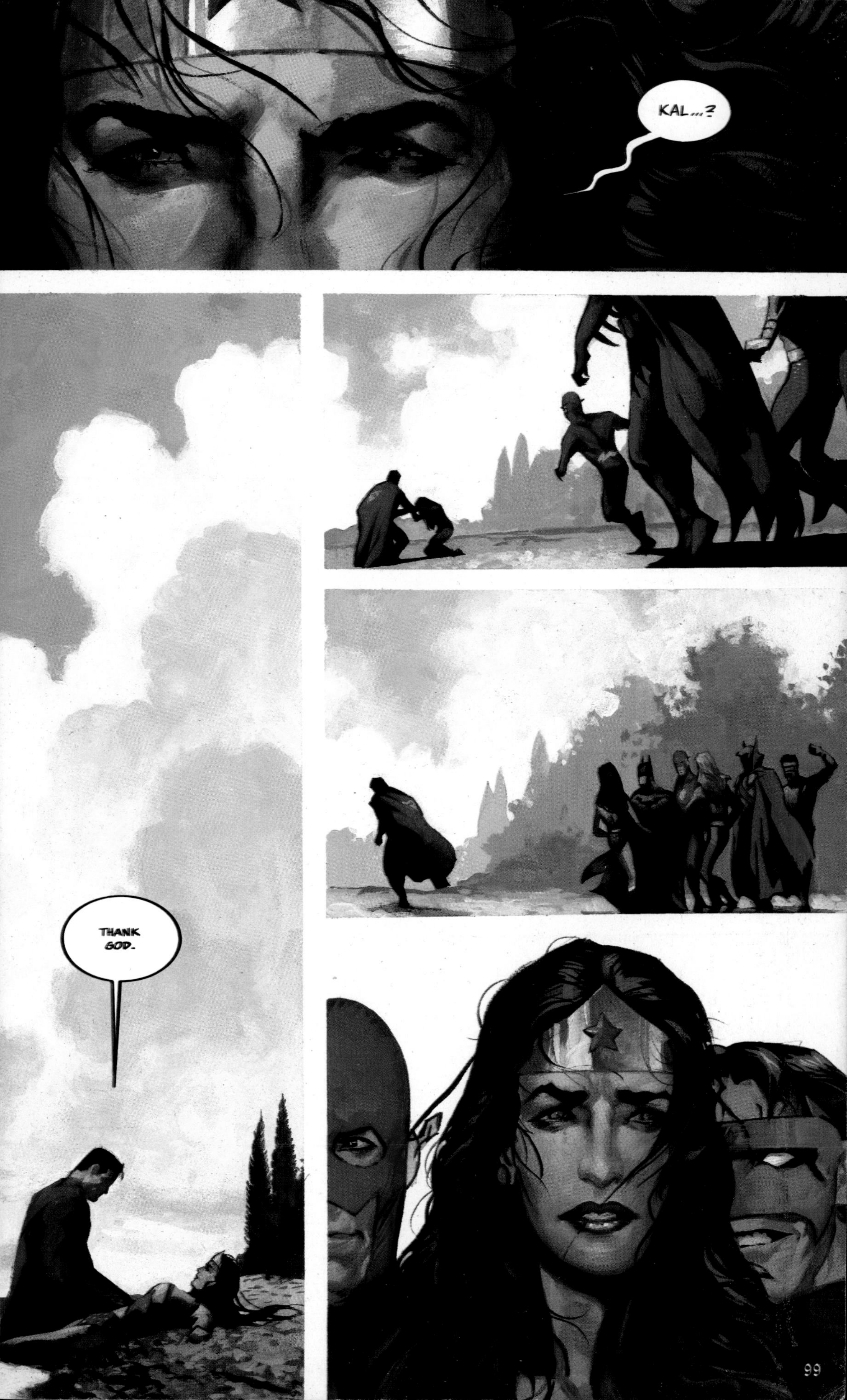
KAL...?
THANK GOD.

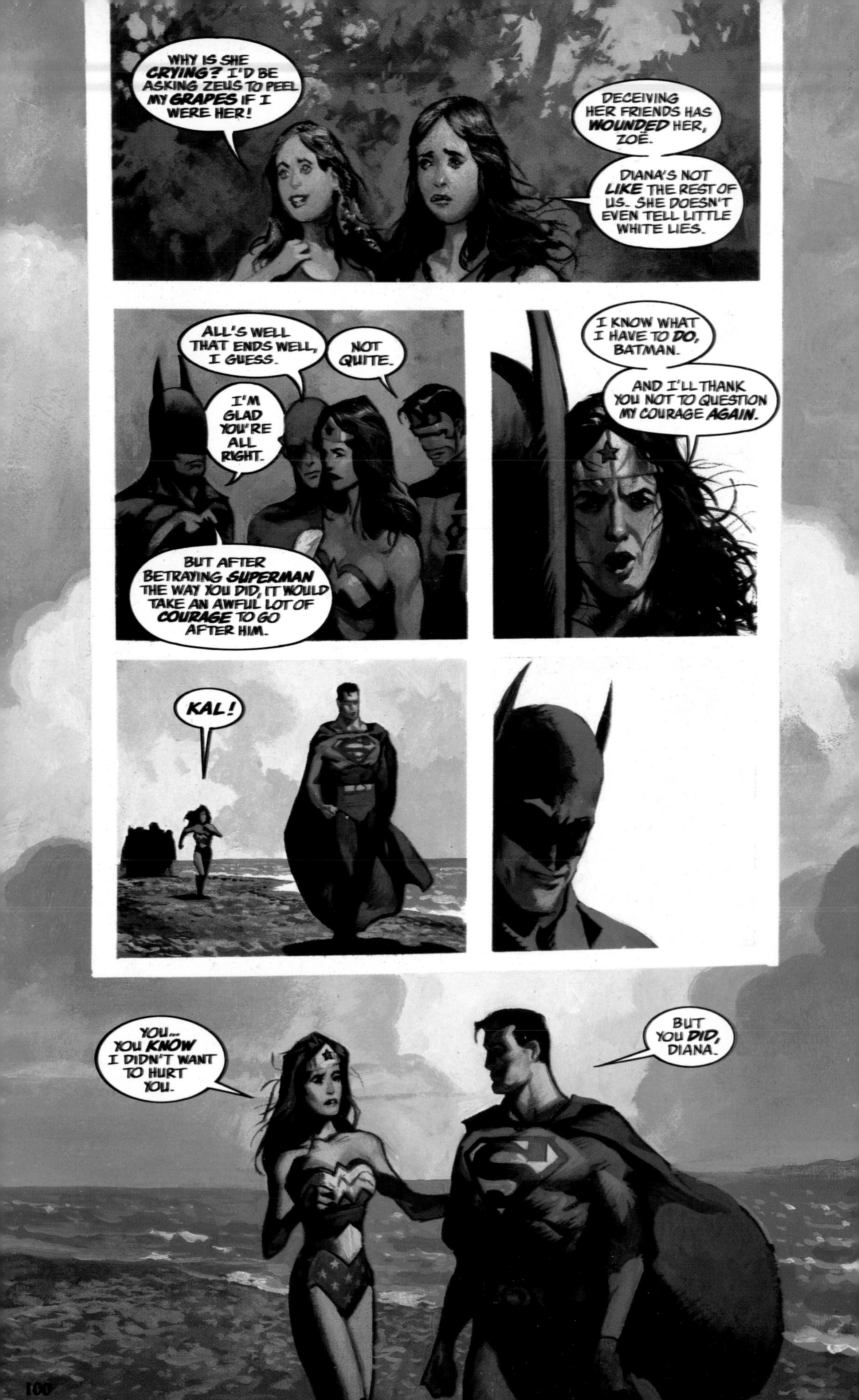
WHY IS SHE CRYING? I'D BE ASKING ZEUS TO PEEL MY GRAPES IF I WERE HER!
DECEIVING HER FRIENDS HAS WOUNDED HER, ZOË.
DIANA'S NOT LIKE THE REST OF US. SHE DOESN'T EVEN TELL LITTLE WHITE LIES.
ALL'S WELL THAT ENDS WELL, I GUESS.
NOT QUITE.
I'M GLAD YOU'RE ALL RIGHT.
BUT AFTER BETRAYING SUPERMAN THE WAY YOU DID, IT WOULD TAKE AN AWFUL LOT OF COURAGE TO GO AFTER HIM.
I KNOW WHAT I HAVE TO DO, BATMAN.
AND I'LL THANK YOU NOT TO QUESTION MY COURAGE AGAIN.
KAL!
YOU... YOU KNOW I DIDN'T WANT TO HURT YOU.
BUT YOU DID, DIANA.

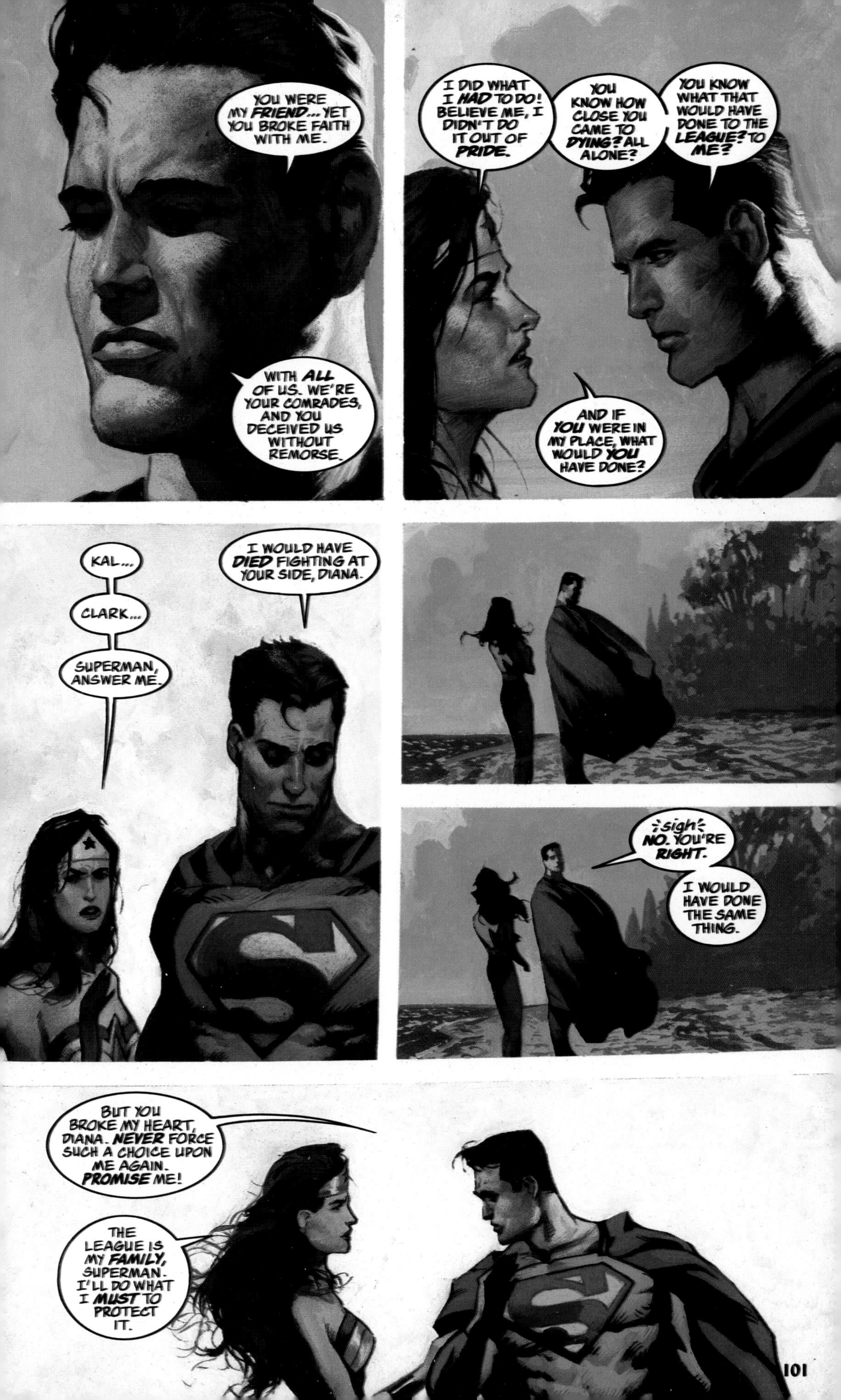

YOU WERE MY FRIEND... YET YOU BROKE FAITH WITH ME.
WITH ALL OF US. WE'RE YOUR COMRADES, AND YOU DECEIVED US WITHOUT REMORSE.
I DID WHAT I HAD TO DO! BELIEVE ME, I DIDN'T DO IT OUT OF PRIDE.
YOU KNOW HOW CLOSE YOU CAME TO DYING? ALL ALONE?
YOU KNOW WHAT THAT WOULD HAVE DONE TO THE LEAGUE? TO ME?
AND IF YOU WERE IN MY PLACE, WHAT WOULD YOU HAVE DONE?
KAL...
CLARK...
SUPERMAN, ANSWER ME.
I WOULD HAVE DIED FIGHTING AT YOUR SIDE, DIANA.
sigh NO. YOU'RE RIGHT.
I WOULD HAVE DONE THE SAME THING.
BUT YOU BROKE MY HEART, DIANA. NEVER FORCE SUCH A CHOICE UPON ME AGAIN. PROMISE ME!
THE LEAGUE IS MY FAMILY, SUPERMAN. I'LL DO WHAT I MUST TO PROTECT IT.

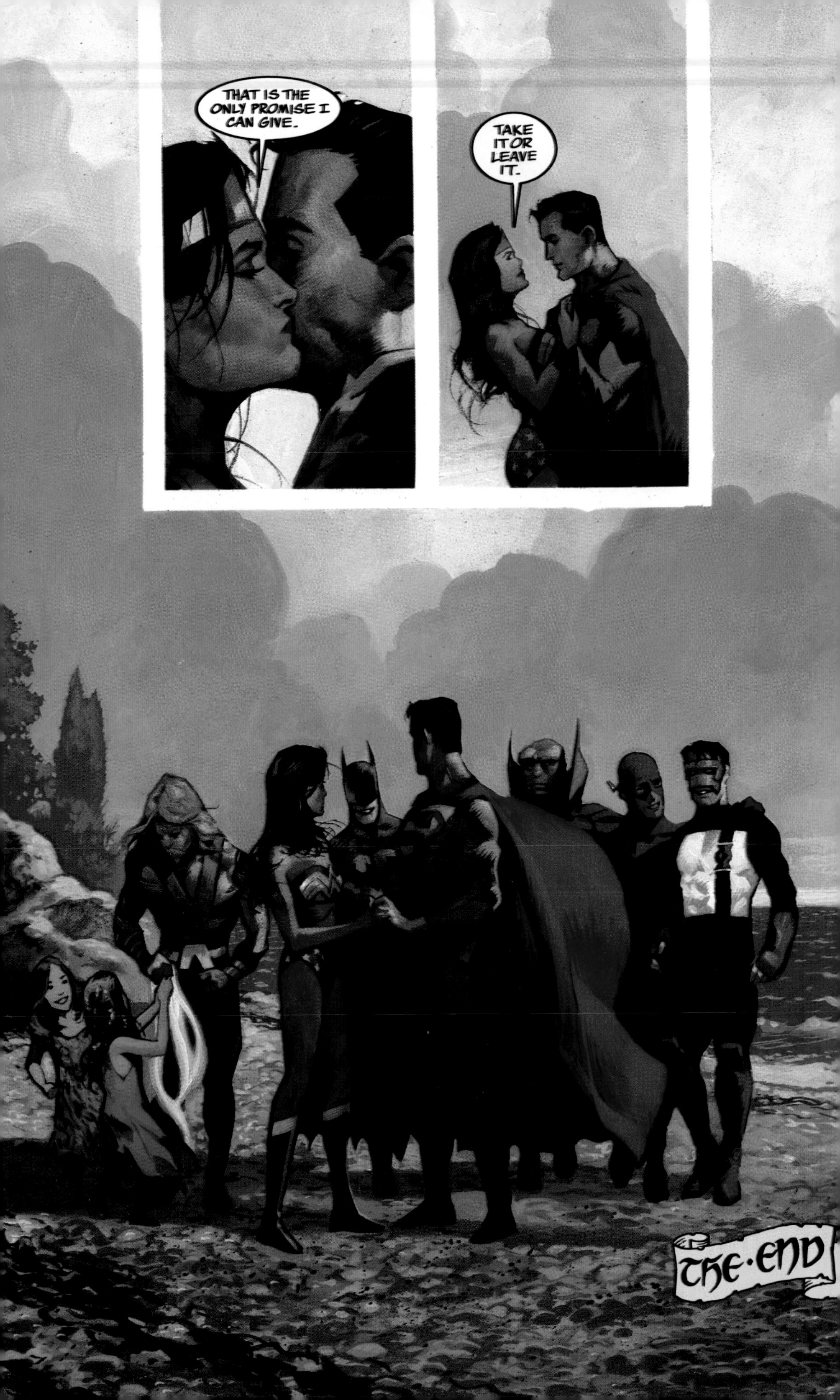
THAT IS THE ONLY PROMISE I CAN GIVE.
TAKE IT OR LEAVE IT.
THE·END

SKETCHBOOK

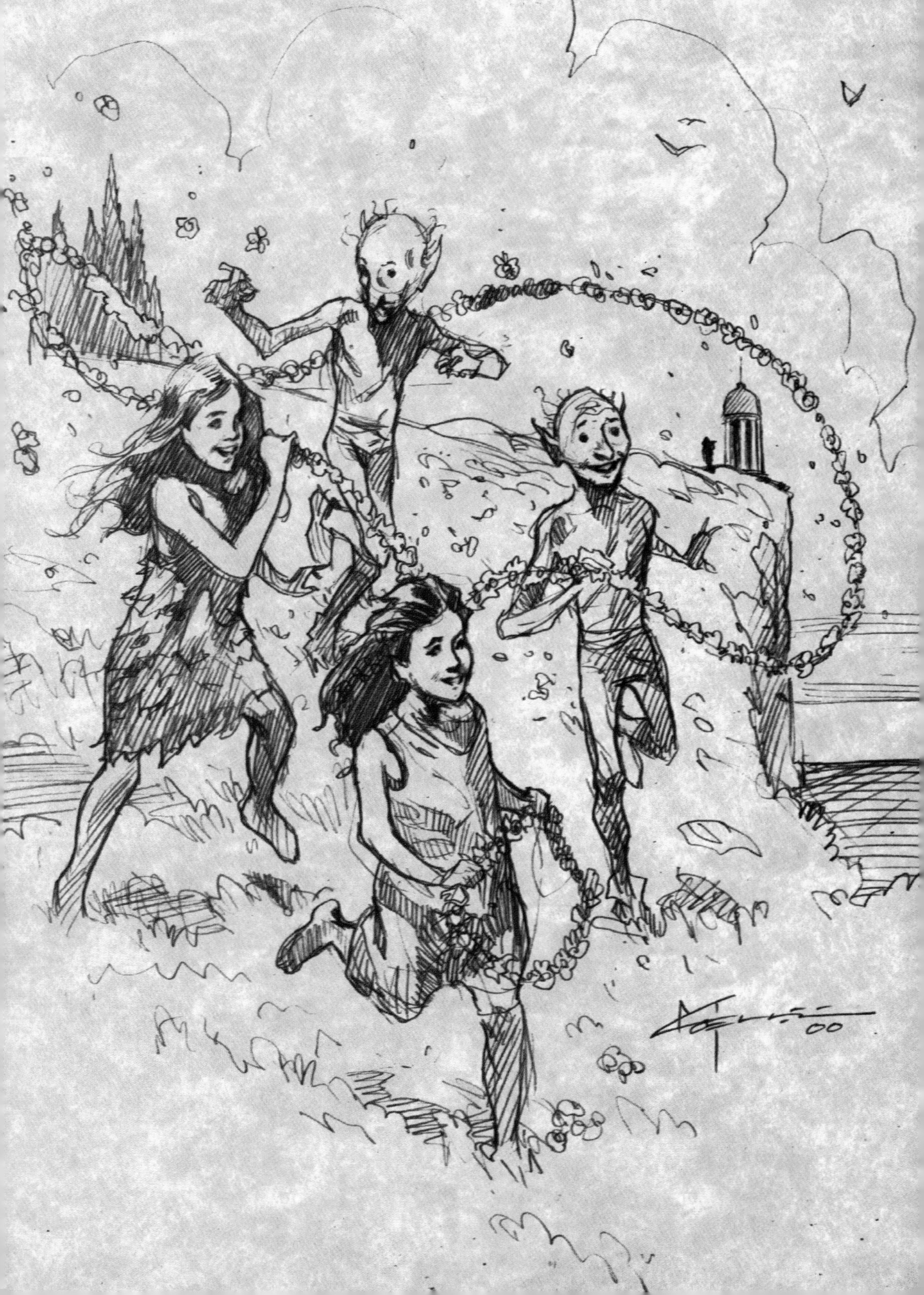

Diana

Diana's Lasso is not just a weapon, but a stern standard of truth. Power corrupts, but through Hephaestus' gift, Wonder Woman has a unique opportunity... to face honestly the self-deceptions from which corruption springs. Diana's Lasso is a beacon, lighting the darkest recesses of her soul.

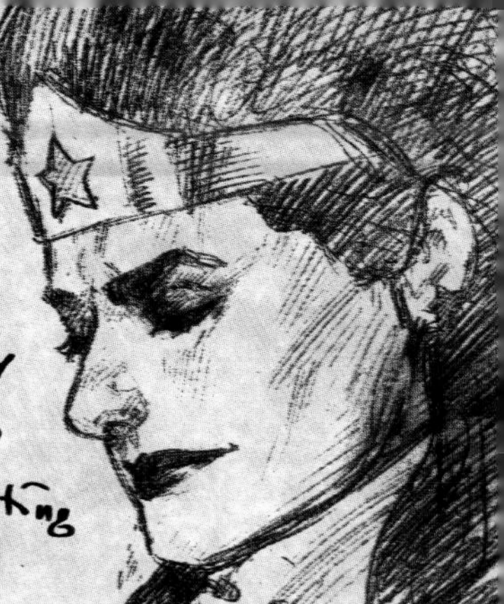

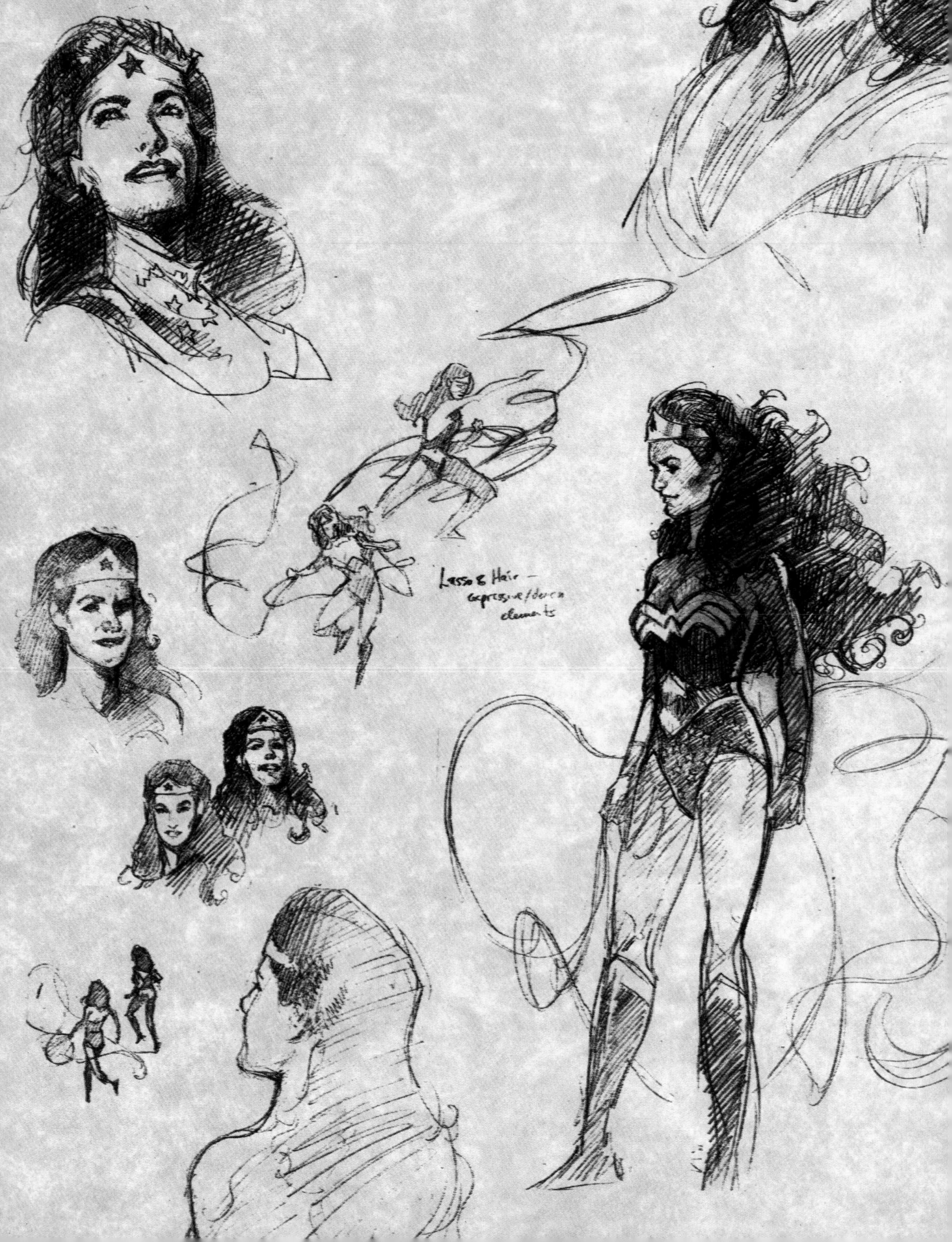
Lasso & Hair —
expressive/dream
elements

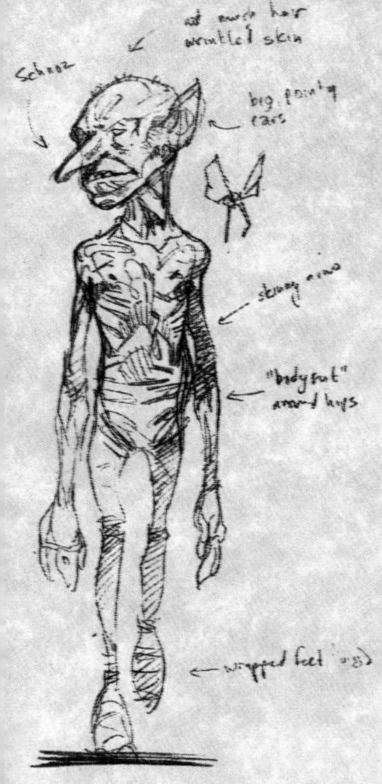
wrinkled skin
Schnoz
big, pointy ears
stringy arms
"bodysuit" around hips
wrapped feet (rags)

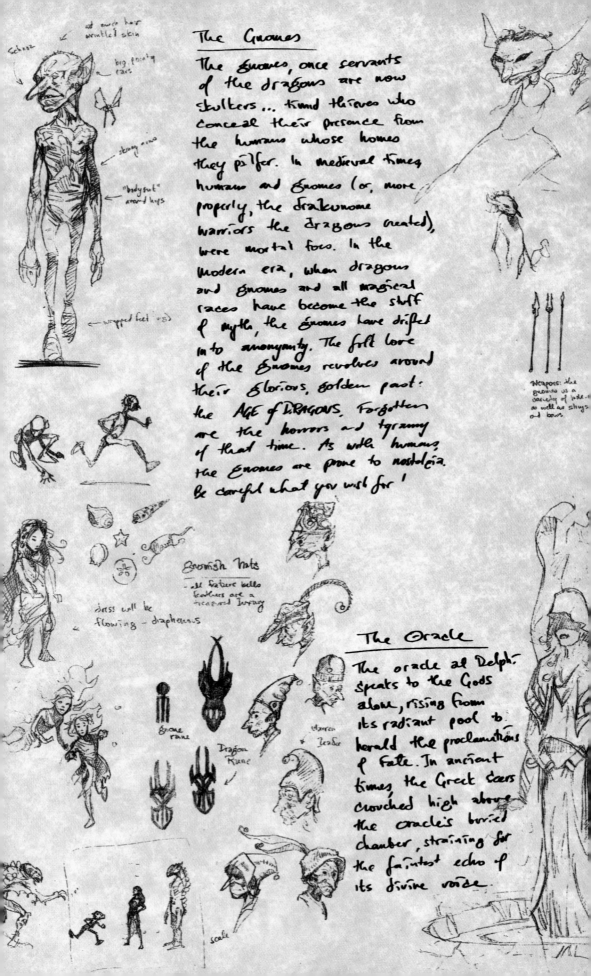

The Gnomes

The gnomes, once servants of the dragons are now skulkers... timid thieves who conceal their presence from the humans whose homes they pilfer. In medieval times humans and gnomes (or, more properly, the drakunome warriors the dragons created), were mortal foes. In the modern era, when dragons and gnomes and all magical races have become the stuff of myth, the gnomes have drifted into anonymity. The folk lore of the gnomes revolves around their glorious, golden past: the AGE of DRAGONS. Forgotten are the horrors and tyranny of that time. As with humans, the gnomes are prone to nostalgia. Be careful what you wish for!

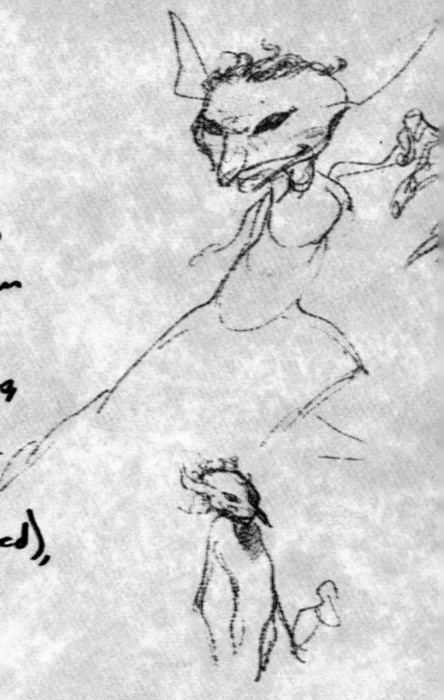

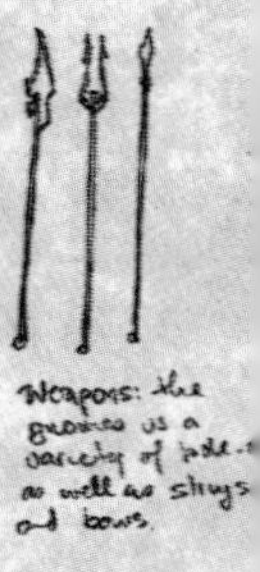
Weapons: the gnomes use a variety of pole-
as well as slings and bows.

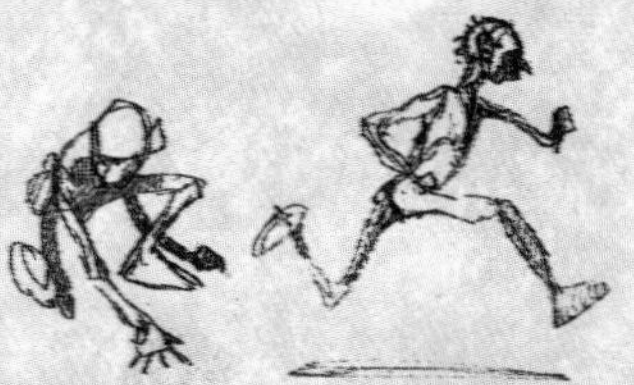

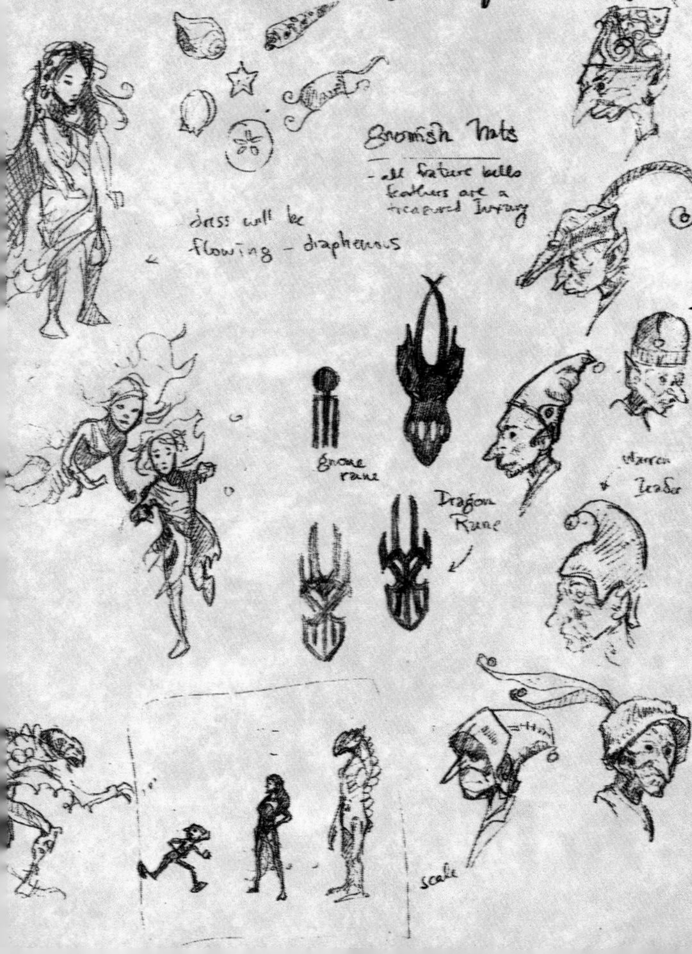
Gnomish Hats
- all feature bells
feathers are a treasured luxury
dress will be flowing - diaphanous
gnome rune
Dragon Rune
scale

The Oracle

The oracle at Delphi speaks to the Gods alone, rising from its radiant pool to herald the proclamations of Fate. In ancient times, the Greek seers crouched high above the oracle's buried chamber, straining for the faintest echo of its divine voice.

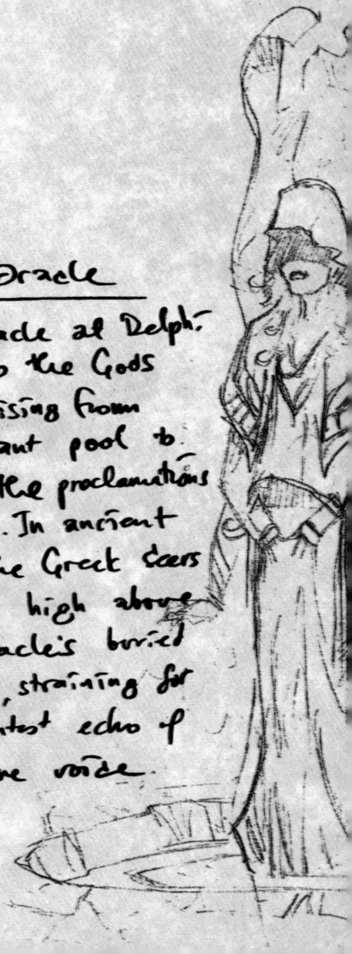

The Dragon's chest, neck and head are based roughly on that of a horse, rather than a snake, or dinosaur. I wanted to create a creature that gave an impression of majesty and proud strength. The horse, with its broad chest and wide, muscular, neck seemed to answer.

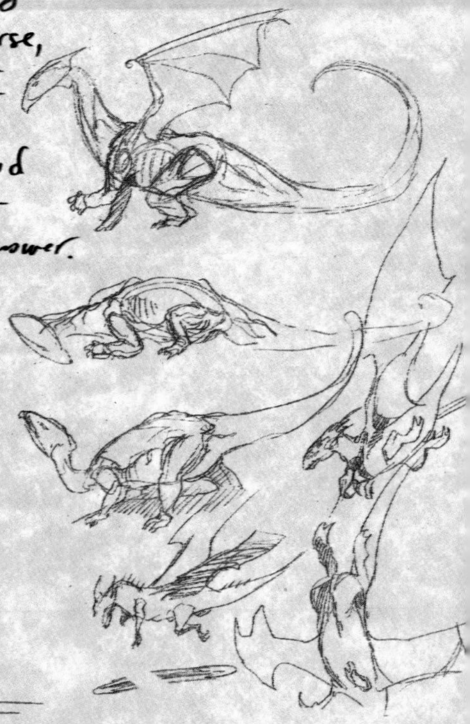

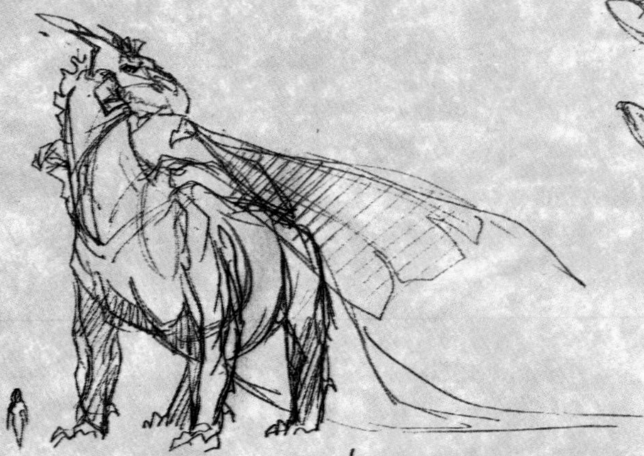

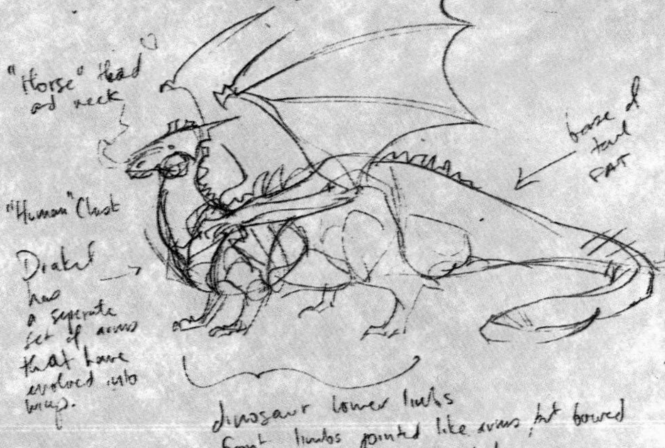
"Horse" head and neck
"Human" Chest
Drake has a seperate set of arms that have evolved into wings.
base of tail FAT
dinosaur lower limbs
- front limbs pointed like arms, but bowed
- rear limbs triple-pointed

I used my dog Cocoa as the model for Karfang's body language. I filmed her jumping, relaxing, walking, and running. Those images became the basis for the dragon.

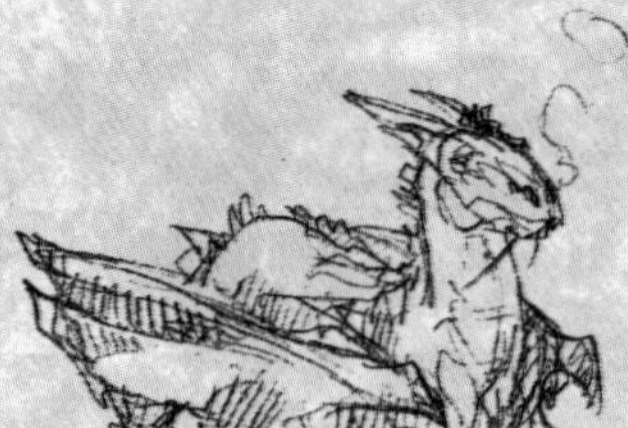
use wings expressively, like superhero's cape.

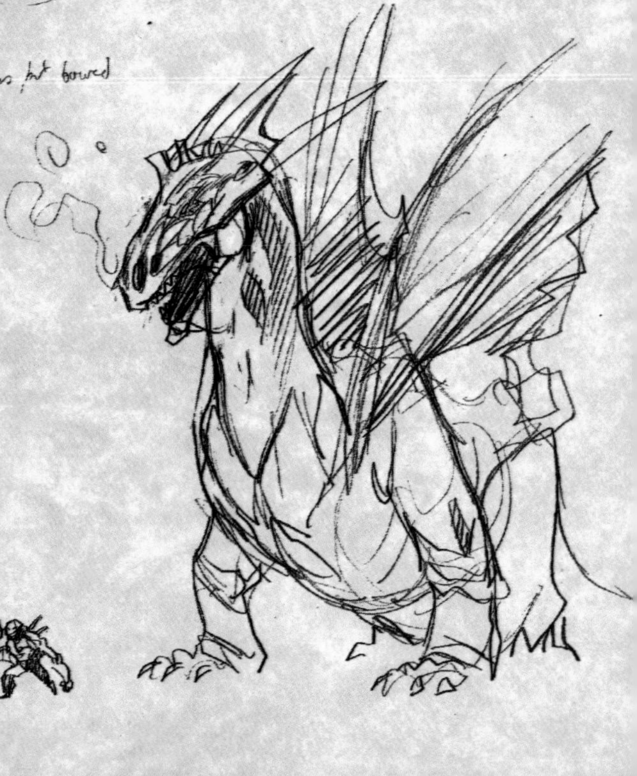

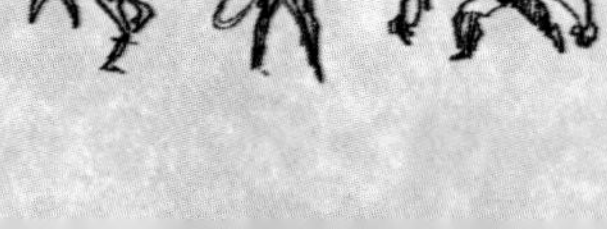

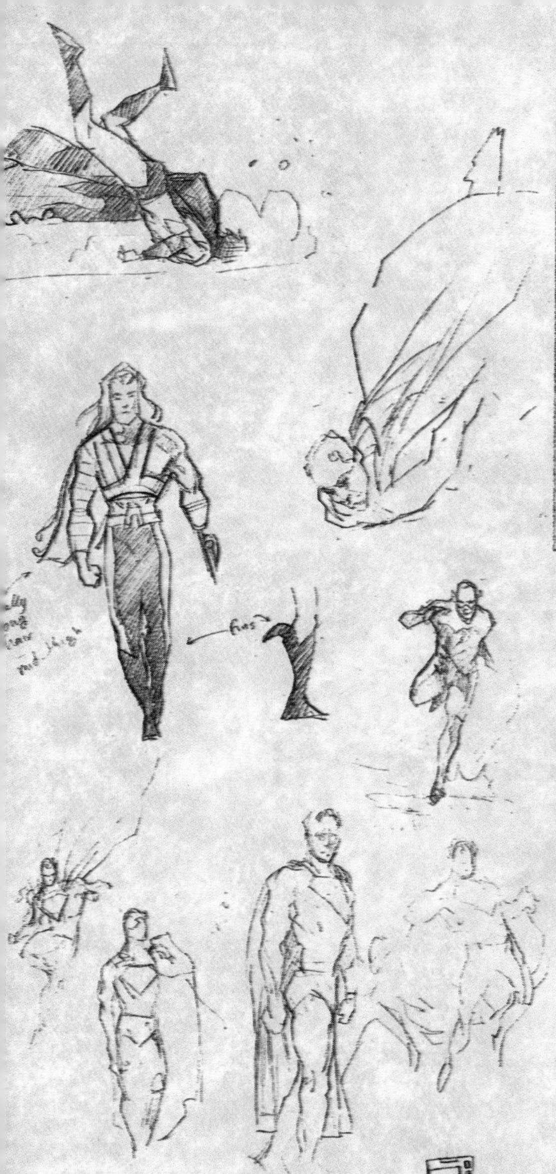
fins

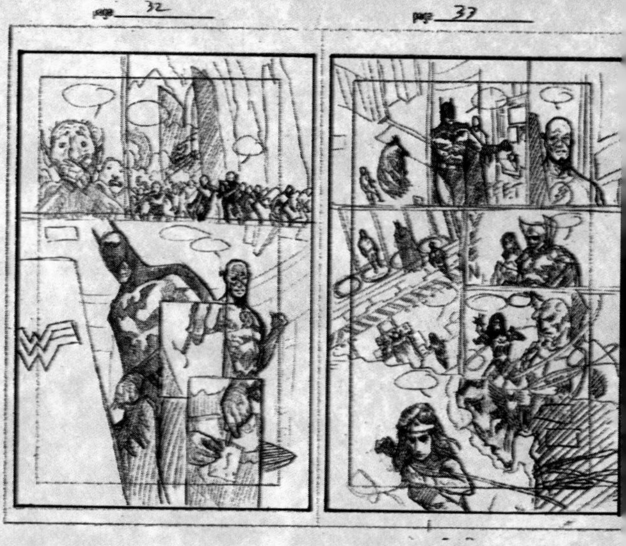
page 32
page 33

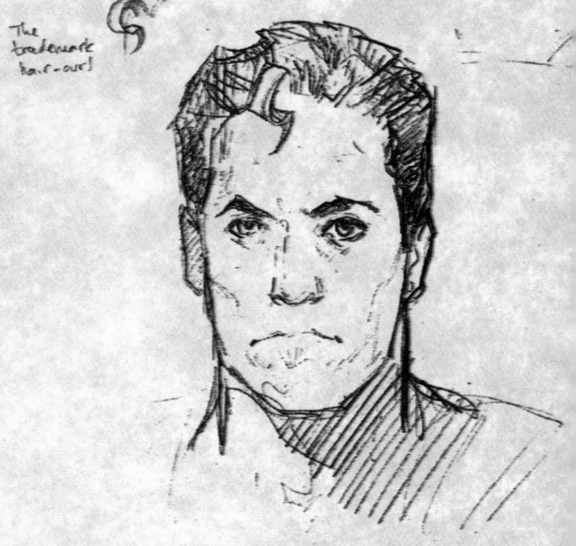
The trademark hair-curl!

The Hall of Justice

The watchtower was my chance to indulge in the "tech" that I find so fascinating. A gritty Watchtower!

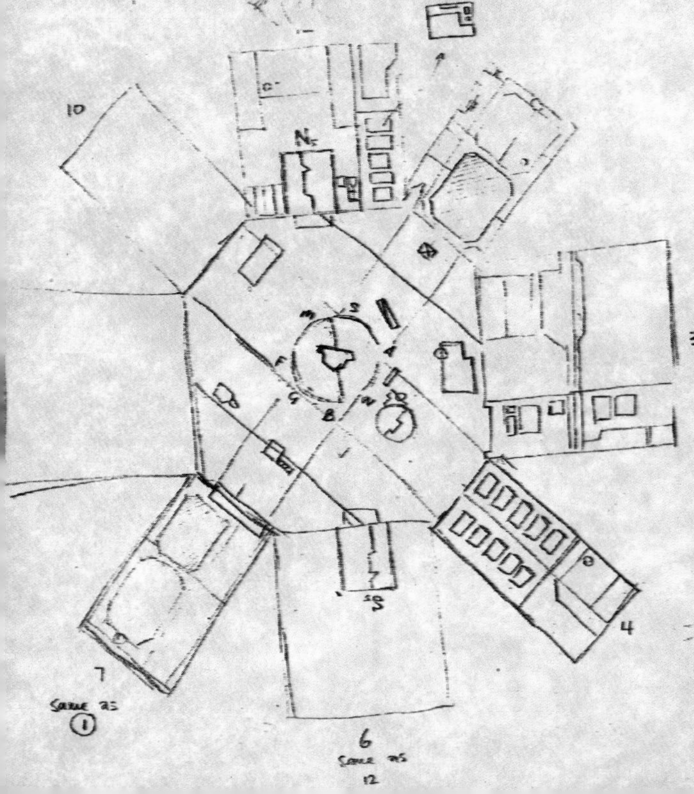
10
3
4
6
Same as 12
7
Same as 1

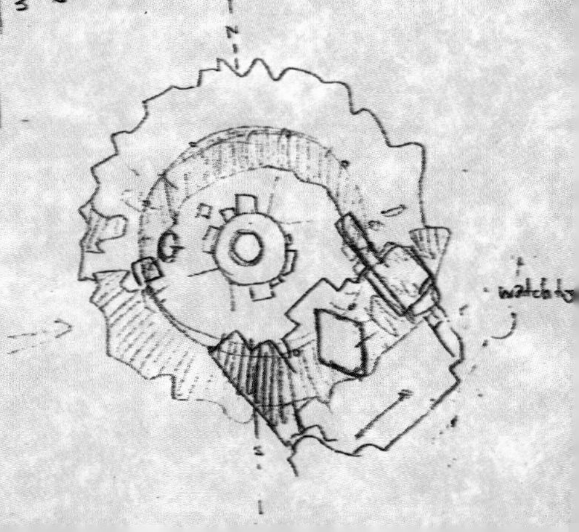
N
S

ACKNOWLEDGMENTS

A few thank-you's...

To Karen Kanuch, my Diana,

to Dave, Scott and Ray, my band of brothers,

to Jeff, for sharing Helen's pierogies,

to Joe, for more than just his scrap file,

to the Freelancers; to Sonia Olivera.

And finally,

forever and always,

to Dawn, Tessa and Eric.

CHRISTOPHER MOELLER

has been working as a writer and painter
in the comics industry since 1990. Moeller's debut
publication, both as a writer and as a painter, was Innovation's
Rocketman: King of the Rocketmen (1991). This was followed in
1991-2 by five issues of artwork for Anne Rice's Interview with the
Vampire, also from Innovation. In 1993, Moeller launched the science
fiction universe Shadow Empires (now Iron Empires) with two stories
from Dark Horse Comics: Faith Conquers, and The Passage.
Moeller was nominated for an Eisner Award in 1994
for his work on Faith Conquers.
In 1996, Moeller created the artwork for the Star Wars
pop-up book from Dark Horse Comics, Star Wars: Battle of the
Bounty Hunters. Moeller's association with the Star Wars property
has included: cover and interior illustrations from the Star Wars
Galaxy Magazine, trading cards for Topps, and covers for various
Star Wars comics and trade paperbacks.

Moeller's most recent work, a second painted Iron Empires story
entitled SHEVA'S WAR, was released from DC Comics under the
Helix imprint in 1998.

In addition to comics work, Moeller has created artwork for posters,
magazines, paperback and hardcover books, game illustrations,
trading cards, advertising and design work.
Moeller currently resides in Pittsburgh, Pennsylvania.